URBAN SPACE

D1674769

Luc Deleu – T.O.P. office
Orban Space

Editors

Wouter Davidts
Guy Châtel
Stefaan Vervoort

Contributors

Guy Châtel
Wouter Davidts
Isabelle De Smet
Hans De Wolf
Maarten Delbeke
Luc Deleu
Marjolijn Dijkman
Kersten Geers
Aglaia Konrad
John Macarthur
Metahaven
Manfred Pernice
Felicity Scott
Teresa Stoppani
UP / Koenraad Dedobbeleer & Kris Kimpe
Steven Van den Bergh
Stefaan Vervoort

Valiz, Amsterdam
Stroom Den Haag

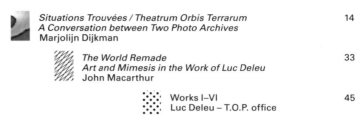

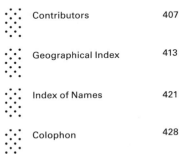

Introduction

Luc Deleu – T.O.P. office: Orban Space

Ever since the founding of the architecture and urban planning firm T.O.P. office in 1970, Antwerp-based architect and
urbanist Luc Deleu (°1944, Duffel, Belgium) has developed a
rich and notable body of work, consisting of architectural and
urban plans, projects, studies and designs, theoretical models and databases, as well as sculptures and monumental
installations for museums, urban piazzas and roundabouts
— navigating, as it were, through the respective fields of architecture, urban planning and the visual arts. Although the
oeuvre can be divided into distinct series of works and discrete types of projects (i.e. container sculptures, cartographic
works, architectural designs, urban planning schemes, etc.),
this book is based on the contention that both the work and
practice of Luc Deleu – T.O.P. office throughout the past four
decades have been marked by an overall conceptual agenda
and a consistent use of a distinct set of operations, actions
and strategies.

The publication *Luc Deleu – T.O.P. office: Orban Space* aims
to trace and explore some of these recurrent operations, actions and strategies. It does not intend to retroactively claim
a position for Luc Deleu – T.O.P. office within postwar art and
architecture, but to assess the theoretical disposition and
critical nature of that work and practice within the perspective of major historical and theoretical developments within
20th-century architecture and urban planning, and global
culture at large. From the very start of his career, Deleu has
developed an architecture and urban planning practice that
takes up the globe as its yardstick: *Orbanism*. He has never
ceased to make critical pleas and concrete efforts to transcend
the local context and to conceive of the practices of architecture and urban planning on a planetary scale, that is, to relate all conceptual schemes and pragmatic solutions to planet
earth – that prime material vessel to which the human race
is allotted. Key to the work and practice of Luc Deleu – T.O.P.

office is the ongoing anguish about the state and development of public space on the globe, a critical concern that at present culminates in the research project *Orban Space* (2006–).

Luc Deleu – T.O.P. office: Orban Space is driven by the aspiration to come up with a material as well as discursive structure that befits the conceptual rigor and material affluence of the work and the practice of Luc Deleu – T.O.P. office of the past four decades. To this end, it has not been organized in an either chronological or thematic manner, but rather by means of a conceptual topography that rests upon seven terms: *Architecture, Imitation, Sculpture, Mobility, Depiction, Scale,* and *Manifesto.* We assumed that this set of terms could cover the array of operative concepts that shaped the work and practice of Luc Deleu – T.O.P. office over time. While we acknowledge that this apparatus is evidently not outright and primarily the outcome of our particular reading, it nevertheless allows for a detailed historical and theoretical exploration of that very work and practice. The seven chosen terms define, respectively, a discipline, a relation, a medium, a condition, a mode of representation, a gauge, and a genre.

Contributors have been invited to draw on a particular term, to navigate through the work and practice of Luc Deleu – T.O.P. office, and to discover new connections and unforeseen affinities among the assorted collections of architectural, urban and artistic works, projects and writings. The resulting contributions are therefore not centered upon a pre-defined subject, a coherent set of projects or a well-established series of works within the oeuvre, but are the outcome of adventurous wanderings throughout the oeuvre as a whole. Contributions either use a term to put the work and practice of Deleu – T.O.P. office in a wider critical, theoretical or historical perspective, or bring the work and practice of Deleu – T.O.P. office into play to reflect upon that very notion that served as a navigation device. Ranging from accounts of a broader zeitgeist to analyses of a single work or project, contributors attempt to broach the various modes of public address, aesthetic strategies, and ethical attitudes that up until today constitute and impel the work and practice of Deleu – T.O.P. office. To conclude, an interview with the present-day members of T.O.P. office offers a tentative view into the future.

This publication brings together an original collection of both *textual* and *visual* essays. Given the central role and importance of image-making, visual data and graphical strategies within the work and practice of Luc Deleu – T.O.P. office, and following our shared credence in the discursive potential of visual research, visual essays have been commissioned to figure parallel to the textual essays. Our basic premise is that both types of contributions serve as equal means of analysis and interpretation. They provide this book with a fascinatingly dual mode of speech.

Luc Deleu – T.O.P. office : Orban Space is unique in that it brings together, for the very first time, an international group of architects, artists, designers and scholars that critically explore and historically contextualize the work and practice of Luc Deleu – T.O.P. office.* In direct correspondence with the 'orban' scope of that very work and practice, we have commissioned people from different parts of the world, working in various countries and on different, even antipodal, continents. All have been commissioned exclusively for this publication to advance a critical reading of the work and practice of Luc Deleu – T.O.P. office, based on their proper field of expertise and on the specific modes and means of their practice. It has been a true privilege to work together with all the people involved in this challenging enterprise. For us, editors, it felt like nothing less than a global conspiracy between like-minded spirits.

Wouter Davidts, Guy Châtel,
and Stefaan Vervoort

* This gathering was not limited to the space of the book but also happened in reality On Wednesday 23 March 2011, the people involved in this book project convened at Stroom Den Haag, the art and architecture center that will host an exhibition on the work of Luc Deleu – T.O.P. office in the spring of 2013. This collective editorial meeting served as the central moment of a week-long Master class on Luc Deleu – T.O.P. office and brought together the majority of the international contributors, as well as Luc Deleu and his colleagues from T.O.P. office, the designers, the editors, the publisher, and the curators of Stroom Den Haag. It rarely happens indeed that, in preparation of an ambitious book such as this, the different parties involved manage to gather around the same table to discuss the future structure and content of that very publication. As editors we share the belief that this unique assembly has marked the nature and shape of this book.

Imitation:

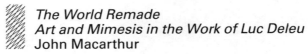

Photo
Marjolijn Dijkman

 Photo
Luc Deleu

 14
Sharjah, United Arab Emirates, 2006
South China, China, 2008

 14
Antwerp, Belgium, 1980

 15
Amsterdam, the Netherlands, 2007
Los Angeles, United States, 2008
Maastricht, the Netherlands, 2008
Porto Alegre, Brazil, 2009

 16
Helpston, United Kingdom, 2010
Maastricht, the Netherlands, 2007
Sharjah, United Arab Emirates, 2007
Weert, the Netherlands, 2005

 17
Shanghai, China, 2009
Weert, the Netherlands, 2005

 17
Antwerp, Belgium, 1979

 18
Salzburg, Austria, 2008
Tbilisi, Georgia, 2006

 18
Antwerp, Belgium, 1980

 19
London, United Kingdom, 2009
Prague, Czech Republic, 2007
Xiamen, China, 2008

 20
Andorra, Andorra, 2007
Palm Springs, United States, 2008

 21
Tokyo, Japan, 2006
Hamilton, Bermuda, 2010

 21
San Francisco, United States, 1980

 22
Musqat, United Arab Emirates, 2007
Sharjah, United Arab Emirates, 2007

 23
Almere, the Netherlands, 2008
Los Angeles, United States, 2006

 23
Antwerp, Belgium, 1977

 24
Batumi, Georgia, 2010
Shanghai, China, 2009
Tazacorte, Las Palmas, 2009

 25
Death Valley, United States, 2006
Sharjah, United Arab Emirates, 2007

 25
Temse, Belgium, 1979

 26
Almere, the Netherlands, 2008
Grand Canyon, United States, 2006

 26
Koksijde, Belgium, 1976

 27
Joshua Tree, United States, 2008
Xiamen, China, 2008

 28
Marnehuizen, the Netherlands, 2005
Rotterdam, the Netherlands, 2008

 28
Antwerp, Belgium, 1980

 29
Aberdeen, Scotland, 2007
Antwerp, Belgium, 2011

Str))m

Luc Deleu - T.O.P. office

Exhibition 20 January thru 24 March 2013

Curators Wouter Davidts & Stefaan Vervoort **Opening** Saturday
19 January 2013 at 5 pm **Stroom Den Haag** The Hague,
The Netherlands *www.stroom.nl*

The project Luc Deleu – T.O.P. office:
Orban Space presents the long-awaited
study and public presentation of the work and
practice of Antwerp-based architect and urban
planner Luc Deleu and T.O.P. office. It consists
of an exhibition at art and architecture center
Stroom Den Haag and a comprehensive
publication by Valiz, Amsterdam.
isbn 978-90-78088-60-8, www.valiz.nl

Later in 2013 the exhibition will travel
to Extra City, Antwerp, Belgium.
www.extracity.org

The project benefited from the generous support of:
Vlaamse Overheid, Flemish-Dutch House deBuren,
Municipality of The Hague, Mondriaan Fund, The
Netherlands Architecture Fund, SNS REAAL Fund,
Fonds BKVB/Mondriaan Fund, VU University
Amsterdam Faculty of Arts, Ghent University
Department of Architecture & Urban Planning,
Duvel Moortgat N.V.

Production partners of the exhibition are:
Flemish Architecture Institute (VAi), Extra City,
LLS 387 and Etablissement d'en face projects.

Hogewal 1-9 | NL-2514 HA The Hague |
t +31 70 3658985 | f +31 70 3617962 |
info@stroom.nl | www.stroom.nl

)enHaag

ULT
STRUC

John Macarthur

The World Remade
Art and Mimesis in the Work of Luc Deleu

'That art, something mimetic, is possible in the midst of rationality, and that it employs its means, is a response to the faulty irrationality of the rational world as an overadministered world.'
Theodor W. Adorno[1]

ART/Oeuvre

The work of Luc Deleu — T.O.P. office combines concerns and objects from multiple registers: electricity pylons make urban spaces, and shipping containers make monuments.[2] The media in which T.O.P. office operates are similarly diverse, combining paper architecture and conceptual art, villas and shops, installations large and small, treatises and teaching— a combination of media that crosses over the disciplinary distinction between architecture and art. Not only the genres and forms of the work are diverse, also their content. For Deleu, there is no single substance or artistic medium. The 'stuff' on which he works ranges from the material to the social, from the concrete to the conceptual. Conducted over decades, clearly this diversity is the result of more than enthusiasm and happy accident.

[1] Theodor W. Adorno, *Aesthetic Theory* (1970) (Minneapolis: University of Minnesota Press, 1997), p. 53.

2 *The Last Stone of Belgium*, Liège, Belgium, 1979.

Superficially, Deleu's oeuvre seems to fall into buildings and architectural projects on the one hand, and installations or conceptual works that are exhibited as 'art' on the other. To a certain extent employing strategies and techniques from the 'visual arts' and thus riding over disciplinary differences is what has distinguished his practice. But this is not to say that he has contested these differences or chosen to recognize them. It would be mistaken to read the diversity and multi-mediality of his work too much in terms of the crossovers between architecture and the visual arts that are in vogue at the present.[3] Deleu's fit to present concerns makes a space for a renewed reception of his work, but the work also presents significant challenges. It has lessons to offer for a time when the relation of art and architecture can seem overly self-conscious

[3] A useful and insightful survey of recent art/architecture crossover practices is: Jane Rendell, *Art and Architecture: A Place Between* (London and New York: I.B. Tauris), 2006.

4 The term is that of Rosalind Krauss, *A Voyage on the North Sea: Art in the Age of the Post–Medium Condition* (London/New York: Thames and Hudson, 2000).

and fall into ritualistic exercises of demonstrating the 'differential specificity' of disciplines and media.[4]

Recently Hal Foster has claimed that the contest of art and architecture forms a complex that structures contemporary culture: 'Not long ago, a near prerequisite for vanguard architecture was an engagement with theory; lately it has become an acquaintance with art.'[5] Architects like Zaha Hadid, Diller Scofidio + Renfro and Herzog & de Meuron, Foster claims, have developed their architectural comportment by learning from and referring to a context in the visual arts: Constructivism, installation, performance, and Minimalism. Foster implies that the concepts and the forms of art seem to have filled the void left by the death of theory—that mixture of Marxism, semiotics, psychoanalysis, phenomenology and deconstruction that used to be the privileged outside of architecture, literature, and indeed, the visual arts.[6]

5 Hal Foster, *The Art–Architecture Complex* (London: Verso, 2011), viii.

6 On this topic see Ian Hunter, 'The history of theory', *Critical Inquiry* 33, no. 1 (2006), pp. 78–112.

In this essay I will claim that Deleu unfolds the strong logic of art as a relation to the world that is anterior to the cultural organization of art into disciplines such as architecture or the visual arts, and that, in doing so, it provides an alternative to the 'complex' that Foster describes.[7] Rather than understanding architecture through differences of medium or institution, Deleu simply asserts its status as art. Hence the difference between the modes of T.O.P. office's practice recedes in relevance. Rather than disciplinarity or interdisciplinarity, Deleu's works have the ambition of a primary relation to the world. We should not understand the diversity of the T.O.P. office oeuvre as a matter of either inclusiveness or differentiation. Neither does it attack the normative definitions of the architecture discipline. It rather asserts each work's identity with the concept of art. From traffic markers to HST stations, each work institutes a complete relation of its content to the world and a logic of arrangement that belongs to that work making it art in a first principles sense, to the (momentary) exclusion of thinking art could be anything else.

7 Throughout the essay, I have drawn freely on Theodor W. Adorno, *Aesthetic Theory*, particularly the section 'Coherence and Meaning', pp. 136–163.

MIMESIS/Manure

Given the variety of materials we might claim for Deleu a grand kind of mastery, his *virtu* being such that he can take anything and give it form; but this is to put the matter the wrong way around. Rather, the contents of the works have made their own demands. The problems of social housing, the red and white code of traffic makers, the nature of precedents in architecture (e.g. Deleu's fascination with Le Corbusier's *Unité d'Habitation*), infrastructure, engineering, a house for a friend—there is something in each of these that compels his attention. Deleu's approach is consistent with the ancient doctrine of mimesis: art imitates the world, but not by whim or choice. As imitation is today seen as a demeaning act it is worth pausing to recall its subtler origins in myth. According to Pliny the Elder, the origins of art lie in tracing shadows of departing loved ones.[8] The first representations presented themselves, and art lay in the observation and recording of what nature had already offered. At stake in mimesis is this desire to copy the world in full knowledge of the inadequacy of possessing a thing through its copy. What is important is not the adequacy of the imitation, but the implication of a contract between an artist and an aspect of the world that has presented itself.

[8] Pliny the Elder, *Natural History*, Books XXXIV and XXXV. The daughter of Butades of Corinth traced the shadow of the profile of her departing lover, which had been thrown on the wall by a lamp, and her father then modeled his face in clay to console her during the young man's absence.

In 1974, Deleu made a manure heap in the garden of the I.C.C. (Internationaal Cultureel Centrum) in Antwerp.[9] An expedient wire and stake fence enclosed the manure as it aerated and decomposed into fertilizer. Despite these material facts, Deleu's *Manure Heap* is, in the larger sense, an imitation. The work does not engage in a game of categories where manure becomes art because it is presented at an art institution, even though it invariably brings to mind Robert Smithson's dialectic of site/non-site.[10] While the garden of the gallery only partially qualifies as a non-site, Deleu's work even so barely gestures at making fertilizer, lacking the scale and workability that the gardeners of Antwerp's parklands would expect. Nevertheless Deleu's imitation is sincere: the very inadequacy of his manure heap connotes the possibilities of urban agriculture and a world where individuals and social groups can feed themselves. In this respect it relates to the activism of Agnes Denes' *Wheatfield—A Confrontation* of 1982,[11] which made something of the same play on the relation of food production and the site/non-site opposition, by planting and harvesting two acres of wheat on a landfill in Battery Park, downtown Manhattan. The actuality of Denes' wheat field, recorded in the tons of wheat produced and later exhibited, is important both to the success of the artwork and to the socio-economic lesson it provides. By contrast, Deleu's *Manure Heap* remains a re-presentation, an attempt to fix and keep some shadow of a world that had presented itself to the artist.

[10] Robert Smithson, 'A Provisional Theory of Non–Sites (1968)', in *Robert Smithson: The Collected Writings*, ed. Jack Flam (Berkeley and Los Angeles: University of California Press, 1996), p. 364.

9 *Manure Heap*, Internationaal Cultureel Centrum (I.C.C.), Antwerp, Belgium, 1974.

11 Agnes Denes, *Wheatfield—A Confrontation*, New York, 1982.

CONTENT/The Unadapted City
In *Manure Heap* and throughout his work Deleu respects the distinction between material and 'content', if by the latter we mean both 'subject matter' and its meaning or significance. Just as bricks, paper, manure and steel are at one level materials

which Deleu manipulates freely and forcefully, so at another level, beyond that of the relation of the artist to the work at hand, these materials have a content that is a significance in and of themselves in relation to their possible uses and the techniques that are available to work them. In older concepts of art we think of content, material, and technique as having a proper relation that defines an art discipline. Sculpture, in past times, had as its privileged concept the human figure, and could be made in either stone or cast metal, by carving or molding. For an architect to make a timber dwelling is still to understand the house as a socio-culturally defined typology that is realized in milled wood and where the technical issues and possibilities for expression reside in tectonics or jointing. We are equally familiar with the idea that the material already constrains or even suggests the content of the work. Frames in reinforced concrete want, in a certain way, to be reproduced at scale so as to make institutional buildings. Yet beyond material and content lies technique. Architecture has been haunted by the continual search for techniques that can overturn the subservience of materials to content—the concrete house, a house that, being made differently, would change in its basic 'content' and thus be inhabited differently, was just such a project across the twentieth century.

Just as the mimetic contract assumes that content gives itself to art and demands a certain attention, so too does Deleu hope to force new contents to reveal themselves through the application of new techniques or through the uptake of novel materials. This approach is that of avant-gardism, a utopian projection of the powers of art to transform society, which has, paradoxically, become a tradition—a kind of content in its own right. Deleu follows in the tradition of the avant-garde in his use of unexpected materials, even when these are less radical than the aerating feces of the *Manure Heap*. The schemes for the HST in Brussels (1986)[12] and Antwerp (1989), for instance, propose to remake those cities using the rail infrastructure that is often hidden and generally assumed

12 *Koude Brug, 1989–93. 'Europe Central Station' (HST Brussels), 1986.*

to be an impediment to the legibility of urban form. In the case of Brussels, the elevated HST tracks cut across the city following the line of the north-south junction, and thus acting as a sign of the extensive demolition of the old city caused by the construction of the earlier rail tunnel in the 1940s. The HST designs are imaginations of an 'other' condition; not a teleological development of the world as it is, but a vision on the world as it might be, or might have been. Historical time as much as rails, pylons, and urban space, as well as the paper on which they are drawn serves as the material of these projects. Whereas the Brussels scheme may appear to lack respect for the scenography of the historic city, it in fact tells the actual history of the violent changes in Brussels' urban morphology.[13] The provocative imagination of a future in which the citizens of Brussels dramatically disturb the scenography of their city, reminds them of the actual eventfulness of the city's history and of the dramatic changes caused by a rapidly integrating Europe (if in a less graspable form). The Brussels and Antwerp HST projects are neither simple avant-gardist reveries nor nostalgic references to the style of technological modernism; rather they activate the contents of architecture history, including its avant-gardism, in a manner that is historically specific. The old contents of architectural culture become a well of fresh and apposite forms.

13 Guy Châtel, 'Luc Deleu', in *Horta and After: 25 Masters of Modern Architecture in Belgium*, ed. Mil De Kooning (Ghent: University of Ghent, 1999), pp. 282–284.

The paradox of avant-gardism is that it requires a present unpopularity in order to show that it is ahead of mainstream culture, but it also tells a story of a future where it will be popular. Avant-gardism is therefore always utopian. Not necessarily in the proposition of positive moral and social values that might be achieved in the future, but in the accusations that people of the future might bring against us for our present failings. Many of T.O.P. office's works have this classic form of the avant-garde project, the HST projects being simpler versions of what is at stake in the series of projects for *The Unadapted City*.[14] Here, linear forms of urban transport are

14 *The Unadapted City: Vipcity*, 2001–03.

strung with tumbling towers like irregular pearls. The project of *The Unadapted City* raises another question of material because its content is not only land, infrastructure and social forms, but also precedents in architectural history. *Usiebenpole*,[15] a design of 1994 for a new city quarter in Vienna and the precursor of *The Unadapted City*, takes a linear infrastructure for a suspended monorail and arrays along it housing blocks that Deleu calls 'unités', referring to Le Corbusier's *Unité d'Habitation* housing blocks for post-war France, just as the linear transport megastructure passing the historic

15 *Usiebenpole*, 1994–96.

16 *The Unadapted City: Dinky Town*, 1998.

city recalls the coastal freeway in Le Corbusier's *Obus* scheme for Algiers (1931). *Dinky Town* (1998)[16] and *Octopus* (1999)[17] show how the line of the struc-

17 *The Unadapted City: Octopus*, 1999.

ture could fatten, developing mat-like structures based on geometries of the intersection of the block and the line. In *Vipcity* (2001–03),[18] the final iteration of *The Unadapted City*, the blocks become a version of T.O.P. office's tumbling tower project for Barcelona (*Housing (&)*

18 *The Unadapted City: Vipcity*, 2001–03.

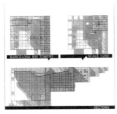

19 *Scale & Perspective: Barcelona Towers (Housing (&) the City)*, 1989.

20 Geoffrey Copcutt, Cumbernauld Town Centre, 1960.

24 Constant Nieuwenhuys, *New Babylon*, 1959–74.

25 Yona Friedman, *Spatial City*, 1958–60.

26 Banham, *Megastructure*: on Nieuwenhuys, pp. 81–82; on Friedman, pp. 60–62; also see Mark Wigley, *Constant's New Babylon: The Hyper–Architecture of Desire* (Rotterdam: 010 Publishers, 1998); and Sabine Lebesque and Helene Fentener van Vlissingen, *Yona Friedman: Structures Serving the Unpredictable* (Rotterdam: NAi Publishers, 1999).

the City, 1989).[19] These projects belong to the architectural family of megastructures, where buildings are proposed at a scale of the city, combining infrastructure and habitable volumes at once. Structures such as Cumbernauld New Town in Scotland (Geoffrey Copcutt, 1955)[20] were built and generally considered to have failed with their time passed by the 1970s.[21] However, T.O.P. office's projects are not concerned with the successes or failures of megastructures but rather with the very concept of megastructure within architectural history. The idea of a horizontal skyscraper, floating on legs above an existing city, goes back to the *Wolkenbügel* devised for Moscow by El Lissitzky[22] and developed by Mart Stam and Emil Roth (1923–25).[23] Using the scale and structural rigidity of tall buildings, the *Wolkenbügel* or 'iron cloud', could be mounted on relatively few legs and make a new ground plane that paralleled the historically developed city beneath it. Constant Nieuwenhuys' *New Babylon* (1959–74)[24] developed this idea into a structure that would spread rhizomatically, while Yona Friedman translated it into an isomorphic variant with his *Spatial City* (from 1960),[25] a universal Cartesian structure nevertheless open to contingency.[26]

The Unadapted City is an admixture made up of as much architectural precedents as it is housing, population demographics and monorails. It does not adhere to a principle of formal synthesis, but rather to an equivalence of social, historical and technical contents. Although these projects refer to and repeat motifs of earlier avant-garde utopias, this does not mean that they are not also utopian. *The Unadapted City* avoids the paradox of neo-avant-gardism in which past utopian impulses are recycled as an internal critical discourse on architecture. This was Manfredo Tafuri's prognosis of the mid-1970s, when he wrote that after a loss of faith in planning for a future, the forms and postures of the avant-garde would be repeated as an empty play of self-reference.[27] But this is not how we should understand *The Unadapted City* series. Here architectural precedents and the issues of social and technical form of cities are

21 Reyner Banham, *Megastructure: Urban Futures of the Recent Past* (London: Thames and Hudson, 1976), pp. 6–11.

22 El Lissitzky, *The Cloud Stirrup (Der Wolkenbügel)*, 1924–25.

23 Sima Ingberman, *ABC: International Constructivist Architecture, 1922–1939* (Cambridge, MIT Press, 1994), pp. 64–65.

27 Manfredo Tafuri, *Architecture and Utopia: Design and Capitalist Development* (Cambridge: MIT Press 1976), see esp. pp. 134–136; and Manfredo Tafuri, *The Sphere and the Labyrinth: Avant–Gardes and Architecture from Piranesi to the 1970s* (Cambridge: MIT Press, 1987), p. 149.

neither situated in different historical series nor the product of different conceptual registers. The Unadapted City does not turn architectural thinking of the past into ossified form, but regards it as content to be freshly deployed.

TECHNIQUE/Scale and Perspective

Deleu employs techniques from Minimalist and Post-Minimalist Art, particularly serial form and rotation, and many of the resulting works are

28 *Principle of a Lesson in Scale with Two Buildings of Identical Volume Featuring the World's Tallest Tower,* 1981.

grouped within the series *Scale & Perspective*. The horizontal skyscraper that has a history in megastructural architecture, discussed above, also has its sources in late twentieth century art. The first project of *Scale & Perspective* involves two highly simplified buildings, a tower and

29 Robert Morris, *Two Columns*, 1961/1973.

its identical twin laid flat (*Principle of a Lesson in Scale with Two Buildings of Identical Volume Featuring the World's Tallest Tower*, 1981).[28] In the documentation, these appear similar to Robert Morris' *Two Columns* (1961),[29] and only the tiny models of people and cars remind us that they represent of large buildings. T.O.P. office's *Housing (&) the City* (1989) has something of the appearance of the gridded tapered form of the sculptures of Sol LeWitt,[30] despite the project being two identical buildings, one prone and one erect, designed in detail for occupation in either orientation. Much of the contemporary interest in megastructure and massive horizontal buildings was in terms of its organizational benefits, its homology with human locomotion and mechanical transport. By contrast, Deleu writes of the

30 Sol LeWitt, *Modular Piece (Double Cube),* 1966.

apprehension of scale that is possible with the horizontal skyscraper that one can walk beside, in a language that is closer to the phenomenology underlying Minimalist practices.[31]

31 Deleu's observations about scale in durational experience are compatible with, but do not refer to, Rosalind Krauss' descriptions of the subjective affects of minimalist sculpture, and indeed, with Michael Fried's problematicization of an overtly affecting 'theatrical' art. Rosalind E. Krauss, *Passages in Modern Sculpture* (London: Thames and Hudson, 1977); Michael Fried, 'Art and Objecthood', *Art Forum V* (June 1967), pp. 12–23.

There are other uptakes of the techniques of the visual arts in Deleu's work. The container works, which I will discuss in more detail shortly, owe much to the concept of serial form, where the putative idealism of art forms is challenged by the simple modularity of industrial products, and ideas of composition are deflated by simple iteration. In the *Ready-made Housing Architecture (Luc Deleu Manifesto to the Board)* (1979–85),[32] Deleu protested against the regu-

32 *Ready–made Housing Architecture (Luc Deleu Manifesto to the Board),* 1979–85.

latory requirement for Belgians to employ architects on domestic housing projects by 'lending' his registration to owners and builders of vernacular villa housing. The documenta-

tion of the resulting buildings recalls Dan Graham's *Homes for America* (1965),[33] and his interest in the serial form of everyday architecture.

33 Dan Graham, *Homes for America*, 1966–67.

Deleu's use of techniques is a matter of neither innocent borrowing nor of explicit appropriation. In their availability he puts them to use, without any overlaid meta-discourse on the relation of the respective art disciplines. To a certain extent, the *oeuvre* of Luc Deleu — T.O.P. office could provide an interesting case to gain a higher level understanding of the 'differential specificity' of art media.[34] However, arguments about the origins of techniques and the property that different disciplines might have in them are neither implicit nor explicit in Deleu's works.

34 Rosalind E. Krauss, *A Voyage on the North Sea: Art in the Age of the Post-Medium Condition* (London/New York: Thames & Hudson, 2000).

The techniques of rotation and seriality involved in the *Scale & Perspective* projects, are objective operations that have their significance exhausted in the content of the works, as we see in the pylons project for Sint-Pietersplein in Ghent (*Scale and Perspective with Two Electricity Pylons*, 1986).[35]

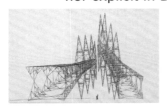

35 *Scale & Perspective with Two Electricity Pylons*, 1983–86.

For this project Deleu laid down two electricity pylons in this city square. Photographed against both St Peter's Church and the parked cars that typically populated the square, the pylons are astonishing in their size. At an immediate level, the pylons are affecting by being laid down, as are the floor works of Minimalist art. Rotation defamiliarizes the pylons, but also makes them less anthropomorphic. What might be understood as their 'arms' and 'legs' become lost in the novel perspective. The steel struts and beams, which, when upright, delineate a form, become an open web that might extend in any direction. However, the meaning of the works goes beyond the phenomenal apprehension of them.

The pylons as structures measure and speak to a larger landscape and the question of changing urban forms. Not only are they familiar objects of the extra-urban landscape, they serve the infrastructure of the national electricity grids and the continent-wide electricity market, which shares load and capacity across Europe. Putting them in Sint-Pietersplein, measures an old urban structure against contemporary Ghent, which is part of a transnational conurbation. What is more, the pylons fit the square; if they were stood upright, they would express a simple contrast of city and extra-urban territory. But laid down as they are, they make a surprising historical connection.

Sint-Pietersplein seems an overly large and unstructured place compared to the other squares of Ghent. It used to be a military parade ground, which explains the 'uncivil' scale of the greater territory.

FORM/Containers
If form were merely the work that an individual did in forming, art works would be mute facts like natural forms. We would directly perceive Deleu's balanced containers as volumes and quantities of steel in space, in their unlikely stasis, and admire them as we would a handsome tree, while being indifferent to Deleu having made them, to the history of the motif of the arch, and so on. This is, in a simple sense, the proposition of aesthetics: the prized immediacy of perceiving and the pleasure of doing so; a contract in which the category of form would be irrelevant. No doubt there is such simple sensual pleasure to be had in experiencing Deleu's container works, but they have a deeper meaning and significance in that they have a recognizable form as *arches*. In the *Manure Heap* and *Scale and Perspective with Two Electricity Pylons*) discussed earlier, the significance of the work opens out of experience through reflection and analysis. In the different iterations of *The Unadapted City* and in the actual built works, the significance (however complex it might be) unfolds with certain self-evidence from the fact that these are ostensibly 'projects' that address explicit problems and situations. The container works require us to recognize their form as arches, and also occasionally, as columns. These works assume, and rightly, that we come to them already knowing the form of the arch and something of its historical significance. Our apprehension of the works will be a matter of what Deleu has done with these known forms. When we say 'form', this greater contract is at stake. Some thing is immediately perceivable, and we recognize it, not merely as a perceptual unity, but as something in which others will recognize the same form. Form is the assumption that the relation of the aesthetic qualities of a work to an individual, who perceives it, necessarily entails the broader inter-subjective implication of art relating to society, and to a society self-aware of its changing ideas of form. What is so eloquent in Deleu's container works is his exploration of both the meaning of the arch in western art history, and the labor of manipulating the containers. It is perhaps trite to say that art is a social labor aimed at creating objects of collective value, but Deleu puts this original social contract of art back into the context of the work and makes it meaningful again.

Deleu's use of containers relates to his wider interest in the role of ratio. From the early treatises measuring the world and urbanization in terms of passenger liners (the entire population of Belgium could live on 5,000 such ships, according to the *Orban Planning Manifesto*) to the complex data-scapes of *Orban Space*, Deleu has been concerned with quantities and the intelligibility of measures. The modularity of the shipping container provides a measure that is close to

36 *Big Triumphal Arch*, Neuchâtel, Switzerland, 1983.

universal. The containers are everywhere apparent in the world, a world that it is their role to unify. While globalization might be measured in the arbitrary units of capital flows, its extent is immediately, almost naturally, apparent in the simple observation of what can fit in a shipping container. Shipping containers are anthropomorphic in their modularity and also in their mobility, their relation to a world of labor, and their purposiveness.[36] The documentation of the container works being assembled by workers with cranes reminds us that they have their own gait, that they are lifted and swung before being shipped, trained, and trucked. They have one scale of spatial extension when moved by winches, cables, and hydraulic jacks, and another on the flat bed of a railway car or the deck of a ship.[37]

37 *Big Triumphal Arch*, Neuchâtel, Switzerland, 1983.

It is this 'orban' scale of the world of containers that is opened for our observation when Deleu stacks them in a manner that lacks purpose but has a recognizable form. In order for the containers to be lifted, stacked, multiply loaded, and constrained against the live forces of a ship at sea, each individual container needs to be vastly stronger than is required to sit on the ground. Thus shipping containers have a rationality derived from their purpose that also can be unfolded in various structural forms that are strictly useless. Deleu recognizes and exploits this structural redundancy when bolting the containers together so they span or cantilever and balance on points and edges: he strips away their purpose, while maintaining their 'purposiveness'.[38] While some of the works such as *MACBA Piece* (1997)[39] have relatively arbitrary geometric forms, and one, *Orbino* (1988–2009),[40] is in fact a building, most of the container works take the form of traditional urban monuments, columns, and most frequently arches.

38 Immanuel Kant, *Kant's Critique of Aesthetic Judgement*, trans. James Creed Meredith, Oxford: Clarendon Press, 1911. See: 'On Purposiveness in General' (§10).

39 *MACBA Piece*, Barcelona, Spain, 1997.

To make a place-specific monument of shipping containers paradoxically celebrates their mobility and ubiquity, but it also refers to the prime architectural forms of the lintel and the arch that have been the basis of architectural thought on movement. It is no accident that the

40 *ORBINO*, Nauerna, Amsterdam, the Netherlands, 2002.

41 *Big Triumphal Arch*, Neuchâtel, 2003.

42 *Porte Ø*, FIAC art fair, Grand Palais, Paris, France, 1991.

documentation of *Big Triumphal Arch* (1983) at Neuchâtel[41] and the *Porte Ø* (1991) at the Grand Palais in Paris,[42] show Deleu's arches against Baroque revival façades. The broken pediment and pedimental arch are symbols of a wider discourse on architectural movement that, from the works of Michelangelo and Vignola, opened out onto the Baroque of the seventeenth century. The Renaissance language of architecture as formalized by Alberti and Bramante reconciled the two spanning techniques of the ancient world, the Greek's colonnade with a flat lintel and the arch and vault of the Romans. But Italian architects of the following centuries and in particular Bernini, Borromini and Da Cortona, found these forms dry, strict and problematically pagan in their symbolism. In the late nineteenth century Heinrich Wölfflin described Baroque architecture as a search for 'massiness' and movement, where the brute materiality of unadorned building would transmute into increasing pictorial overlays of the architectural orders and figurative ornament.[43] Not only the fashion for Neo-Baroque that swept Europe in the last decades of the Nineteenth Century, but also modern concepts of architectural space arose from the German *Kunstwissenschaft* discourse of this period. Wölfflin's student, Sigfried Giedion, popularized these ideas by identifying his teacher's aesthetic psychology of movement with industrialization and the increasing speed and extent of mechanized transport.[44]

43 Heinrich Wölfflin, *Renaissance and Baroque*, trans. Kathrin Simon (Ithaca NY: Cornell University Press, 1966).

44 Sigfried Giedion, *Space, Time and Architecture: The Growth of a New Tradition* (Cambridge: Harvard University Press, 1941); and Sigfried Giedion, *Mechanization Takes Command: A Contribution to Anonymous History* (New York: Oxford University Press, 1948).

Deleu's container works may not immediately communicate this cultural content but it is fundamentally at stake and demands interpretation. It can be unfolded from a simple recognition of their form as arches and the ur-form of building in western architecture. Placed against the grand Baroque revival façades the container arches possess all the brute materiality of the Baroque formal contract without the balancing exuberant imagistic play of moving layers. The acuteness of Deleu's work lies in the missing term, the sense of movement which is not present perceptually, but which is nevertheless present in the 'content' or significance of the shipping container. Just as the purposeless logicality of Deleu's stacking hints at the global nature of containerization, the palpable 'massiness' of the containers points to another kind of movement—a common language of forms having been coded into the built environment over centuries and turned familiar.

Deleu's Content and Content today

There is, at present, a culture-wide anxiety about 'content', a term that has changed its popular meaning because of the Internet. It is common to observe that the success of an individual's blog or a newspaper's business is a matter of content management, of filling the gaping maw of a medium that can hold any amount of content and distribute it infinitely, but with no apparent recognition of the content in the older sense of meaning, rarity, truth or significance. This situation has its corollaries in art and architecture, where the dialectic between form and content is going through another iteration. Form becomes a matter of acquiring content, where the flows, perturbations and novelties of the everything-that-is-out-there are data-mined for novel formal resources. T.O.P. office can remind us of some older artistic values. Deleu's work maintains a distinction of artistic materials from the greater issue of content. Contents, whether manure and the responsibility of feeding ourselves in a shrinking world, or a cultural motif like the arch, are matters of significance, not merely capacities and resistances to the artist's will to form.

45 *Journey Around the World in 80 Days (Madrid–Weber–Madrid),* 1992–93.

Deleu moves containers as a sculptor models clay: as a material to be manipulated according to the internal logic of the artwork. But the relation of triumphal arches built of containers to our shared culture of art and architecture, respects both the concept of the arch and the container as having a content that is properly theirs, transcending what Deleu has done with them. Like all art worthy of the name, Deleu's practice is in the first instance mimetic. It is a genuine impulse to draw closer to the stuff of the world, and indeed the world itself, and to recognize our place in it through imitation.[45] Form is not a power in excess of a given content; it is the struggle to hold the mimetic impulse in a thing; to overcome, for a moment, the world's indifference to us.

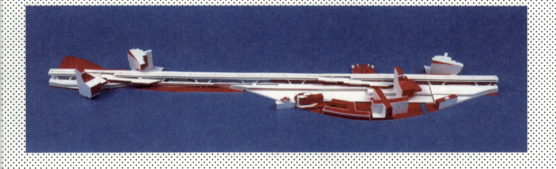

Madrid–Madrid en 80 jours par son antipode, 40°25S 176°17E (Weber), 1993

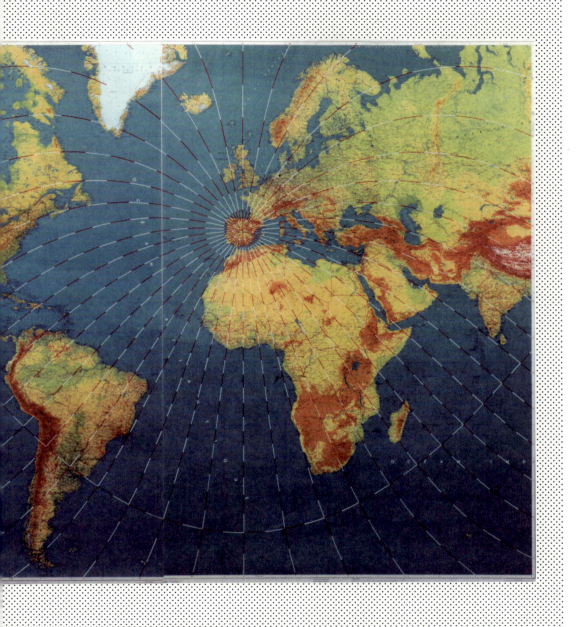

Luc Deleu – T.O.P. office

50

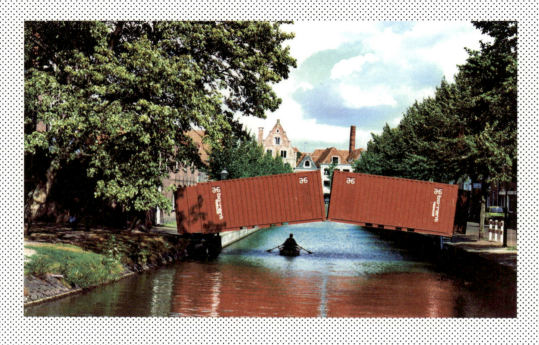

Container Bridge over the Venidse, Hoorn, the Netherlands, 1990

V

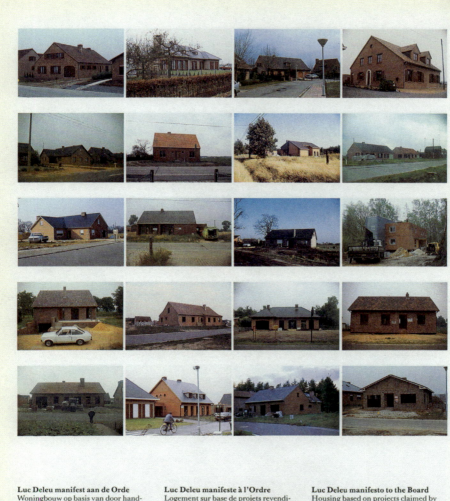

Luc Deleu manifest aan de Orde
Woningbouw op basis van door hand-
tekening toegeëigende ontwerpen,
voorbeelden, 1979-85
(foto's T.O.P. office)

Luc Deleu manifeste à l'Ordre
Logement sur base de projets revendi-
qués par signature, examples, 1979-85
(photos T.O.P. office)

Luc Deleu manifesto to the Board
Housing based on projects claimed by
signature, examples, 1979-85
(photos T.O.P. office)

Luc Deleu – T.O.P. office

Obelisk, Antwerp, Belgium, 1987

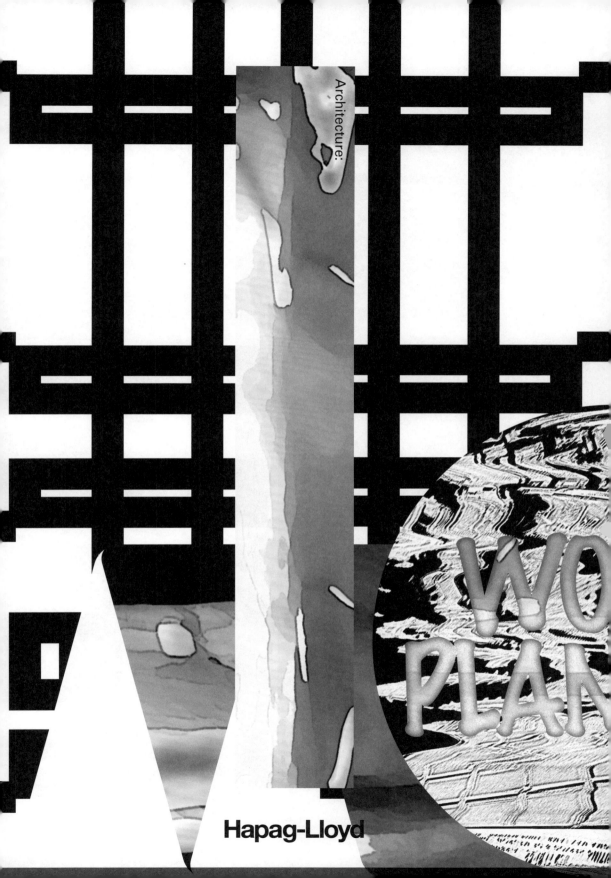

Architecture:

WO
PLAN

Hapag-Lloyd

Architecture:

Entrance to the Office of Luc Deleu – T.O.P. office
Koenraad Dedobbeleer & Kris Kimpe

*Being an Architect, Producing Theory,
Making Architecture*
Maarten Delbeke

Works VII–XIII
Luc Deleu – T.O.P. office

Maarten Delbeke

Being an Architect, Producing Theory, Making Architecture

'S'il est assez aisé de définir, à l'échelle universelle, l'architecture, c'est l'architecte dont l'existence ne se laisse pas aisément caractériser.'
Pierre Francastel[1]

Luc Deleu is an architect: he went to architecture school, has designed and constructed buildings and runs an office. His writings, the architecture theory course he taught for 20-odd years at the St-Lucas School of Architecture, his installations and buildings all address the question of what architecture is and how it relates to the profession of the architect and the act of building. His work is underpinned by a view of architecture as an art form performed by the architect, much according to the principles that have been laid down by Vitruvius, were developed in the Renaissance and found their apogee in Modernism. At the same time, Deleu recognizes that architecture has been affected fundamentally by the conditions imposed by the architect's contemporary working environment: on a global scale and as much in other media as in brick and concrete. The disciplinary basis of architecture remains intact but its practice has been transformed since the advent of modernity. This conclusion is evident in the entire oeuvre of Luc Deleu — T.O.P. office, including the architecture projects. As resolute as they are fragile, simultaneously self-confident explorations of architectural principles and minute attempts at transforming their own small universe, these projects set the stage for Deleu's research into what could be termed, without any hint of irony, the substance of architecture.

1 Pierre Francastel, *Les architectes célèbres* (Paris: L.Mazenod, 1958), Introduction.

2 'Luc Deleu says farewell to architecture' (invitation card), Vacuum voor nieuwe dimensies, 1970.
The gallery was housed on the ground floor of the house Les Nenuphars that the families of Luc Deleu and the artist Filip Francis shared. This space is now used as the offices of T.O.P. office.

A Farewell to What?

Luc Deleu's first statement as an architect was the exhibition 'Luc Deleu says farewell to architecture' of 1970 in the gallery Vacuum voor nieuwe dimensies in Antwerp.[2] He showed projects from his student days at the St-Lucas School of Architecture in Brussels together with brutally crossed-out pictures of Archigram's *Plug-in City*, Moshe

3 *Crossed-out Collage,* 1970.

Safdie's *Habitat* and Le Corbusier's *Unité d'Habitation.*[3] In this exhibition Deleu seemed to turn his back on architecture. With an almost childish gesture he killed his fathers while bestowing the status of fully-fledged exhibits to such objects as architecture models, suggesting that their critical and artistic potential far outstripped their original status as residues of the architectural design process.

Upon closer inspection, however, Deleu's 'Farewell to architecture' was less a turning away from architecture per se than a criticism of architectural education and the fictions it entertains in order to shape future architects. The exhibition called attention to the objects of education: models, both in the sense of scale models and examples. If scale models are by-products in 'real' architectural practice, which aspires to building, they are the very substance of students' work. And Deleu could consider Archigram, Safdie and Le Corbusier as his examples only because his education had told him so. Manipulating these objects in the exhibition opened up a margin between the practices and institutions that shape the profession and the possibilities inherent to the discipline. The objects are presented as a primary matter ready for further exploration, not mere instruments to assume the cloak of a profession recognized and legitimized by society. The education of architects is identified as a process where these possibilities are at once made available to the student and subjected to the demands of the profession. The real question the exhibition posed was: what does being an architect really mean?

This question became explicit in Deleu's first show in an art gallery, at the Spectrum Gallery in Antwerp in 1978. It presented his 'Proposal for the abolishment of the law protecting the title and profession of the architect' in the form of black graffiti on a gallery wall partly covered with four sets of framed photos, together with a construction of Lego blocks (one of a series of such constructions executed between 1977 and 1983) and a carefully assembled bird's nest. The admonition to lift the protection of the architectural profession in Belgium belongs to a larger series of 'proposals'. Since the early 1970s, Deleu had been circulating 'proposals and advices' that typically consisted of straightforward, one-shot interventions jotted down or sketched on a T.O.P. office file sheet and abundantly rubberstamped for authentication and approval.[4] They investigated the ecology of modern life by offering solutions for the contemporary city that subverted the deeply engrained social and legal conventions regulating our relation with urban space. In so

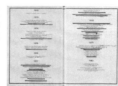

4 Spread from exhibition catalogue *Vrije Ruimte — Espace Libre — Open Space* (Luc Deleu, Antwerp: Internationaal Cultureel Centrum (I.C.C.)/Ministerie van Nationale Opvoeding en Nederlandse Cultuur) with *Proposals* (1972–80), 1980. Annotated version, reproduced in Luc Deleu, *Luc Deleu: Postfuturismus?* (Antwerp: DeSingel, 1987).

doing, the proposals extended the architect's field of operation to every occasion where mass society represents itself, be it in public space, monuments, infrastructure or through communal practices, a preoccupation that is a central theme in his architecture theory course and would feed straight

into the infrastructural projects developed from the 1980s onwards, such as the proposal to install windmills on top of power pylons (*Worldwide Windmill Network*, 1981) or a project to suspend the new high speed train line over the Brussels' city center ('*Europe Central Station*', *1986–89*).[5]

5 *Proposal for a Worldwide Windmill Network*, 1981.

Compared to these propositions, the *Proposal for the abolishment* was more particular in form and kind. It targeted the Belgian law of 20 February 1939 stipulating that only those trained at a recognized institution of architectural education—i.e. underwent the process that Deleu had dissected in his first exhibition—could be granted access to the profession. Since architects are responsible for all building activity in Belgium, this law excluded actors without architectural education from shaping the built environment. The

6 See e.g. Luc Deleu, 'Alles ist Architektur', in: *Das letze Haus im Steir* (Graz: Haus der Architektur, 1995), pp. 36-48.

obvious inference, which Deleu has relished to draw, is that every building in Belgium is at least nominally designed by architects and, therefore, architecture. Architects authored the present, often deplorable state of the built environment.[6] At the same time, granting the architect the monopoly over the design of buildings allowed the Belgian state to devolve its responsibility for the built environment to a professional class that spends most of its time working on small, individual commissions. This pulverization of responsibility was only exacerbated by the fact that the Order of Architects, the corporation representing all qualified architects, was more interested in policing the protection of the profession than developing and promoting substantive views on architecture and urban planning.[7]

7 Geert Bekaert, 'Wie over architectuur wil spreken sta op en zwijge. Bedenkingen van een buitenstaander— buitenstaanders hebben gemakkelijk spreken', in: *Verzamelde opstellen 4: De kromme weg 1981–1985* (Vlees & Beton 75) (Ghent: WZW Productions & Productions, 2008), pp. 305-331 deals with exactly this problem. It had been commissioned in 1981 for publication in *A+*, the architecture journal sponsored by the Order, and was refused because of its critical content.

Deleu's criticism of the current state of the profession was very much of its time. In an essay tracing the debates amongst architects in Belgium around 1970, Geert Bekaert quotes an assessment of the profession by architect Peter Callebout (1916–1970), a fine exponent of the acculturated modernism practiced in Belgium since the 1950s, which smolders with spite and self-hate. In Callebout's view architects are blind for the real needs of their clients and society at large because of their artistic pretentions and navel-gazing. Callebout calls himself and his fellow architects cheaters, liars and thieves, concluding that 'Architecture [with capital A] should disappear

8 Geert Bekaert, 'Het einde van de architectuur', in: Verzamelde opstellen 5: Spoorloos 1986–1990, (*Vlees & Beton* 77) (Ghent: WZW Productions & Productions, 2008), pp. 558-559. The full quote runs as follows: 'In my view Architecture should disappear before one could once again speak of architecture. (...) We can in fact, morally speaking, regard the current situation as an enormous cheating of clients, as organized villainy, since we consciously deliver inferior goods. (...) We still have much to learn if we are to serve our clients properly. At present we are in fact ... bunglers. We should be constructors first, not architects producing only self-portraits.' 'Mijns inziens moet "Architectuur" verdwijnen eer er weer van architectuur sprake kan zijn. (...) We kunnen eigenlijk de huidige situatie beschouwen als een ontzaglijk bedrog van de cliënten, moreel beschouwd, een georganiseerde smeerlapperij, vermits we bewust slechte waar leveren. (...) We moeten nog allerlei leren om goed te dienen, nu zijn we eigenlijk ... knoeiers. We moeten eerst constructeurs worden en geen architecten die slechts zelfportretten bouwen.'

11 Maarten Delbeke, 'Roadside Museums. The "Little Gardens of Eden"', in: Harald Szeemann, Bart De Baere and Maarten Delbeke, *Johan van Geluwe (The Museum of Museums)* (Ghent: Ludion, 2004), pp. 23-24. Van Geluwe himself has declared Deleu and T.O.P. office an influence, see Annie Gentils, 'Johan Van Geluwe: ART-chitect', in: *Johan Van Geluwe: The Museum of Museums* (Antwerpen: ICC, 1981), p. 3.

12 See Luc Deleu, *Theorie van de Architectuur* (Hogeschool voor wetenschap voor wetenschap en kunst, Departement Architectuur Sint-Lucas Brussel-Gent, 2000–2001), pp. 104-106. For a very similar statement, published around the same time, see Dick Higgins and Wolf Vostell, Pop Architektur: Concept Art (Düsseldorf: Droste, 1969).

before one could once again speak of architecture.'[8] Architects should unlearn architecture and re-educate themselves from the bottom up. A similar discontent pervades the book *Bouwen in België 1945–1970* (1971) by Bekaert and Francis Strauven, a landmark state-of-the-question about Belgian architecture after the Second World War.[9] The authors' deliberate choice for 'bouwen' or 'building' in the title rather than 'architecture' represents their view that architecture is not just a matter for architects but for a multitude of actors with equal responsibility and capabilities; buildings only assume their full potential when architecture enters into a meaningful dialogue with these actors. Finally, Deleu's proposals resonate with the early work of Johan Van Geluwe, another trained architect whose examination of the Belgian context triggered a sustained critique of mainly artistic institutions. More in particular, in the 1970s

9 Geert Bekaert and Francis Strauven, *Bouwen in België 1945–1979* (Brussel: Nationale Federatie van het Bouwbedrijf, 1971).

Van Geluwe and his architecture students at St-Lucas made a series of photographs of private roadside gardens where the individual imagination was let loose.[10] Dubbed the *Little gardens of Eden*, to Van Geluwe they represented the last vestiges of individual architectural expression in an era when

10 Johan van Geluwe, *Gardens of Eden*, 1981.

'building is in danger of becoming an impersonal matter.' This 'primitive architecture,' says Van Geluwe, stems from pure spontaneity and is inspired only by a desire to be surrounded by beauty; as such, it acquires a far greater legitimacy than 'authored' architecture.[11]

Deleu's 'Proposal' certainly has some affinity with this strain of discourse but it is directed elsewhere. If Hans Hollein's statement that 'Alles ist Architektur', raucously explored in the January 1968 issue of the journal *Bau*, was understood by Van Geluwe as in incitement to explore 'architecture without architects', to Deleu it signified that the discipline of architecture is not confined to the media, regimes and institutions associated with the profession of the architect and building practice.[12] Architects, Deleu conveyed, are impeded not so much by the nature of their discipline but by the social and institutional embedding of its practice in contemporary—Belgian—society. The 'Proposal' would rectify this situation not only by giving non-experts the opportunity to act upon the built environment but also by liberating architects from their subservience to unwilling, mostly individual clients that prevented them from addressing the real issues of the day and age. Architecture is not the problem; the modalities of being an architect are. Removing architecture from its institutional straightjacket would reinstate—rather than annihilate—the architect as its primary agent.

A Recovery of Origins

This position distinguishes Deleu's criticism of Belgian architecture from for instance Callebout's loathing of contemporary practice or Van Geluwe's fascination with architecture without architects. The eminently local concerns that underpin their advocacy of an original, pure form of building tinge it with the provincialism that has characterized the discourse on Belgian architecture ever since the modernist Renaat Braem declared Belgium the ugliest country in the world. This criticism tends to define the ambitions and agenda of contemporary architecture in terms of a 'typical' or 'particular' Belgian situation. Deleu, to the contrary, aims to liberate the art of architecture from irrelevant constrictions in order to refocus its purpose and address its essential, universal principles; the 'Belgian condition' is not the target of his criticism but its catalyst.

13 'Voorstel tot afschaffing van de wet van 20 februari 1939', Spectrum Gallery, Antwerp, Belgium, 1978.

The presentation of the 'Proposal' at the Spectrum Gallery illustrates this: at first, scrawling it on the gallery wall seems an act of vandalism addressed against architecture.[13] But because it is applied to a wall, and neatly framed at that, the sprayed text also draws attention to the fact that the gallery, too, is (part of) a building. The flat picture frames hung over the graffiti emphasize the materiality and texture of the wall. The photos in the picture frames in turn show architectural elements: building blocks, walls, columns, found in the streets and ready to receive the imprint of whichever message an interested party may want to express, including the proposal itself. Combined with the content of the proposal, the installation thus emphasized the ineluctable presence of the architectural artifact, an object that has been designed, built and used regardless of institutionalized agency or authorship. Deleu's criticism of the profession shapes up to affirm the being of architecture. Such a thing as architecture exists; the real question is how to approach it.

This question is the topic of the exhibition as a whole. The 'Proposal' combined with the Lego construction and the bird's nest stages the tension between architecture as a practice bound to contingencies and local circumstances and as an art form based on essential laws, elementary components and higher principles. They can in fact be read as an almost literal return to Vitruvius' original definition of architecture in his treatise De architectura. In the treatise's first book Vitruvius defined architecture in terms of the knowledge it involves; by portraying its ideal practitioner; through the definition of design principles; by describing its scope of action; and finally according to the three qualities to which all architecture should aspire, *firmitas, utilitas* and *venustas*.[14] These descriptors of architecture, which will be examined in some more detail in what follows, are rooted in a myth of origin given in the second book.

14 Vitruvius, *Ten Books on Architecture*, ed. and trans. Ingrid Rowland and Thomas Noble Howe (Cambridge: Cambridge University Press, 1999), 1.1-3.

Be it intentional or unintentional, the exhibits cover Vitruvius' constituting elements of architecture—the definitions and the myth. However, far from being an illustration of a venerable theoretical position they treat the foundational definition of architecture both as an ideal and a problem. The 'Proposal' is a case in point, as it addresses the intellectual status of the architect discussed in Vitruvius' first book. There, from the list of competences that one should master to practice architecture emerges a picture of the architect as a particular *persona*, 'who [is] educated from an early age in the various types of study [and therefore] recognize[s] the same salient points in all types of writing, and the relationship of all the branches of knowledge, and because of this (...) come[s] to know all matter of subjects with a greater ease.'[15] By attacking the enshrinement of 'professionalism' in a profession, the 'Proposal' implicitly translates this ability to find the generic in specialized knowledge into an incitement to amateurism, to adopt Stefaan Vervoort's characterization of Deleu's practice.[16] Being an architect is not a matter of institutionalized schooling or corporate membership but of an attitude towards knowledge and a stance in the world.

15 Vitruvius, *Ten Books on Architecture*, 1.1.12, p. 23b.

16 Stefaan Vervoort, *From architecture to sculpture (and back again). Three essays on the sculptural phenomenon in the work and practice of Luc Deleu — T.O.P. office* (MA thesis, VU Amsterdam, 2011) p. 123.

17 *Bird's Nest*, 1978.

The bird's nest recalls the origin of architecture.[17] According to Vitruvius a first step towards architecture was taken when primitive society took the constructions of animals as models for its first habitations. At this stage man relied on *fabrica*, knowledge born from experience and making.[18] In a second step specialization came about and the arts emerged. Man became truly civilized and 'progressed from haphazard and uncertain opinions to the stable principles of symmetry.'[19] Symmetry is a key notion with Vitruvius. It signifies proportion based on the application of a single measuring unit and involves abstract reasoning and drawing. The human body is the paradigm of symmetry, visualized in the famous Vitruvian man whose body is circumscribed by the square and the circle.[20] The myth of origin suggests that symmetry

18 Vitruvius, *Ten Books on Architecture*, 1.1.1, p. 21b.

19 Vitruvius, *Ten Books on Architecture*, 2.1, pp. 34-35, with the citation at 2.1.6, p. 35a.

20 Vitruvius, *Ten Books on Architecture*, 1.2.4, 25a; 3.1.1-3, 47.

distinguishes architecture from mere construction. Copying a birds' nest involves a degree of dexterity and experiential insight but no knowledge of principles that would lead the application of units of measure and proportion, ratiocinatio in Vitruvius' terms. Not until man discovered the principle of symmetry was there question of architecture. Since such a discovery could only come about in a complex and developed society, good architecture expresses the perfected state of society and helps to sustain it. With this in mind Deleu's bird's nest is a kind of reverse engineering: an architect reconstructing the primitive origins of his own art or rather returning to the moment right before his art was born, by doing away with the formal principle whose establishment defined that very art. The nest is a form of building before architecture, without symmetry and therefore without design. The nest could only exist as an artefact whose form was the product of a process of making, not of plans and sections.

At the same time, principles of measure and composition—of symmetry—were embodied in the Lego construction.[21] Lego blocks conjure up the promise of endless and universal applicability because of their unity of measure. These blocks allowed Deleu to engage with issues of form: the overall shape of the Lego construction was symmetrical in plan (in the contemporary sense of the word) but color had been applied according to a divergent pattern. If the result referenced modernist and minimal

21 *Lego Construction,* 1979.

painting, not in the least because of the modernist slant in the Lego color scheme of the 1970s, it was also—to paraphrase Deleu himself—proof that making architecture is not bound up with making buildings. Architecture exists regardless of the imperatives of practice and its real principles are easily detached from building to find expression in any system that is apposite to their application, such as Lego blocks.

The *Bird's Nest* and the *Lego Constructions* express the original elements of architecture but also their segregation. According to Vitruvius, architecture became established when primitive construction and design principles were combined; the exhibits show them separate, as unwound DNA strains. Moreover, they are miniatures. If the nest represents the origin of architecture it does so at a reduced scale. The same is true for the Lego construction: the size as well as the matter of the blocks inevitably cast the objects they produce as models, regardless of their size or shape, an effect enhanced by the scattering of color across the surface. In sum, like the student work in 'A Farewell to Architecture' the exhibits assume the double sense of the word 'model': ideals as well as reductions. The idealized and reduced object is architecture itself; the exhibits are scale models of what the discipline is about. With these objects Deleu casts himself as a producer of theory. After all, the carefully assembled objects and handwritten text on the wall carry the indelible imprint of their maker. The production of theory takes place in an art institution in a laboratory setting. The research question here is not whether the theory generates good and culturally valid buildings—whether it is operative—but rather which conditions allow it to exist. As in all experiments, the exhibition eliminates some parameters while transmogrifying others. The most obvious transformation concerns the human body: it isn't positioned as the origin and organizing principle of measure, as in Vitruvius, but mobilized to determine the viewer's relation to the exhibits, defining them as models in the first place.

It is this shift—moving the body outside of architecture, as performed within the space of the gallery—that enables Deleu to determine architecture's presence in the world. After all, it not only affects notions like scale and measure but also position and place. In the Vitruvian canon the erect body marks the universal unity of measure as well as the position from which to fathom the universe. Man was predisposed to civilize himself because 'they walked, not prone, but upright, [and] therefore could look upon the magnificence of the universe and the stars.'[22] According to Deleu the view of the universe is no longer afforded by inhabiting an upright body but by watching planet Earth from a distance, an experience available only to few but made accessible by means of many different media.

22 Vitruvius, *Ten Books on Architecture*, 2.1.2, p. 34a.

This raises the question of architecture's place in the world. If in a Vitruvian scheme buildings are the embodiment of man's central position in the universe, the telescopic worldview constructed in the gallery installation and facilitated by space travel seems to dissolve any remaining reference points in favor of an indistinct global sphere. Deleu's competition entry for an architecture museum in Ghent (1983) appears to make this point: it consisted of a collage of the globe on a black background with the inscription *The Museum of Architecture*.[23] The proposal thus declared any form of building across the globe as worthy of collection and display; there is no center or authority that could impose a limit or taxonomy onto this global patrimony. At the same time it emphasized that architecture cannot be collected in any other form than its contingent and ephemeral 'reality'. Buildings are irreducible; only the telescopic view—from so far away as to render actual buildings invisible—is able to transform them into exhibits. What the *Museum* suggests, in other words, is that while all buildings participate in architecture's global field of action, and this field of action is a legitimate object of study in its own right, buildings only acquire their true value as specimens distinguished by dint of their particular articulation in a singular place and time.

23 It is worth noting that Johan van Geluwe received an honorable mention in the competition with a strikingly similar proposal to consider the world as the true museum of architecture, the *World Architecture Museum*. Contrary to Deleu, van Geluwe did propose to erect a building on the designated site.

The Place of Architecture

Deleu's engagement with infrastructure exemplifies this reciprocity between architecture's global field of action and the particularity of the building. The aircraft carriers of the *Mobile Medium University* (1972/1989) but also the high tension pylons, drilling rigs and freight containers derive from a globalized economy.[24] As commodities extracted from the global economy—much like the raw materials of minimalist sculpture—the containers stacked and assembled into obelisks and triumphal arches are monuments to a virtual empire without ruler or nation. But the monuments also harness the sheer power of number and scale-less nature of this economy into an archetypal form, suggesting the local presence of a global yet formless order. As imperceptible as this order is, in each particular locus its presence will take on a singular shape, a mechanism perhaps made most explicit in one of the first of the Triumphal Arch projects, the two small container constructions crowning an unfinished highway exit in Basel, Switzerland (*Two Small Triumphal Arches*, 1981).[25] Even in this setting the triumphal arches assume an ineluctable 'thereness' that seems to precede any attempt at putting them into discourse, as Guy Châtel has observed.[26] These monuments as well as the exercises in scale and perspective that employ similar primary matter testify to the fact that place retains its singularity both as the subject of perception and the marker of a universal order, despite the global dimension of architecture—in terms of its intended reach, its worldwide dissemination in different media and its potential dissolution into mobile infrastructure and networks.

25 *Two Small Triumphal Arches,* 1983.

24 See, for instance, Marc Mer and Thomas Feuerstein, 'Translocation. Interview with Luc Deleu',' typescript dated summer 1993.

26 Guy Châtel, 'Luc Deleu', in: Mil De Kooning (ed.), *Horta and After. 25 Masters of Modern Architecture in Belgium* (Ghent: Universiteit Gent, 1999), pp. 277-288 (278).

Projecting visual order into a world teetering on the edge of chaos and escaping perceptibility reintroduces the measure and scale that Deleu evacuated from the architectural object in the setting of the Spectrum Gallery and other exhibitions such as 'Perspective and Scale' of 1981 at the Zeno X gallery, which also consisted of scale models.[27] Deleu's outdoor experiments investigate these notions less by means of different media such as models and drawings than by *performing* them for the viewing subject in a particular setting (in his architecture theory course, Deleu argues that the fundamental shift operated by modernist architecture but initiated in painting and photography is the abolishment of perspectival space in favor of a layered space that can only be understood by means of a sequential exploration). As such these experiments inevitably

27 'perspective and scale' (exhibition poster), Zeno X Gallery, Antwerp, Belgium, 1981.

28 *Promenade Pier*, 1985; *Tent for Napoleon (Waterloo)*, 1986. *Scale & Perspective with Two Electricity Pylons*, Ghent, Belgium, 1986.

invoke a symbolical dimension. The container constructions as well as the experiment in scale and perspective with the two electricity pylons on Sint-Pietersplein in Ghent, or the proposal to recycle an oil rig on the beach of Flushing play on human perception to explore the tension not only between quantity, measure and proportion but also the viewer's expectations about what a singular place should mean and represent.[28]

The question of how the *implementation* of measure and scale affects a symbolical order is at stake in the *Tent for Napoleon* designed for Waterloo in Belgium in 1986 and built on a smaller scale in La-Roche-sur-Yon in France in 1989. In Waterloo the tent was envisioned as an ephemeral theater at the foot of the hill commemorating Napoleon's historical defeat where Abel Gance's silent movie *Napoleon* would have been shown.[29] In La-Roche-sur-Yon the tent stood at the base of the equestrian statue in the center of a city that Napoleon had built in his own name.[30] In both cases the tent was

29 *Tent for Napoleon (La-Roche-sur-Yon)*, 1989.

mounted on cables suspended from a cage-like structure built around the central figure of the monument, the Waterloo lion and the equestrian. The structure was kept in place by other cables attached to the ground in a circular pattern, emphasizing the *locus* of the monument.

30 *Tent for Napoleon (La-Roche-sur-Yon)*, 1989.

The Waterloo installation as a whole superimposed an ephemeral image of primitive shelter and contemporary construction technology onto eminently readable historical monuments while staging a confrontation between the static sculptural images and the fleeting moving image of the film. It proclaimed the obsoleteness of old imperial strategies of representation but recognized their material traces as valid points of departure for reinvesting places with new forms of signification. The appearance of the new monument was shaped by scaffoldings and cables, standardized elements derived from the demands of contemporary construction techniques and independent from the human or animal forms within. In this sense, the volume and structure supporting the tent are close cousins of the container monuments. At the same time, the enclosed sculptures as well as the layout of the sites remind the viewer of the old order that is still present in these places. The *Tent for Napoleon* does not annihilate order

31 *Tent for Napoleon (Waterloo),* 1986.

32 *Tracés Régulateurs on Villa Schwob (Le Corbusier),* Le-Chaux-de-Fonds, Switzerland, 1987.

but complicates it by layering different systems, both placeless and indigenous. Any sense of measure or scale is at once produced and complicated by switching between different media and registers of the imagination.[31]

Similarly, Deleu's installation of the *tracés regulateurs* on the façade of Le Corbusier's Villa Schwob in La-Chaux-de-Fonds (1987) made real the geometrical figures that Le Corbusier composed on paper—in drawings but also superimposed on often manipulated photos—in order to root his architecture in what he argued was a universal, primitive order, an axiom that Deleu discussed at length in his architecture theory course.[32] Just like the spectacular manipulation of huge yet eminently unremarkable pieces of infrastructure suddenly renders them and their surroundings strikingly real, so the a *posteriori* application of what is supposedly the genetic code of a building—yet another form of reverse engineering—ties timeless and placeless principles to a particular object and site.[33]

33 Stefaan Vervoort, *From architecture to sculpture (and back again),* p. 101; Deleu, *Theorie van de Architectuur,* pp. 59-61.

The handling of found objects and the articulation of abstract principles in reality meet in the design and construction of buildings by Deleu and T.O.P. office. The architecture projects seek to impose systems and rigid order on a particular commission while graciously giving way to circumstantial contingencies and accidents. If the container arches or the tents seem to depend on an order rendered ineffective or unintelligible by its unreality, the architecture projects lay bare the fleeting and momentary nature of all forms of order by pitting design systems against the surplus of reality represented by clients, regulations, the building process and so on. This confrontation reveals the measure of inevitable chaos, irrationality and subconsciousness in any attempt at producing order. In the Medical Practice A.P.C. in Hoogvliet (1993), for instance, the figure of the plan is defined by a pentagonal central space giving access to four doctor's offices, with the entrance to the clinic on the fifth side.[34] The plan of the offices was to be rectangular but building regulations sliced off a corner of one office. The irregular form was

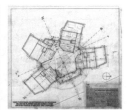

34 *Medical Practice A.P.C.,* Hoogvliet, the Netherlands, 1995.

repeated throughout. Rather than making a show of the incident the project simply incorporates it as a means to vary the appearance and visual experience of the building. This is a small example of how in the projects of Deleu and T.O.P. office architectural forms derived from particular expectations, desires or regimes (such as building regulations) detach themselves from their original cause to establish a new reality. The

35 *Belle Epoque Center,* Blankenberge, Belgium, 2010.

tangible presence of an intentional order prevents architecture from being reduced to mere subservience. This strategy is very apparent when the office tackles existing buildings. The transformation of three derelict Belle Epoque houses in Blankenberge into a museum (2010) required a considerable new volume containing circulation, office space and meeting rooms.[35] Fully acknowledging the scale of the intervention, the project never seeks to blend in with the historical structure nor does it act as a serviceable attached piece of infrastructure. It presents itself as an accumulation of possibilities on a par with the elements of the existing structure, whose value is thus emphasized by the same token that reveals its contingency.

36 *Casa Roja,* Tervuren, Belgium, 2005.

The same dialectic pervades the Casa Roja in Tervuren near Brussels (1998–2005).[36] In essence the house consists of a volume facing south set on a sloping building site and installed on a grid of columns aligned with the street. But it also puts a montage of modernist tropes like the *promenade architecturale* in the service of highly particular requests and desires such as the convenient arrangement of the furniture from the clients' previous home. The modernist phantasm of total design is relinquished in favor of a persistent intelligence that attaches equal importance to the system that governs the whole project as to the innumerable incidents that contribute to the feasibility, quality and experience of the building. The relation of Casa Roja to its modernist antecedents is perhaps best exemplified by its red color. The striking substitute for the purist white was desired by the client's wife as a reminiscence of her Mexican origins, a particular anecdote that proceeds to determine and indeed dominate the overall appearance of the building. In this, as in all other micro decisions pervading the house, the design intelligence does not coagulate into an overall system but discovers the new forms that speak to the inhabitant or the viewer from between order and contingency. The sheer density of these decisions requires extreme precision and craftsmanship as well as the mastery of an ever-accruing repertory of forms, such as, for instance, the shape derived from the golden section rectangle that repeatedly figures as a cutout in surfaces to optimize views.

The procedures applied in the design of the Casa Roja recall *The Unadapted City,* but now on the at once larger and smaller scale of a real building. If *The Unadapted City* is a gigantic structure only existing in documents, drawings and models that fit the art gallery, the Casa Roja is a pilot model of a fragment placed in a hostile environment, almost a prototype subjected to a crash test.[37] The purpose of the experiment here is not to control the environment and collect hard data. After all, collecting data and the

37 See Guy Châtel's essay in this volume.

concomitant evacuation of reality precedes the formal operations that give shape to the City and its components. Emerging from the transformation and adaption of such data, the Casa Roja is an enlarged model where the design principles shaping *The Unadapted City* are subjected to the strains of reality.

Architecture with Architects

Deleu's preoccupation with order and its at once unadapted and appropriate articulation in a given situation enables him to restate architecture's original global field of action. It is also the fundamental design principle in his oeuvre. As Deleu himself points out in, for instance, *Urbi et Orbi* (a reference to the imperial order adopted by the Roman church), the chaos that people need and sustain to live in community requires to be balanced by an image or a system of a larger order. This order is only visible from a distance or within the logic of a numerical system but guarantees the life and the relevance of the chaos developing within.[38]

38 Luc Deleu, 'Urbi et Orbi (D.O.S. XXI)', in: Luc Deleu and Hans Theys, *Urbi et Orbi: De Onaangepaste Stad* (Ghent: Ludion, 2002), pp. 21-138 (43-44).

The architecture theory course that Luc Deleu has taught at the St-Lucas School of Architecture is a systematic analysis of works that exemplify possible principles of such an order, such as the oeuvre of Le Corbusier and Peter Eisenman.[39] In Deleu's view such analysis is exactly what architecture theory should provide: lay bare the code of design of projects and recover the often simple systems that generate an intricate involvement with space and the formal language of architecture. Such analysis is projective: it allows one to think about architecture in future and ideal conditions without postulating a fixed image or a final state, a program that Deleu sees exemplified in Japanese Metabolism. It also enables architects to choose their distance with regard to the program of architecture. In Deleu's view, Le Corbusier's and Eisenman's engagement

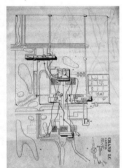

39 Le Modulor over Chandigarh; slide from Architecture Theory course.

with society and its needs are polar opposites, but the fact that Le Corbusier exemplifies the architect's social responsibility so valued by Deleu in no way diminishes his appreciation for Eisenman's ability to allow a limited set of operations (such as scaling, shifting, copying, ...) literally invent new architectural forms.[40]

40 On Eisenman, see Deleu, *Theorie van de Architectuur*, pp. 161-168.

Deleu believes that architecture is held to exploring the modernist agenda of discovering systems to approach space and form; there is no way back. His course builds its canon of great architects accordingly. The classicist modernism of Behrens does not fit in, while regionalism and historicist postmodernism receive short thrift. Perhaps more strikingly, the postwar restatement of modernism by Team X and affiliated architects is barely mentioned at all, despite the fact that Deleu does consider the crisis of the discipline in the 1960s and 1970s a historical turning point that determined the contemporary condition of architecture. In his reading, statements like Hollein's declaration of architecture's ubiquity are the ultimate consequence rather than the abnegation of the high modernist telos: the early twentieth-century expansion of the architect's field of action to society in its entirety allowed all forms of cultural production affecting modern life to claim the status of architecture. At the same time, it condemned architecture and society to each other, as in a shotgun wedding. In Deleu's reading, architecture has attempted to escape this deadlock either by withdrawing into autonomy or by borrowing strategies from other media and the visual arts. The structuralist approach and the participation movement that stemmed from the modernist self-critique were stillborn attempts at mending fences.

Deleu's course deliberately does not discuss his own work and barely pays attention to Belgian architecture, but it outlines the historical and international horizon of the orbanist agenda, *The Unadapted City* and his own practice as an architect working in Belgium. This practice, in turn, stands at the center of Deleu's reflection on the discipline developed in his teaching course and his other work. After all, working as an architect necessarily tests the consequence of distinguishing architecture as an art form from a professional practice bound to legal and social conditions. This distinction lay at the heart of the 'Proposal'-exhibition, as we have seen. It was expressed in the graffiti but also embodied in the bird's nest. If making a nest does not amount to formulating a working design theory (quite to the contrary), *separating* the nest from architecture's other constituting elements, as the exhibition did, is operative. In fact, Deleu viewed the nest less as a reflection on the origins of the art form than as a metaphor for the home. As a representation of the private realm the *Bird's Nest* marks the outer limits of architecture's sphere of action. Designing the home belongs to those who are best aware of what it should look like and how it should feel: its inhabitants. Accordingly, in the private home architecture may devolve into a primitive, pre-reflexive form of building. Still, the nest proved to Deleu that even birds work like architects when tackling questions of construction, comfort and functionality, the domestic version of the Vitruvian triad. The instinct that takes over in the building of a house does equally well as the architect.

As we have seen, the Belgian law that the 1978 exhibition proposed to abolish demands that houses, too, be designed by architects. Starting in 1979 Deleu openly attacked this provision by selling his signature to around 150 private builders so that they could fulfill their legal obligation to work with an architect. In so doing he publicly adopted a widespread but illegal practice of architects only nominally supervising projects designed and built by their future inhabitants, the inevitable side effect of such a law in a country with a venerable DIY tradition. The

Order of Architects puts great effort in detecting and punishing this abuse of the professional dignity. As Deleu intended, it became suspicious of the sheer number of building permits submitted in his name. The ensuing disciplinary procedure ended in a stalemate. Deleu's account of the dispute was published in 1983 in his *Luc Deleu Manifesto to the Board*, together with pictures of houses built under his name.[41]

41 Luc Deleu, *Luc Deleu Manifest aan de Orde*, Antwerp: Guy Schraenen (front cover), 1980.

The *Manifesto* has often (and rightly) been interpreted in terms of the local Belgian context.[42] It indicted Belgian urban planning and the attempts of the profession to pass off aesthetic and ethical judgments about popular domestic architecture

42 See, for instance, Geert Bekaert, 'Luc Deleu: A Self-power Man', p. 62.

as the application of objective standards regarding professionalism and architectural quality. Indeed, most of the houses that Deleu helped to have built were small freestanding villas designed in one of the several generic idioms encountered across suburbia. The problem with these houses, Deleu conveyed, is not their architecture but the kind of wasteful urban planning that produces endless allotments and building zones inappropriate for good housing, a practice that he already had symbolically ended by installing the 'Last stone of Belgium' in 1979. In more general terms the *Manifesto* forms part of Deleu's inquiry into the relation between small-scale objects and large-scale order, but also—like the Spectrum Gallery exhibition—into the entanglement of the professional and artistic personas of the architect. The 150 houses are like the nest in that they are authored versions of otherwise authorless artifacts. Indeed, what distinguishes these 150 from the literally thousands of houses that came about in exactly the same way, is their inclusion in the *Manifesto*, a gesture emphasized by the conspicuous inclusion of 'Luc Deleu' in the title of the work. As a book that accompanied an eponymous gallery exhibition, the *Manifesto* is not only a political but also an artistic statement. It deals with issues of authorship and creativity as much as it attacks Belgian law. The legal obligations that Deleu seeks to unmask as absurdities also provide a mechanism to test the limits of authorial involvement in architecture without devolving in architecture without architects.

43 *Plan for a Terrace House*, 1970.

The *Manifesto* thus exemplifies an important strategy in Deleu's architectural work. When freely distributing a generic plan of a house, as Deleu has done at the opening of the show in the Vacuum gallery in 1970, the architect transformed what could be termed a collective good into the object of an artistic practice, an operation made possible by the legal constrictions imposed on that same collective good.[43] The legal enshrinement of the architect's authorship enables Deleu to make existing designs his own, such as the slightly

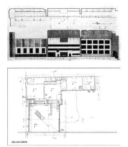

44 *Antique shop J. Dirven*, 1987. *Clinckx House and Studio*, 1998.

altered façade of Villa Stein in the antique shop of J. Dirven (1986–87) or Le Corbusier's and Jeanneret's Mass-Production Artisans' dwelling in Clinckx House and Studio (1998–2001).[44]

In other words, the Spectrum Gallery exhibition or the *Manifesto* distinguished the artistic and professional identity of the architect not to declare their mutual independence but to explore their inevitable resonance. Between artistic and professional identity the architect finds the space to treat the most trivial circumstances as an opportunity for artistic production while enabling the same architect to treat the very substance of his art as a mere collective good. Authorship and its articulation in the signature, both in terms of legal authentication and a stylistic mark, are therefore yet another medium Deleu employs to research the relation between the individual and the collective, the theme of his analysis of order as a design principle. It is no coincidence that Deleu considers Le Corbusier's famous perspective view of the Plan Obus,[45] which represents exactly

45 Le Corbusier, *Plan Obus (Algiers)*, 1930–33.

46 *Hôtel Stok*, 1992.

a plethora of manifestations of this relation, as the best architecture drawing ever made.

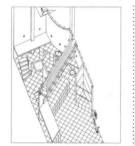

47 *Flower Shop Mergits*, 1981.

48 Fig. 29: *Belle Epoque Center*, Blankenberge, Belgium, 2010.

49 *Casa Roja*, Tervuren, Belgium, 2005.

The vindication of the complexity of authorship also evacuates the apparent paradox produced by Deleu's orbanist stance, that the futility of small-scale architecture would render meaningless the designing of houses and other small buildings. As an architect Deleu takes full advantage of the liberties afforded by the conglomerate of professional and artistic practice. Idiosyncrasies of the client, such as their emotional attachment to a vintage Alfa Romeo in the case of Hôtel Stok (1992–95),[46] are combined with gregarious explorations of patterns and screens, in works ranging from the Flower Shop Mergits (1981–82)[47] to the Belle Epoque Center,[48] or materials and colors, as in the Casa Roja.[49] There is no holding back in this architecture, rather an overinvestment of design intentions. As a consequence, from early on Deleu's architecture projects seem to turn inward, a movement already exemplified in early projects such as Bentley House (1977),[50] which

50 *Bentley House*, Malaga, Spain, 1977.

consisted of an undulating interior tent, or the interior of De Skipper (1973–75), a pub in Antwerp.[51] In the interior, almost as in a gallery space, architecture can impose its presence onto an attentive subject, temporarily disengaged from the world yet made aware of the intricacies and complexities that exist outside, as in a *cabinet de curiosités* or a *Wunderkammer*.

51 *De Skipper*, Antwerp, Belgium, 1975.

Luc Deleu — T.O.P. office

Crossed-out Collage, 1970

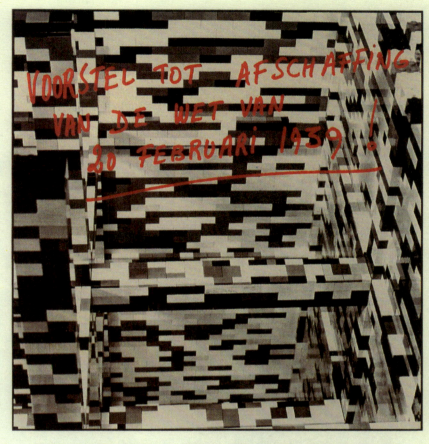

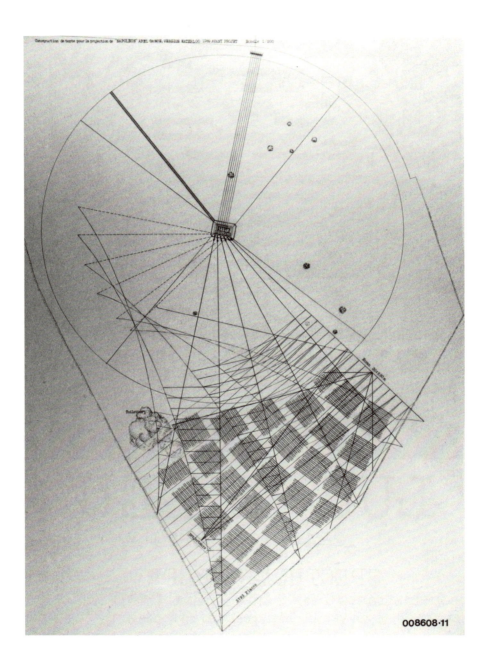

008608·11

X

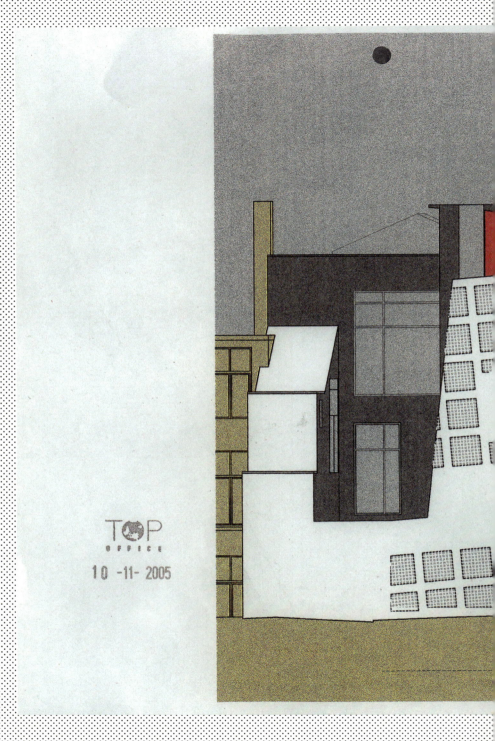

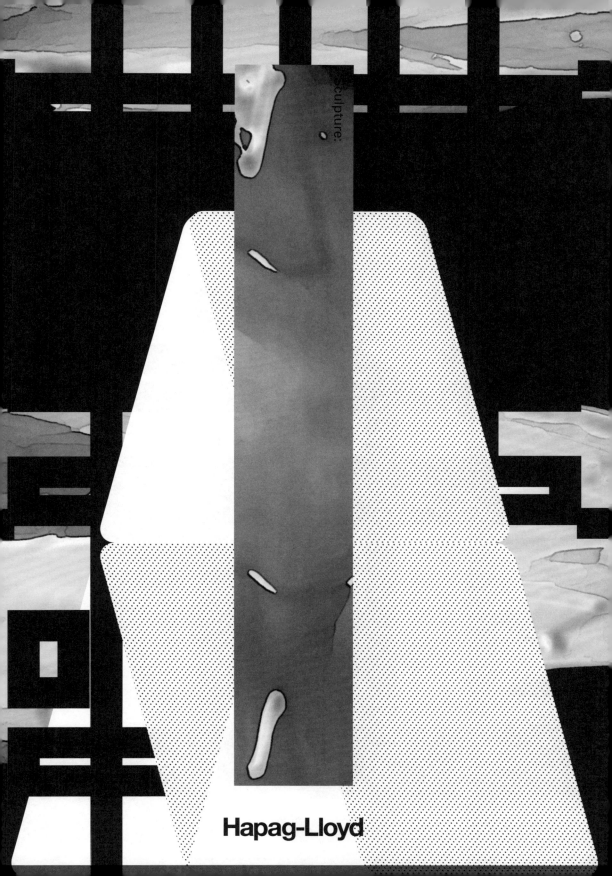

sculpture:

Hapag-Lloyd

Sculpture:

Promenade
Manfred Pernice

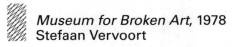
Museum for Broken Art, 1978
Stefaan Vervoort

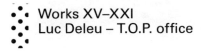
Works XV–XXI
Luc Deleu – T.O.P. office

promenade

horizon, stairs and bicycles

handling space, disruptions and
architectures resulting in this process,
reflect signals, impressions and voids.

Mc Bernie's

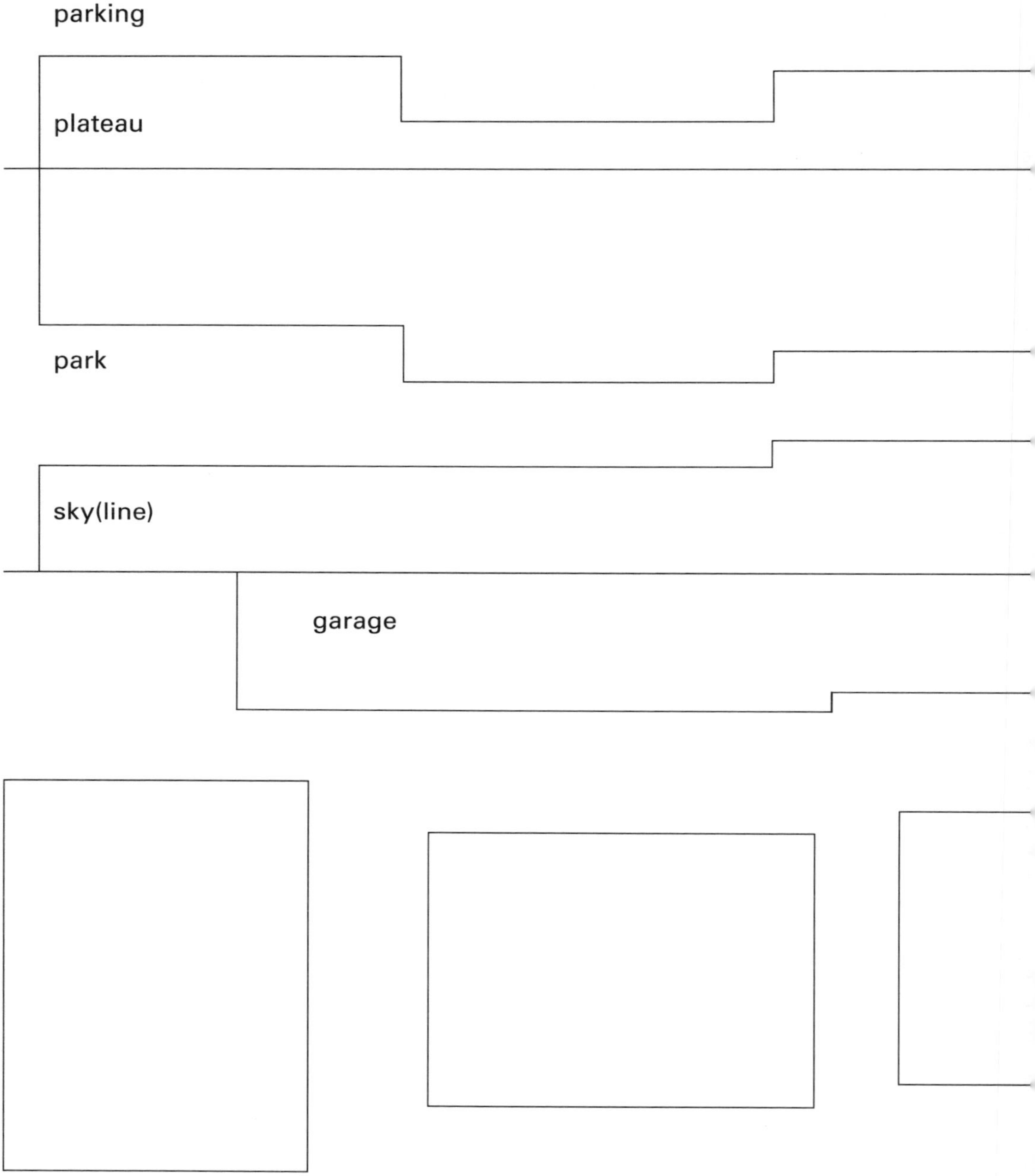

parking

plateau

park

sky(line)

garage

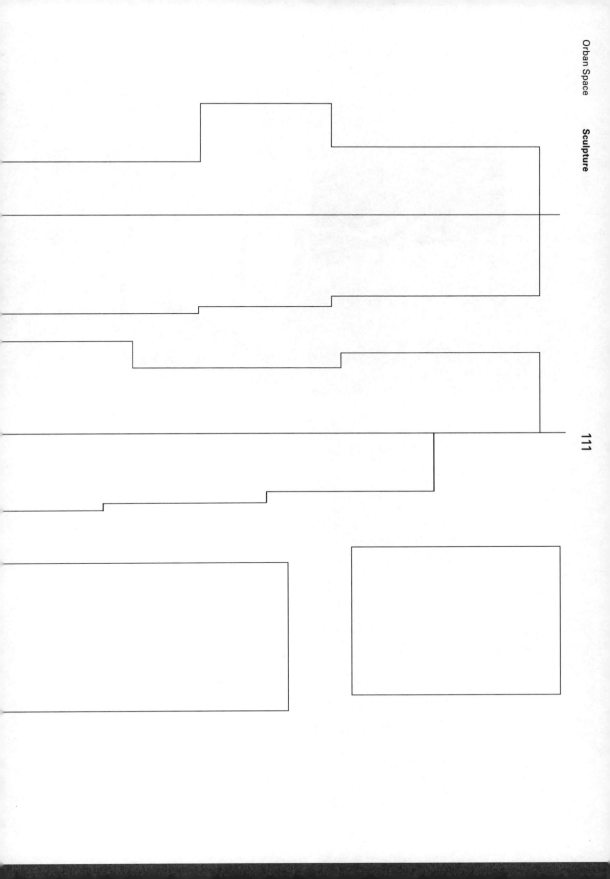

Badonviller

Meck-Pom.

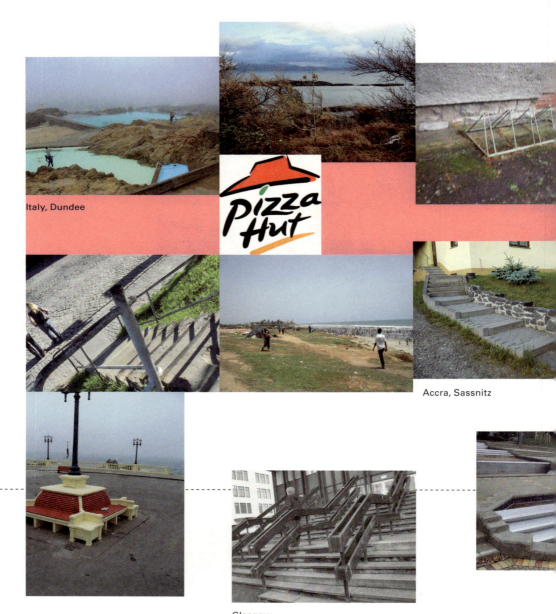

Italy, Dundee

Accra, Sassnitz

Glasgow

Edinburgh

Neuzelle

2002

Tegel

Ostia

CapeCoast

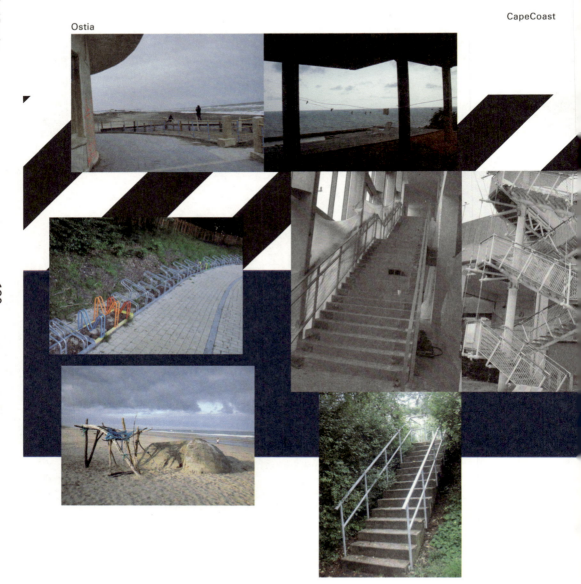

Charleroi

2007

Stefaan Vervoort

Museum for Broken Art, 1978

'However, more important than conscious and controlled associations seem to me the unconscious, uncontrolled (and sometimes unwanted) associations that are produced by our subconscious. C.G. Jung termed this—as opposed to the "causality" principle—the "synchronicity" principle, which does not consider the concurrence of events in time and space as mere coincidence but attributes deeper meaning to it.'
Luc Deleu[1]

'In the 1980s it was always like this. When nobody knew anymore what to do with a building, everyone eventually said: museum!'
Luc Deleu[2]

In December 1978 Luc Deleu participated in a group exhibition at De Warande, a cultural center in the provincial capital of Turnhout. Curated by artistic director Annie Gentils, the show addressed the relativity of 'time and space' and presented three artists: Deleu and his Antwerp colleagues Wout Vercammen and Filip Francis.[3] With the intent of displaying both new and existing work, each artist was commissioned to create a piece that specifically engaged the institutional context of De Warande.[4] Vercammen and Francis did so quite literally: the former stretched canvasses and a kilometer-long wire through the exhibition spaces, emphasizing the contingency of his aesthetic constructs; the latter composed a site-specific version of his *Tumbling Wood-blocks* (1975–76)—a domino-brick performance alluding to societal uprooting. Deleu's vista, however, was set wider.[5] Knowing Turnhout through his collaboration with architect Jan Groenen on a local youth canter, the artist-architect had his eye on a building site on the outskirts of the

1 'Belangrijker echter dan de bewuste, gecontroleerde associatie lijken mij de onbewuste, niet gecontroleerde (en soms ongewilde) associaties die ons onderbewustzijn tot stand brengt. (…) C.G. Jung noemde dit, in tegenstelling tot het "causaliteitsprincipe", het "synchroniteitsprincipe", dat coïncidentie van gebeurtenissen in tijd en ruimte niet als louter toeval beschouwt doch er een diepere betekenis aan toekent.' Luc Deleu, *Associatief Ontwerpen*, 21 November, 1991 (unpublished), T.O.P. office archives, s.p. (author's translation).

4 *Museum for Broken Art* aside, Deleu presented *Antwerp Caravan City* (1978), a model and photos of *Lego Constructions* (1977–83), a series of proposals (including *Design for a City Fontain* (1978) and *Proposal to Legalise Graffiti* (1978)), and several video works.

2 'In de jaren tachtig is het toch voortdurend zo geweest dat, als men met een gebouw geen raad meer wist, uiteindelijk iedereen riep: Museum!' Hans Baaij, 'Luc Deleu en het geweten van de architect: Interview met Luc Deleu', *Het Gebaar* no. 2 (June 1990), p. 5 (author's translation).

3 Annie Gentils, *Luc Deleu, Filip Francis, Wout Vercammen* (Turnhout: Cultuur- en ontmoetingcentrum De Warande, 1978), s.p.

5 Having worked closely with Deleu in joint collaborations, happenings, the practices of Francis and Vercammen were of obvious influence to the work and practice of Luc Deleu – T.O.P. office. The resurgence of the contemporary art scene in Antwerp around 1970 via collectives as the Artworker Foundation and Ercola, and through newly founded public institutions as the I.C.C. (International Cultural Centre) undoubtedly amounted to an atmosphere of in-crowd cross-fertilisation. In the case of the exhibition at De Warande, Francis's tumbling domino-blocks and 'card house' setup of his installation as well as Vercammen's metric system are echoed in later work by Deleu – T.O.P. office.

8 Daan Dellanoy, 'Humo sprak met Luc Deleu', *Humo* 2 May, 1985, p. 67.

9 Deleu, *The Ethics of Architecture*, p. 7.

11 'Dit project zou ik realizeren van 16.12.78 tot 7.1.79. Naarmate echter de tijd kortte werd ik bang voor de massa werk van deze realizatie. Mijn opluchting was dan ook groot toen ik vernam dat de afbraakwerken in nov '78 gestart waren. Een kapot museum van kapotte kunst vergemakkelijkte de zaak aanzienlijk om enkele stedebouwkundige accenten te (ver)leggen.' Luc Deleu, *Museum for Broken Art*, 2 December, 1978 (my translation).

town. Here, in full dereliction, stood a decommissioned waterworks building, its reinforced concrete framework dating back to 1904. Wanting 'to see recycled every built structure (= human energy) to the very limit,' Deleu, in an all but clear gesture, declared the former purification plant *Museum for Broken Art* (1978).[6] His intention was to fill the run-down premises with dilapidated art-works—'broken paintings and sculptures of friends'—so that the building 'would visually reflect its function.'[7] With paintings 'fallen down or punctuated by a foot,' the exhibition mounted in the institution was going to be *'magnificent'*.[8] Yet the project remained 'under pressure of circumstances', and Deleu's intentions never saw the light of day.[9] Shortly before the opening of the show at De Warande the building was demolished, lengthening the project's title to 'Broken Museum for Broken Art'. Hardly taken off balance by the mishap, Deleu displayed a multifaceted work at De Warande that ingeniously accumulated its various temporal and physical stages.

6 Luc Deleu, *Museum for Broken Art*, 2 December, 1978, s.p.

7 Luc Deleu, *The Ethics of Architecture,* April 1988 (unpublished), T.O.P. office archives, s.p., p. 7. Deleu continues: 'Although a museum for broken art might seem strange at first thought, I want to point out that Cairo, Athens, Rome, (...) are full of museums for broken art.'

Museum for Broken Art consists of a text-based proposal, a building site, a series of photographs, a video, sculptural reinforced concrete debris, and a live performance.[10] The objects encompass the ramshackle waterworks plant both before and after the demolition, thus joining hands to represent the project. The handwritten text, dated December 2, 1978, functions as a cryptic game plan or state of intent:

10 *Museum for Broken Art*, 1978.

'I would realize this project from 16 December '78 to 7 January '79. As the deadline approached, however, I became nervous about the loads of work this project would take. Therefore, I was greatly relieved when I heard that demolition had begun in November '78. A broken museum for broken art made it significantly easier to shift some urban emphases. P.S. proposal for safety in Turnhout: increase use of horn.'[11]

The project's rather hazy intent is visualized by the various photos and the video.[12] Scanning both the interior and exterior of the concrete skeleton, the snapshots show empty and abandoned

12 *Museum for Broken Art*, 1978.

13 *Museum for Broken Art,* film still, 1978. Translated 'Power Plant' from German, Kraftwerk surely was a well-chosen band to soundtrack the video. The technological determinism of architectural 'progress' addressed in Deleu's project reverberates with the attitude and lyrics of the German electro-pop sensation. As the excavator stands on top of the wreckage, the music is blasting: 'We're functioning automatik/ And we are dancing mechanik/ We are the robots.'

15 Jack van Gils, 'Zwevend met de voeten op de grond', *De Morgen* 29 December, 1978.

16 Ibidem.

17 Marc Callewaert, 'Speelse kritiek en kritisch spel', *Gazet van Antwerpen* 27 December, 1978.

rooms, missing doors and windows, cracked and molded walls, all indications of the ruinesque state of the building. The video follows up on this image sequence with a recording of the demolished building site. Guided through the various scenes by the music of Kraftwerk's 1978 album *The Man-Machine*, we watch Deleu as he carefully selects pieces of debris from the site, has them loaded onto a truck, and dumps them on the doorstep of De Warande later.[13] Scattered across the lawn and exhibition spaces there, the steel rods and pointy concrete angles delivered material proof of the nonfulfillment or 'failure' of the project— a corpse of a museum that was never meant to be.[14] To top it all off, Deleu delivered a flabbergasting performance at the opening of the show. Blasting away at the rubble with a jackhammer, his 'Sonata with Hammer and Building' undoubtedly left visitors boggled over what the artists were after.

14 *Museum for Broken Art*, De Warande, Turnhout, Belgium, 1978.

The response to the show was mixed. 'People said that both the artists and the organizers at De Warande "have lost their minds",' journalist Jack van Gils recounted; 'three Antwerp weirdo's that have come to soil the cultural center of the small province town of Turnhout.'[15] Partially because of the show's dumb-striking experience, the critical corollaries and the historical grounds of Deleu's project were hardly discerned. The 'sharp indictment' and 'harsh realities' noted in the work by some critics were just as vague as the arcane 'urban emphasises' in Deleu's handwritten proposal.[16] 'You need to know something of the artists' intentions beforehand,' critic Marc Callewaert pinpointed the problem, 'because if you approach their work strictly visually (...) you will miss the main point, the grounds upon which it was all founded.'[17] Nevertheless, the critic remained vaguely positive about the nature of such possible grounds. 'In short,' he wrote, 'it's all about societal critique.'

18 Cover of *CJP-Maandblad*, 7, no. 57 (1980) with Gordon Matta-Clark, *Office Baroque*, Antwerp, Belgium, 1977.

1977

Nearly a year before the making of *Museum for Broken Art,* in October 1977, American artist Gordon Matta-Clark created *Office Baroque* in an abandoned office building in Antwerp, across the historical hotspot of the medieval fortress 'Steen'.[18] This was the last building he

Gordon Matta-Clark, *Office Baroque*, 1977.

19 The cuttings in fact went all the way from the basement up and through the roof, as Matta–Clark wanted to 'extend the building (...) below as much as above, like an alchemical motif where there is that definite dichotomy—or balance—between the above and below.' Matta-Clark's original suggestion, to cut out partly a large spherical shape at the exterior corner of the building, was declined by local authorities on the ground of being 'too public'. See Johan Pas, 'Een ruïne als kunstwerk', in: *Beeldenstorm in een spiegelzaal: Het ICC en de actuele kunst 1970–1990* (Leuven: Lannoocampus, 2005), pp. 199–228.

21 Flor Bex and numerous leading figures in the Belgian art scene founded the Foundation Gordon Matta-Clark February 12, 1979. Motivated by Crawford, some 230 artists, including Vito Acconci, Robert Rauschenberg, Christo, Sol LeWitt, Isamu Noguchi, and Deleu himself, agreed to donate works for either budget accumulation or to sway local authorities. See Pas, *Beeldenstorm in een spiegelzaal*, p. 279.

cut before dying of cancer at the early age of 35 and the work consisted of a complex rhythm of elliptical cuts across the five interior floors of the premises.[19] Due to the invisibility of the piece from the street and Matta-Clark's relative anonymity in Belgium at that time, few people saw *Office Baroque*. While the concurrent exhibition in the International Centre for Culture (I.C.C.) lured in some 7000 visitors, the site-specific installation, although one of the artist's most ambitious works, counted a mere couple of hundreds enthusiasts. Nevertheless, *Office Baroque* did write history indeed. Shortly after the artist's death, in August 1978, commissioner and I.C.C.-director Flor Bex and Matta-Clark's wife Jane Crawford formulated a plan to preserve the installation, integrating it into a new contemporary art museum to be allocated in the surrounding compounds.[20] To gather sufficient funds they initiated the Gordon Matta-Clark Foundation, and both local and internationally renowned artists agreed to donate artworks in support of the project.[21] These numerous and collective efforts notwithstanding, *Office Baroque* could not be saved. After a lengthy administrative battle with city, province and state authorities, the owner

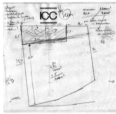

20 Flor Bex, Sketch for a Museum of Contemporary Art, behind the building with the work *Office Baroque* (Gordon Matta-Clark, 1977), undated. This drawing and other documents about the plans to build a museum on the plot behind *Office Baroque* were presented for the first time in 2007 in the Exhibition *Beginners & Begetters*, curated by Wouter Davidts, at Extra City Kunsthal Antwerp.

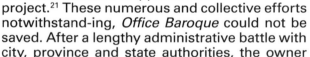

and project developer Marcel Peeters demolished the building, unannounced, in the summer of 1980.[22]

22 In 1985, the Antwerp Museum for Contemporary Art (MUHKA) was eventually housed in a refurbished warehouse not far from the demolished site, opening most tellingly, as homage, with a Matta-Clark retrospective.

Deleu's appreciation of *Office Baroque* was varied from the start. While it is safe to say that he has never been a fan of slick city branding and corporate project developments, he did not approve of Matta-Clark's destructive treatment of the office building either. In a letter to Flor Bex of May 1977, a month before the actual production of *Office Baroque*, he directly linked Matta-Clark's intervention to the premises' imminent demolition. 'With this inappropriate act, you are clearly supporting big capital,' he charged, adding cynically: 'why not saw an egg out of the I.C.C., the Rubens House, etc.' Hoping to avoid 'Charlie De Pauw's scenario in Brussels', namely, 'the erection of parking lots', the artist-architect exhorted Bex to cancel the commission:

'I feel urged to protest against this [the plan to realize *Office Baroque*, S.V.], and to advise you to distance yourself from such an undertaking. Art here is clearly being used to give developers

23 Ik voel mij gedwongen hiertegen te protesteren, en je de raad te geven je van een dergelijke onderneming te distanciëren. De kunst wordt hier duidelijk gebruikt om promotors zoals M. Peeters de kans te geven de pil te verzachten, en zo de aftakeling van de stad vlotjes te laten verlopen. (…) Het bewuste pand is in goede staat en het geld dat tegen deze act zal gegooid worden is beter besteed aan renovatie. (…) Je steunt met deze act dus duidelijk het groot kapitaal (waarom geen ei zagen uit het I.C.C., het Rubenshuis, enz.)' All quotes above originate from: Luc Deleu, 'Letter to Flor Bex', unpublished letter, dated 2 May, 1977, T.O.P. office archives (author's translation).

26 Luc Deleu, 'Paris, Les Halles', unpublished project text for *Idée pour la transformation du chantier 'Les Halles' en paysage urbain en évolution*, 1979–80, T.O.P. office archives, s.p.

27 *Principle of a Lesson in Perspective Featuring the World's Tallest Twin Towers*, 1980.

28 Gordon Matta-Clark, photograph from *Anarchitecture*, 1974.

like M. Peeters the opportunity to sugarcoat the pill and thereby help smoothen the decline of the city. (…) The property in question is in good order and the money spent on this act is better invested in renovation.'[23]

Deleu's resolute disapproval of *Office Baroque* is nothing less than surprising at first. Not only did he know and appreciate the artist's work through their mutual connection Flor Bex, he also shared a number of common interests with Matta-Clark. Roughly around the same time, both architects by training protested against amnesic urban renewal and the symbolism of neoliberal architecture. Deleu's urban design for Les Halles of 1979–80[24] for instance was marked by a sensibility very akin to Matta-Clark's photographic series of Paris's subsoil in *Soussols de Paris: Les Halles* (1977).[25] While Deleu transformed the existing construction pit into an integrated 'open space' of town, Matta-Clark connected the underground layers of the city to urban structures such as the Eiffel Tower, 'expanding' as it were the geographical structure of the city.[26] Another example of kinship is Deleu's *Principle of a Lesson in Scale with Two Buildings of Identical Volume Featuring the World's Tallest Tower* (1980)[27] and Matta-Clark's black-and-white photographs of the Twin Towers (photographs from *Anarchitecture,* 1974).[28] Deleu's proposal to topple one of two towers follows up on Matta-Clark's suggestion to contribute 'some positive and interesting insights into the new scale and complexity of the World Trade Center.'[29] Nevertheless, when the two artists met for dinner in 1977, the conversation turned out a legendary dialogue of the

24 *Idée pour la transformation du chantier 'Les Halles' en paysage urbain en évolution*, 1979–80.

25 Gordon Matta-Clark, *Sous-sols de Paris: Les Halles*, collage, 1977.

29 Gordon Matta-Clark, as cited in: Pamela M. Lee, *Object to be Destroyed: The Work of Gordon Matta-Clark* (Cambridge, MA: MIT Press, 2000), p. 109. One could here equally juxtapose *Museum for Broken Art* with Matta-Clark's bio-degrading *Museum* (1970–71).

30 Office Baroque was een elegante manier om het ding weg te krijgen. Ik was ideologisch onbuigzamer en vond het niet te verschonen een huis zomaar af te breken. Matta-Clark was op dat moment even weinig ingewerkt in de Antwerpse stadsproblematiek als ik in zijn werk.' Luc Deleu as cited in: Pas, *Beeldenstorm in een Spiegelzaal*, p. 225 (author's translation).

deaf. According to Deleu, the meeting was too late, badly timed, and thus, a failure. Some 30 years later, in 2005, he looked back on the artists' verbal grapple:

'*Office Baroque* was an elegant way of disposing of the thing [the office building, S.V.]. I was ideologically less flexible, and found the random demolition of a house unjustifiable. At that time, Matta-Clark was as little acquainted with the urban problematic of Antwerp as I was with his work.'[30]

I would like to argue that instead of quarrelling with words, Deleu resolved his discontent with actions. Strictly through a polemical project would he respond to *Office Baroque*,

31 Gordon Matta-Clark, as cited in: Pas, *Beeldenstorm in een Spiegelzaal*, p. 223.

and, in one fell swoop, ratify the nickname 'Filip Francis's polemical architect friend' that Matta-Clark gave him.[31] With *Museum for Broken Art*, made one year after the facts, Deleu delivered his response to the methods and themes addressed by Matta-Clark, both in the artist's Antwerp project as well as more broadly in his oeuvre.

1978–79

Looking back upon *Museum for Broken Art* and *Office Baroque*, in retrospect the numerous parallels are almost hard to miss. Firstly, on a formal and scenographic level, Deleu's varying documentation of the former purification plant echoes the split nature of Matta-Clark's cuttings. Here too the project is disintegrated in various material and temporal stages, setting up a complex dialogue between the work in situ and its synecdochal displacement within the gallery space, between the 'before' and 'after' of the project. In addition, Robert Smithson's concepts of site-nonsite and entropy come to mind as well: *Museum for Broken Art* is at once documentary photo series and speculative proposal, a future art institution and a bygone ruin, and an architectural and sculptural endeavor. Secondly, on a conceptual level, the genesis of *Museum for Broken Art* remarkably correlates with the 1977 turn of events in Antwerp. Much like *Office Baroque*, the Turnhout project involves degenerated property that is about to be sold to private investors, and in which an artist is temporarily allowed to 'intervene'. Subsequently, to save either building or artwork, the edifice is declared a museum—instantly by Deleu, posthumously on behalf of Matta-Clark—yet, in both cases, the efforts are in vain. The building is destroyed, leaving only 'souvenirs' of the actual intervention. One would be inclined to think, then, that the concrete refuse, leftovers of some non-specific sawing, and the voluntary transformation of the down-at-heel environment into museum of *Museum for Broken Art* is a facetious jest directed at *Office Baroque*. Having protested against the realization of Matta-Clark's installation, in 1978, Deleu

32 *Museum for Broken Art*, 1978. As if these allusions would not suffice Deleu even threw in a visual reference. In a gloomy snapshot of the building's cellar three similarly shaped holes give shape to a horizontal, 'bootleg' Matta-Clark.

33 Robert Smithson, *Hotel Palenque*, collage, 1969.

35 Deleu speaks in Smithson–like terms about the project for planning 'Les Halles' (1979): 'Instead of aiming at a bewildering result, I have chosen as main theme the process of urban changes (the building-site). In other words, my point of view is that a town is constantly transforming its own ruins; that a town is a decaying building-site.' Deleu, 'Paris Les Halles', s.p.

restaged the Antwerp events in a wry and vulgar sketch, now entitled 'Office Baraque'.[32]

Yet to disdain *Museum for Broken Art* as a Matta-Clark spoof would surpass the work's critical faculty. For unlike the ruins of Smithson and Matta-Clark, Deleu's power plant fundamentally contains a positive message for the discipline of architecture. It suffices here to make the comparison between *Museum for Broken Art* and Smithson's *Hotel Palenque* (1969–72).[33] While the various snapshots of the waterworks plant strongly resemble those of Smithson's dilapidated Mexican hotel—the missing chamber roofs, broken pool or protruding reinforcement bars having turned into missing windows, sand-covered floors, and overgrown courtyards—the differences between the works are fundamental. Smithson's milestone artwork, as art historian Wouter Davidts has noted, obliquely criticizes architecture for being 'too slow to assimilate experiments.'[34] Due to architecture's inability to cope with entropy the hotel 'evolves in a gradual, consistent and, above all, conceited manner into a state of self-obliterating equilibrium.' The work of Smithson, in other words, *registers* architecture's surrender to the inevitable force of entropy. *Museum for Broken Art*, on the other hand, converts this capitulation into an advantage. It does not so much demarcate the failure of architecture to keep up with changes as actively wield entropy as a programmatic and structural catalyst—the whole foundation, in fact, of the broken art museum. As the bare concrete structure sits 'in between jobs', in limbo between power plant and art institution, the photos and film footage capture and suspend the moment upon which the building may accommodate programmatic transformations and alternative afterlives. In *Museum for Broken Art* architecture thus not only acknowledges and consumes its own entropic state—it consciously and conscientiously *acts upon it.* Without lapsing into overtly romantic views, Deleu points to the potential that lies within decay. He envisioned *Museum for Broken Art* less in Matta-Clark's and Smithson's terms of disintegration but rather delivered his own version of a 'ruin in reverse'—exploiting the open-ended potential of the ruin-cum-construction-site.[35] Retracting the architectural antagonism from the sculptural concepts of his peers, for Deleu the notion of entropy denotes a positive, non-destructive and, especially, functional project.

34 Wouter Davidts, 'Operative Entropy: Robert Smithson's Hotel Palenque (1969–72)', in: Katja Grillner, Per Glembrandt and Sven-Olov Wallenstein (eds.), *01.AKAD: Experimental Research in Architecture and Design, Beginnings* (Stockholm: AKAD, 2005), pp. 128–135 (133).

The point thus is clear: Deleu envisioned a different correlation between sculpture and architecture. The collage with a 1979 newspaper clipping on the Gordon Matta-Clark Foundation, pasted on T.O.P. office company paper similar to the *Proposals* (1972–82, 2000, 2002), demonstrates that the attempts to save the Antwerp installation brought him an epiphany. Far from preparing the building for demolition, Deleu now understood, *Office Baroque* had set in motion a three-headed apparatus of institution, artwork, and architecture that might possibly save it instead. In the Antwerp saga, that is, these three players compare forces and flaws, strengths as well as weaknesses. Set out in an arena, they each play out their potential, the overarching goal of which was to save *Office Baroque* from annihilation. As the institution would 'conserve' the artwork, the artwork in turn would 'save' the building—and, in turn, this building would 'house' and thus ground the institution. Consisting of the same basic ingredients, *Museum for Broken Art* repeats this exact play. Against all preconceptions of architecture or sculpture proper, or devoid of any bias towards the art institution, it occupies and instrumentalizes all three fields simultaneously. It does not 'choose' between a sculptural or architectural regime, but cleverly spreads the aesthetic construct over concurrent platforms that enforce as well as contradict each other, diverge as well as overlap. As such, disciplines neither 'expand' nor 'contract' per se, but they oscillate, change, and adapt when necessary. They negotiate their mutual positions as elements of a triangular force field, in which preset hierarchies or conventionalist claims, on either the level of art or architecture, do not exist. In *Museum for Broken Art*, as an early exploration of Deleu's very own 'expanded field', the registers of sculpture, architecture, and art institution are tested, worked through, and evaluated at the end.[36]

36 See Rosalind Krauss, 'Sculpture in the Expanded Field' (1979) in: *The Originality of the Avant–Garde and Other Modernist Myths* (Cambridge, MA: MIT Press, 1986), pp. 276–290.

37 An explicit fan of Eisenman, Deleu respects the architect's attempts to unground the discipline of architecture, yet he does not endorse his poststructuralist program. The 'bland and literal translation' of society's instability into the formal aspects of deconstructivist architecture, Deleu wrote in his teaching course, hollows out architecture into a fragile and redundant discipline, transforming the architect into 'a city harlequin who merely designs suits for buildings.' Further on, he noted rationally: 'The strange thing about Deconstructivism is that, while everything is oblique and slanted, the floors remain horizontal. This immediately implies the petit bourgeois character of the movement, for if one utterly aims to express instability, if one really wants to provoke, one must surely place the floors crooked.' Luc Deleu, 'Teaching Course St-Lukas' (unpublished manuscript), 2010, T.O.P. office archives, p. 173. For the art-architecture scrimmage over the meta-structure, see for instance Richard Serra, 'Interview with Peter Eisenman (1982)', in: *Writings, Interviews* (Chicago: University of Chicago Press, 1994), pp. 141–156.

1980s

Going into the next decade, in many of his works Deleu further developed his enlightened disciplinary attitude. On the one hand, the artist-architect refuted the essentialist stance of architects and artists such as Peter Eisenman and Richard Serra. Their respective obstinacy to the alleged cores of architecture and sculpture—a battle settled via claims over the system of systems, the card house—struck Deleu merely as 'a petit-bourgeois interpretation' that neglected 'the societal problematic discovered by Modernism.'[37] *Big Card House Castle* (1986), a three-decked glass card house mounted on two wooden beams, is an obvious pun

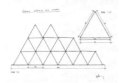

38 *Big Card House Castle*, 1986.

at such discussions on disciplinary 'essence'.[38] Composed of 32 glass playing cards—rounded corners and all—the transparent structure hints both at Serra's 1969 steel-sheet sculpture *One-Ton Prop (House of Cards)*[39] and at the first six villas by Eisenman, named 'Houses of Cards' (1969–76).[40] 'As does the rest of my work,' Deleu writes in the project description, '*Big Card House Castle* owes multiple ambiguities and references to the borderline between architecture and the plastic arts, and this is where it derives its singularity from.'[41] With humorous lucidity, then, Serra's material-driven and Eisenman's poststructuralist positions are rendered

39 Richard Serra, *One Ton Prop (House of Cards)*, 1969.

40 Peter Eisenman, model of *House II*, 1970.

41 'Zoals mijn ander werk heeft het "Groot kaartenhuis" meerdere dubbelzinnigheden en referenties in het randgebied tussen architectuur en plastische kunsten en hieraan ontleent het ook zijn eigenheid.' Luc Deleu, '"Groot Kaartenhuis", 1986', unpublished text for *Big Card House Castle*, 1986, T.O.P. office archives, s.p. (author's translation).

43 A mentor to Peter Eisenman at Cornell, Colin Rowe's comparison of Palladio's Villa Foscari (c. 1550–60) and Le Corbusier's Villa Stein may well be considered the germ into the search for architecture's 'core'. See: Colin Rowe, 'The Mathematics of the Ideal Villa', in: *Mathematics of the Ideal Villa and Other Essays* (Cambridge, MA: MIT Press, 1976), pp. 1–28.

into precarious and overtly donnish affairs. A similar claim may be made for Deleu's refurbishment of J. Dirven Antique shop (1986–87).[42] Here, the inclusion of Le Corbusier's Villa Stein (Garches, 1927) in the interior of the showroom indicates how a strictly formalist focus, as in Colin Rowe's description of the suburban modernist villa, transforms architecture into vapid decoration.[44] Deleu integrated a scaled-down version of the façade, equipped with Rowe's 'ideal' proportions, in a showcase that displayed various antiques (the balcony and windows) and also contained a radiator and a speaker system (the carport and entrance respectively). Siding hermetic formalism with two-dimensional retail or shop design, the quest for architectural truth thus was stripped of highbrow parley, exposed as a crude joke. As early as 1986, Deleu noted that it is 'obvious' that 'autonomous architecture is a defense mechanism, created by designers to protect their social conformism and apathy.'[44]

42 *Antique Shop J. Dirven*, Antwerp, Belgium, 1987.

44 'In de neo-conservatieve jaren tachtig ligt het voor de hand op te werpen dat autonome architectuur een verdedigingsbolwerk is, opgeworpen door de ontwerpers ter bescherming van hun sociaal conformisme en apathie.' Luc Deleu, *Over de belangrijkheid en onbelangrijkheid van de architectuur*, February 1985 (unpublished), T.O.P. office archives, p.7 (author's translation).

On the other hand the artist-architect has no interest in radical eclecticism either. While he often notes that architecture is an art form as much as, say, sculpture—his oft-repeated maxim being 'I am an artist *because* I am an architect'—several of his works object to the mindless broadening of disciplinary fields. *Manifesto to the Board* (1979–85), a project in which Deleu signed and built some 150 houses designed by their owners, is such a protest against an all-inclusive regime of architecture. As the Belgian law states that all buildings equal architecture—or that, as architect Hans Hollein quipped in 1967, 'Alles ist Architektur'—Deleu aimed to prove the opposite. By granting popular building wishes he made clear that architecture is a specific and singular regime, not to be applied to every spatial construction. Apart from the work's local agenda, then, *Ready-made Housing Architecture (Luc Deleu Manifesto to the Board)* revised the 1960s interdisciplinarity of Hollein and contemporaries, according to Deleu, to 'put architecture theory with both feet back on the ground.'[45] However, things are not that simple. When Deleu publicly presented the project at Spectrum Gallery in Antwerp in 1987, he made, among other

45 Luc Deleu, 'Alles ist Architektur', in: *Das letze Haus im Steir* (Graz: Haus der Architektur, 1995).

objects, a 1:100 scale model. Packed in an open flight case mounted on a mobile base, the model is pivoted vertically, providing the viewer with a zenithal perspective on the suburban housing plots. The small houses, gardens, and sidewalks all are restrained to the zone demarcated by a thick canvas frame, nudging the work into a register between painting and sculpture—a quirky version, as it were, of Donald Judd's 'specific object.' Accordingly, the singularity

46 *Untitled (Installation with Windsocks and Rulers)* (1986) & *Untitled (Red-white Mast Project)* (1990): 1987–90.

predicated elsewhere in the project is here détourned into its final and most sophisticated form. Instead of being form-related, the pictorial model testifies, architectural specificity for Deleu is an ideological attitude, a professional and ethical stance that has nothing to do with the physical properties conventionally grounding media such as sculpture and painting. Put differently, Deleu's position in the artistic circuit was a most nifty sleight of hand. With painting and sculpture appended to his architectural vocabularium, in the sphere of the arts, the artist-architect could demonstrate precisely what architecture was *not* about.

Museum!

If this disciplinary differentiation was to come into play, however, in the aforementioned as well as in other works, Deleu needed the museum or gallery. Only via the institutional regime of art could he set up a clinch between sculpture and architecture, articulating the conventions and limits of both fields from there. Several exhibition scenographies by Deleu confirm this operativity of the institutional sphere. While a presentation of the *Red-white Mast Projects* (Furkapasshohe 1986, Tel Hai 1990) shows a scale model alongside a photograph of a realized work,[46] Deleu's model of De Hef (Rotterdam, 1989–90) is placed against the backdrop of a Kümmerly+Frey world map.[47]

47 *De Hef* (1989–90) & world map Kummerly + Frey, Galerie Christine & Isy Brachot, Brussels, Belgium, 1990.

Partly inside, partly outside the institution, these installations declare a space in which the work hovers between the regime of sculpture and architecture proper, indeed, where it obtains meaning fundamentally from a place where it is not.

48 *Studs*, École Supérieure d'Art Visuel, Geneva, Switzerland, 1990.

Deleu's *Studs* (1990) testify to a similar position.[48] Turned 90 degrees much like the *Manifesto* model, the studs are installed in the hallway of a Geneva art school. Although they push out against the exhibition space horizontally, they hardly reiterate the oft-quoted tenets of institutional critique.

49 Chris Burden, *Samson*, 1985.

In sharp contrast to Chris Burden's *Samson* (1985), *Studs*'s artistic sibling, Deleu does not break down the museum nor does he 'expose' the physical or discursive constitution of its institutional apparatus.[49] Instead, he finds a partner in these walls, clamping between them an exemplary object of building practice both literally and figuratively. The art institution thus is the regime *par excellence* enabling him to think through his architectural positioning, as he confirmed in a 1987 interview:

'Architects build their frustrations. I too build mine, but I rather build them on St. Peter's Square [where *Scale & Perspective with Two Electricity Pylons*) was installed, S.V.]. Those two poles are very important in my work. By realizing a project like these power pylons, I can build a house unprejudiced, and vice versa.'[50]

50 'Architecten bouwen hun frustraties. Ik bouw ook mijn frustraties, maar ik bouw ze liever op het Sint-Pietersplein. Die twee polen in mijn werk zijn zeer belangrijk. Door de mogelijkheid een project als deze hoogspanningsmasten te realiseren kan ik heel onbevooroordeeld een huisje bouwen en vice versa.' Luc Deleu, 'Interview with Katrien Vandermarliere', in: *Luc Deleu Postfuturismus?* (Antwerp: deSingel/Wommelgem: Den Gulden Engel, 1987), p. 16 (author's translation). Here again, the link with Matta-Clark is revealing. 'I think that… architects would be fascinated,' Matta-Clark declared, 'because they spend so much time being so totally frustrated by having that kind of stuff…in their heads… and then not getting a chance to ever execute it.' Gordon Matta-Clark, as cited in: Lee, *Object to be Destroyed*, p. 215.

Since the modus operandi of T.O.P office thus depended on institutional regimes, Deleu would not shy away from installing them himself. Indeed, through numerous operations and on various levels, the artist-architect has often declared his own musealization, even up until today. He is not so much condemned to work inside the art institution, as is often stated, but rather creates for himself a museological atmosphere to ensure architecture's ungrounding. One could even trace back this strategy all the way to the founding of T.O.P. office. Having 'formalized' the firm in a company name and logo—itself an embryonic form of institutional management—in 1970, Deleu self-commissioned his first solo-exhibition. Set in the alternative exhibition space Vacuum voor nieuwe dimensies [Vacuum for New Dimensions] (1970–71), run by Filip Francis and Deleu himself, the 'Luc Deleu says farewell to architecture' show opened his eyes as to 'the conceptual openings the art space offered him as

51 'Luc Deleu says farewell to architecture' exhibition, Vacuum voor nieuwe dimensies, Antwerp, Belgium, 1970; Johan Pas, *Vacuum 1970–1971* (Antwerp: Kunstgalerie Rode Zeven, 2006), s.p.

52 *Flagging of the Cogels Osylei*, Antwerp, Belgium, 1971.

53 Lut Pil, 'Luc Deleu: Postfuturismus?', *Kultuurleven* no. 2 (1987).

an architect.'[51] Later, in 1972, these very same spaces came to house the studio and home of Deleu – T.O.P. office—again a claim put on the art institution, made official by Deleu's ceremonial installation of flags leading up to the building a year earlier.[52] Then, after almost two decades of exhibitions in various art institutions across the globe, the titles of which Deleu describes as 'elements of a story,' T.O.P. office created its own exhibition apparatus in 1988.[53] Named after the concept of *Orban Planning*, ORBINO (1988, 2002, 2004, 2007, 2009) is a viewpoint-cum-exhibition space made from three stacked and two cantilevered containers, equipped with a door, staircase, and two small windows on the back.[54] On the front, a wall-to-wall glass curtain window opens up onto a vast panorama of the surroundings. In this highly specific space, the artist-architect has regularly presented the products of his self-commissioned research project *The Unadapted City* (1995-2006). On the walls, shelves, and even on the ceiling, he staged his speculative models and drawings, using the

54 *ORBINO*, 1988.

world as a large visual backdrop.[55] With *ORBINO* Deleu thus hints at the beneficial dialectic offered to him by an exhibition space. A semi-secluded and pseudo-autonomous sphere, the museum is the primordial space which allows for architectural (self-)reflection, while concurrently linking those products of thought to the real world. T.O.P. office's very own

55 *ORBINO* with interior presentation of *The Unadapted City* (1995–2002) (1st realization), Nauerna, Amsterdam, the Netherlands, 2002.

56 Only recently the artist-architect made a comment regarding Duchamp's *Boîte-en-Valise* (1935–41). Discussing his design for a travelling De Stijl exhibition—an expanding flightcase holding paintings, objects, and furniture of the movement—Deleu significantly claimed that 'T.O.P. office should do something similar as well.' Luc Deleu, interview with the author, 20 December, 2011.

'boîte-en-valise', *ORBINO* is a transportable and easy-to-build materialization of Deleu's institutional idiosyncrasy.[56]

When it comes to museums, however, the most insistent of Deleu's claims lies within a sole image. In 1983, the artist-architect entered a polemical design for the competition for a museum of architecture in Ghent. A collage, depicting the globe as a worldwide *Museum of Architecture,* confirms the aforementioned operative status of the institutional sphere to Deleu. It follows up on Le Corbusier's statement that 'the true museum is the one that contains everything,' yet transposes this argument onto an automatic process of overall institutionalization. In this respect, Museum of Architecture strikes a chord with Deleu's earlier *Orban Planning Manifesto* (1980). Since architecture 'underwent an important change of

57 Luc Deleu, 'Introduction', in: *Vrije Ruimte—Espace Libre—Open Space* (Antwerp: Internationaal Cultureel Centrum [I.C.C.]/Ministerie van Nationale Opvoeding en Nederlandse Cultuur, 1980) (exh. cat.), p. 3.

function and meaning' as did 'painting (...) after the invention of photography,' *Orban Planning* no longer condemns architecture to the strict domain many still consider it to be.[57] Instead, it institutes architecture's logic and conventions within a broad and interdisciplinary field.

58 'Men zou kunnen stellen dat de theoretische architectuur, die niet ontworpen is in een direct relatie met een opdracht, opdrachtgever, reële situatie of uitvoering, de ideale ivoren toren is om zich als een autonoom architect in terug te trekken. Daar kan de architect-kunstenaar zich vrijblijvend bezighouden met het ontwerpen van theoretisch en ideale modellen. Hij maakt papieren, conceptuele of geschreven architectuur voor een ideale wereld en een utopische maatschappij.' Deleu, 'Over de belangrijkheid en onbelangrijkheid van de architectuur', p. 8 (author's translation).

'One could argue that theoretical architecture, which is not designed in direct relationship to an assignment, contractor, real situation or execution, is the ideal ivory tower for an autonomous architect to retreat to', writes Deleu. 'There the artist-architect (...) creates paper, conceptual, or written architecture for an ideal world and utopic society.'[58] *Orban Planning,* in other words, denotes the modus operandi resulting from architecture's institutionalization. It is the expanded and experimental way of working that ensues from museological interdisciplinarity, secluding architecture from the world while simultaneously reconnecting it to other domains of cultural production. In such a realm, architecture is both autonomous and socially embedded, both singular and multivalent. Within the age-old debate of art versus life, it chooses both sides, forging a work ethics out of their oxymoronic merger. If Rem Koolhaas successfully affixes Dali's irrationalism to Le Corbusier's rationalism, as Hal Foster has argued, Deleu mediates dialectically opposing

59 Hal Foster, 'Architecture and Empire', in: *Design and Crime (And Other Diatribes)* (London and New York, NY: Verso Books, 2002), pp. 43–64, esp. 60.

avant-gardes of his own.[59] Merging 1960s pluralism with 1980s autonomy in the 'Orban Space' of the museum, he there installs for architecture a conditional, experimental, and above all self-critical sphere.

Back in 1978, then, *Museum for Broken Art* marked the moment when Deleu contemplated the direction his practice was heading. After nearly a decade of architectural practice and with his first gallery exhibition (Spectrum Gallery, Antwerp, Spring 1978) just behind him, it had become clear that the art institution could be of the utmost convenience to him. In the sphere of the arts, Deleu not only could present works as diverse as the *Lego Constructions* (1977–83) or *The Unadapted City* (1995–2006), but he could strengthen his 'objective atti-

60 Deleu, *The Ethics of Architecture*, p. 6.

tude towards architecture' as well.[60] The 1977 confrontation with Matta-Clark contributed to this 'objective attitude', be it via the causality of historical trajectories or through a more Jungian zeitgeist. As opposed to the antagonist position taken up by the American artist—once portrayed as 'the outlaw artist against good taste and Mr. Right Architect'—Deleu never wanted to choose sides. In and through the Turnhout project, he considered the conventions and limits of his working terrain afresh, negotiating the link between architecture and sculpture for the era to come. As such, if the modern art institution was proclaimed extinct at the end of the 1970s, its 'single, perfect similitude' of objects signaling the alleged end of art, *Museum for Broken Art* is its antipode.[61] A phoenix risen from the museum's ashes, its scruffy remains indicated that the art institution, although on the verge of being obsolete, still had a story of objecthood to tell.

[61] See for example Douglas Crimp, *On the Museum's Ruins* (Cambridge, MA: MIT Press, 2000), here p. 54.

luc deleu

stedebouwkundige - architect
cogels-osylei 42
2600 berchem-antwerpen
tel. 031/30 40 67
bank : brussel lambert nr. 320-0295854-74
b.t.w. 509.535.753

...gne ...erligen worden ver-
acht, om zich te bezinnen over
et tema «Wat met Brussel en
laams Brabant in het kader
n de staatshervorming ?» dat
een paneelgesprek behan-
ld zal worden m.m.v. de hh.
em De Ridder, Van Waeg en
urgeois.
Aan de vergezellende echtge-
tes en kinderen wordt onder-
ssen de kans gegeven om
.v. een gids het Afrikaans
useum te bezoeken.
Na de koffietafel wordt het
rogramma afgesloten met het
treden van een kleinkunst-
oep.
Voor meer inlichtingen : Da-
sfonds, provinciaal sekreta-
at, Blijde Inkomststraat 79,
00 Leuven. Tel. (016)23.23.34.

Hans Radloff te Gent

insdag 16 oktober is Hans
dloff van de Brechtgroep bij
staatsteater van Weimar
DR) te gast in teater Arena,
evaarstraat te Gent. Hij
ngt, begeleid door een vijf-
muzikanten, balladen, be-
hten, chansons, gesprekken,
deren, brieven en citaten
o.a. Brecht, Tucholsky,
ruda, Heine, Dessau. De
ziek is van Hans Eisler en
a aantal hedendaagse kom-
isten uit de DDR.

Voor hedendaags museum te Antwerpen

Stichting Gordon Matta - Clark

Een gebouw aan de Ernest
Van Dijckkaai te Antwerpen,
met het kunstwerk «Office baroque», is het enige ter wereld
nog bestaande en in werkelijkheid uitgevoerde werk van de
jonge Amerikaanse kunstenaar
Gordon Matta - Clark, die op
32-jarige leeftijd te New York
overleed. Omdat dit gebouw
met sloping bedreigd wordt,
werd een vereniging gesticht
met het doel, het werk van
Gordon Matta - Clark, dat hij
realizeerde in 1977, in stand te
houden.
De stichting heeft echter een
ruimer doel : beoogd wordt het
kunstwerk op te nemen in een
museum voor hedendaagse
kunst, waarvoor aanpalend de
nodige ruimte beschikbaar is,
en waarvoor de ligging uiterst
geschikt is in de oude stads-
kern. Het projekt kan gereali-
zeerd worden in twee tijden.
Vooreerst moet het huis met
het werk van Matta - Clark
veilig gesteld worden, en later
kan het museumgedeelte ge-
bouwd worden.
Het plan wordt gesteund door
personaliteiten uit binnen- en
buitenland. Het kan uitgevoerd
worden door de staat, de provincie en de stad, samen of
afzonderlijk, maar ook door
een tijdelijke vereniging. Deze
vereniging zou met overheids-
steun of waarborg en met
privé-steun het pand kunnen
kopen, herstellen en bewaren.
De stichting ontving reeds
schenkingen van kunstenaars
voor meer dan veertig miljoen
B.fr., die de kern van een
verzameling vormen. Instellin-
gen zoals de Kunsthalle te
Düsseldorf hebben een tentoonstelling Matta - Clark inge-
richt, teneinde steun voor het
Antwerpse projekt te ver-
werven.
De vereniging doet een be-
roep op de overheid en het
privé-initiatief om de nodige
financiële middelen te verza-
melen. (Men kan lid worden van
de vereniging door storting of
overschrijving van minimum
duizend frank en maximum
tienduizend fr. op bankreke-
ning 551-2521500-54 bij de Bank
van Parijs en de Nederlanden.)

Gazet van Antwerpen 16. oct. 79

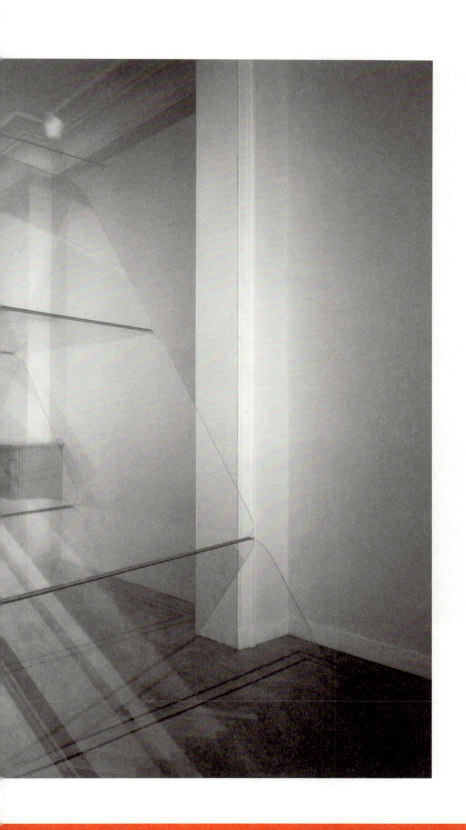

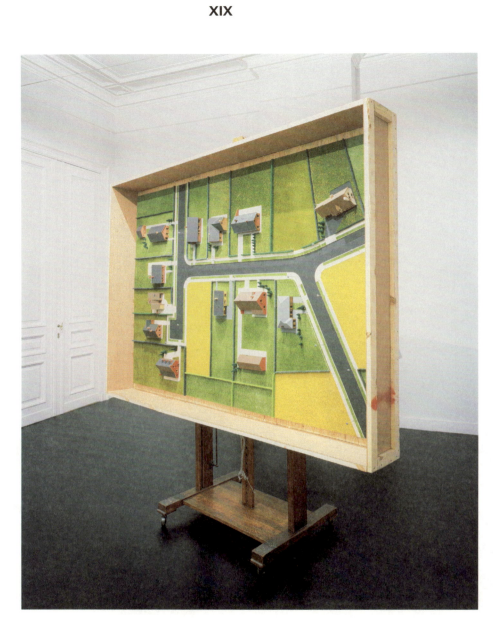

Ready-made Housing Architecture (Luc Deleu Manifesto to the Board), 1987

THE MUSEUM OF ARCHITECTURE

Mobility:

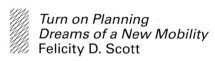

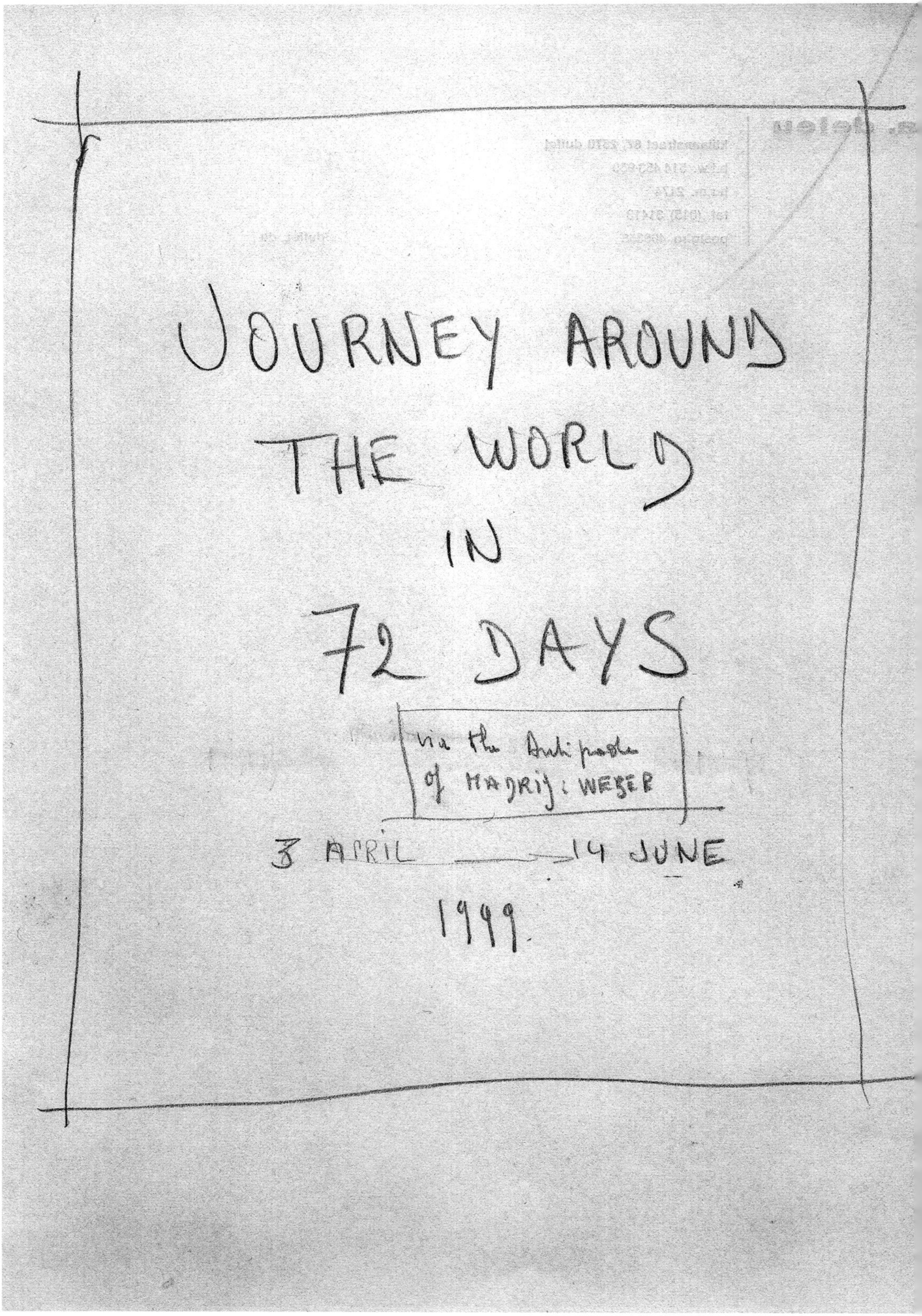

JOURNEY AROUND

THE WORLD

IN

72 DAYS

via the Antipodes
of MADRID : WEBER

3 APRIL ———→ 14 JUNE

1999

Pango Pango

Australia, Sydney and the Blue Mountains

Felicity D. Scott

Turn on Planning
Dreams of a New Mobility

'You are confronted with architecture,
whether you like it or not.'
Luc Deleu[1]

Spaceship Earth

In a short reflection entitled *Spaceship Earth* of 1997, Luc Deleu returned to a theme dating back many decades, a theme appearing in his earliest speculations as T.O.P. office: the rapid reduction of space—both 'untouched' and urban 'open space'—available per inhabitant on planet Earth. Supporting his point with statistics on the ongoing decrease of hectares per earthling as calculated within a global framework (total surface area of earth/world population), he read the rapid erosion of open or undeveloped land as both a product of population growth, urbanization, and what he called 'an historically unprecedented pathological mania for building' during the 20th century.[2] In 1970, the year T.O.P office was founded in Antwerp, questions of population growth, environmental destruction, and the foreclosure of the last remnants of a global commons—such as the sea, desert, jungles, and mountain ranges to which he pointed in this text—were at the forefront of public debate. Widespread discussions about (and fear of) population growth and environmental catastrophe had been fueled, for instance within the United States, by charismatic figures like R. Buckminster Fuller, who in 1969 published two key texts on the subject—*Utopia or Oblivion: The Prospects for Humanity* and *Operating Manual for Spaceship Earth.* The Belgian architect's response to such discourses, which extends far beyond the citation of Fuller's rhetoric in his title, situates his practice as a cogent engagement with environmental debates as they struggled to come to terms with the impact of a transforming modernity, for which the US remained a driving force.

In 1968, the year before Fuller's much-celebrated books appeared, Stanford University Biology professor Paul Ehrlich had published *The Population Bomb*, which had also quickly

1 Luc Deleu, *The Ethics of Architecture*, April 1988 (unpublished), T.O.P. office archives, s.p.

2 Luc Deleu, *Spaceship Earth*, 18 July, 1997 (unpublished) T.O.P. office archives, s.p. As Deleu explained, 'In 1970 (when T.O.P. office was set up) there were on earth still 4.1 ha of land, or 5.6 football pitches, per inhabitant. Now, 27 years later, the population has grown from 2,000,000,000 to about 5,600,000,000 and only 2.66 ha. per inhabitant remain, or 3.6 football pitches.'

3 See R. Buckminster Fuller, *Utopia or Oblivion: The Prospects for Humanity* (New York: Bantam Books, 1969); R. Buckminster Fuller, *Operating Manual for Spaceship Earth* (Carbondale: Southern Illinois University Press, 1969); and Paul Ehrlich, *The Population Bomb* (New York: Ballantine, 1968).

become a bestseller.[3] It was, furthermore, the year Stewart Brand, a former student of Ehrlich and avowed disciple of Fuller, launched his legendary *Whole Earth Catalog*, a large-format print publication, the cover of which featured an iconic image of Earth from outer space.[4] *The Catalog* served as an important access-to-tools and information vehicle within the American counter-culture, promoting alternative lifestyles and rendering Brand another counter-cultural celebrity. Bringing together diverse topics and sales items— ranging from organic gardening, environmentalism, self-hypnosis, Tantra art, Indian teepees, the *Dome Cookbook*, kibbutzum, nomadics and other alternative architectural technologies to psycho-cybernetics, documentary film-making, computers, *National Geographic* and, of course, population control—it also fueled survivalist anxieties. Two years earlier, Brand had campaigned the United States' National Aeronautics and Space Administration (NASA) to release photographs of Earth from outer space taken by astronauts during its Apollo missions.[5] The subsequent circulation of a series of haunting photographs of Earth as a fragile globe, with its land masses and extensive water bodies wrapped in clouds and floating alone in space, soon became affiliated with the world-thinking of the *Whole Earth Catalog* and with that of Fuller and Marshall McLuhan. Deleu retains two issues of the *Whole Earth Catalog* in his personal library, and both Fuller and McLuhan appear repeatedly in his writings.[6] In what follows I want to trace the impact of Deleu's highly mediated encounter with this North American trio as it played out in his reflections on the interrelated notions of mobility and globalization. This rather particular focus is not intended to displace the priority of his distinctly local formation as an architect and the very precise geographical and linguistic terms informing his critical stakes. Rather, it is an attempt to trace the contours of a complex topology emerging within Deleu's work and thinking as he gradually constructed his own mode of 'world thinking', manifest for instance in his notion of 'orbanism', the theorization of which coincided with his eventually setting foot in America in 1980.[7]

4 *Whole Earth Catalog*, Fall 1968 (cover).

5 Stewart Brand, *Why haven't we seen a photograph of the whole Earth yet?*, button.

6 I thank the editors for pointing out to me that Deleu retains to this day two issues of the *Catalog*, namely *The (updated) last Whole Earth Catalog*, 16th edition, June 1975 and *The Next Whole Earth Catalog*, 1st edition, 1980, as well as a the first issue of Shelter, edited by Lloyd Kahn and published in 1973. On the history of the *Whole Earth Catalog* and its legacy, see Andrew G Kirk, *Counterculture Green: The Whole Earth Catalog and American Environmentalism* (Lawrence: University Press of Kansas, 2007) and; Fred Turner, *From Counterculture to Cyberculture: Stewart Brand, the Whole Earth Network, and the Rise of Digital Utopianism* (Chicago: University of Chicago Press, 2006).

7 As pointed out by the editors of this volume, prior to his visit to the US in 1980 Deleu had access to American culture only through the media. The effect of this limited knowledge, they suggest, is nicely encapsulated in a comment by Gordon Matta-Clark following a disastrous meeting of the two in 1977. As recounted to them by Deleu in 2011, Matta-Clark had indicated that 'it was time for him to come to New York.' Correspondence with editors, November 7, 2011.

This focus also attempts to situate Deleu's work as another important moment in the reception of the universalism pervading the 'world thinking' of Fuller et al, to identify a moment of critical reception that renders significant the emergence of contingencies, vicissitudes, and departures from that universalism that were born of its translation into local contexts.

8 *Tribune,* 1972–75 (spread 33).

NASA's images of Earth from outer space left a profound mark on Deleu and the convictions driving his work.[8] We find traces of them, including clippings from the *Whole Earth Catalog*, in his remarkable collage book, begun around 1972 and completed three years later (to which I will return), and the architect continues, to this day, to open public lectures with Apollo images and the epiphany regarding the global character of Earth's environment which they initially provoked. They are even inscribed or embodied, albeit it abstractly, in the graphic identity of his firm.[9] As he explained in 1988, connecting the power of NASA images not only to their circulation in print but also to their dissemination via electronic media,

9 *T.O.P. office logo* (c. 1970) on window of *Les Nénuphars*, Cogels Oyslei, Antwerp, Belgium. Photo Dominique Stroobandt, 1989.

'The "O" in T.O.P. office is the globe, upside-down and in reverse. This is because, on July 16, 1969 [sic], shortly after I finished my studies, Apollo 11 landed on the moon, shown in a direct T.V. broadcast. I then realized very clearly that the earth would never be the same again. For the first time, man had seen the earth from an other planet. [sic] Buckminster Fuller's idea "Spaceship Earth" and the resulting awareness of its passengers' common destiny, was to become a day-to-day fact.[10]

10 Deleu, *The Ethics of Architecture,* s.p. The moon is not, of course, a planet. The Apollo 11 spaceflight left earth on July 16, 1969, but the first humans landed on the Moon on July 20.

For Deleu this shift in aspect and understanding meant that architecture and urbanism could no longer operate solely at the scale of housing or even the town, as had characterized the domain of modernism. Rather, he argued, 'architecture would now have to be treated on a global scale.'[11] **11** Ibid.

This foundational moment of Deleu's practice coincided with the height of the environmental movement's radical energy and its popular appeal during this period. Environmental debates were soon after re-codified in largely managerial and regulatory terms, for instance at the 1972 United Nations Conference on the Human Environment in Stockholm and through the Club of Rome's neo-Malthusian report the same year, *Limits to Growth*, an enormously popular but in retrospect highly problematic treatise that informed the period's arguments regarding the need to limit growth in the developing world.[12] Deleu referenced *Limits to Growth* in his 1995 text, 'A Task for Contemporary Architecture'. But the architect's conceptual and political framework, I want to argue, remained more critical and nuanced than that of this think-tank derived appeal to the need for (Euro-American led) global management of populations and world resources.

12 Donella H. Meadows et al., *The Limits to Growth: A Report of the Club of Rome's Project on the Predicament of Mankind* (New York: Universe Books, 1972). Reiterating Robert Malthus's claim in the late 18th century that the growth of human populations was not sustainable on account of limited food resources, neo-Malthusian thinkers in the late 1960s and early 70s called for population control, particularly in the Third World or Global South. On the centrality of *Limits to Growth* in this respect, see Paul Neurath, *From Malthus to the Club of Rome and Back: Problems of Limits to Growth, Population Control, and Migrations* (Armonk, NY: M. E. Sharpe, 1994).

Deleu argued, in the first instance, that it had become 'obvious that the pressure of human space on earth had increased enormously on account of population growth and, chiefly, consumption patterns, with all its consequences for the environment.' Yet, in the second instance, he inflected these problems with regard to the vicissitudes of modern architecture.[13] Continuing, he explained, indicating a historical transition away from modernist topoi,

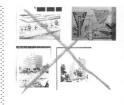

13 *Crossed–Out Collage*, 1970.

'The consumer society requires a different approach than the production society of the beginning of this century. The mid-sixties and early seventies was a period full of changes —social and technical as well as artistic. Le Corbusier and Mies died. The first communication satellites were launched, enabling us to see events from all over the world in "real time" on our home TV screen. Concepts such as "Global Village" and "Spaceship Earth" were in use. The concept "ecology" (thinking about the earth) was in general use by the time of the Club of Rome report, which emphasized the limits of the earth and its mineral resources. And, it should not be forgotten that in 1969 a human being set foot on the moon and could contemplate the earth for the very first time from an other planet! [sic].'[14]

14 Luc Deleu, 'A Task for Contemporary Architecture', in: *Sites & Stations: Provisional Utopias* (Lusitania 7), ed. by Stan Allen with Kyong Park, New York: Lusitania Press, 1995, pp. 234–242 (236–237).

As mentioned above, Deleu invoked the popular duo of 'World Thinking'—McLuhan's Global Village and Fuller's Spaceship Earth—on a number of occasions, making clear that what he called 'world planning' or 'orbanism' was indebted to both and hence inextricably connected the so-called communication revolution.[15] He also repeatedly clarified, however, that orbanism was not directed toward designing or managing the Earth at a global scale (as in Fuller's World Game) but rather to conceiving of a model of design that was attentive to the scale of the earth and its interconnectedness.[16] Hence the ironic commentary on global ecological interdependence appearing in *Proposal for an*

15 On the relation of Fuller and McLuhan see Mark Wigley, 'Network Fever', *Grey Room* 4 (Summer 2001), pp. 82–122.

16 'The World Game', *Whole Earth Catalog*, March 1971 (cover).

International Dunghill on the Sahara of 1975 and *Proposal to Shoot Nuclear Waste to the Sun* of 1976.[17] As he wryly explained, 'The proposal for an international compost heap in the Sahara is, for instance, an ecological project on a planetary scale. By shipping all vegetable waste to the Sahara, where it dehydrates quickly and becomes dust, the winds from the Sahara will carry particles that will automatically fertilize our farmland in Europe. I wrote a proposal to shoot nuclear waste to the sun. Obviously the sun is the best location to dump our nuclear

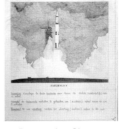

17 *Proposal to Shoot Nuclear Waste to the Sun*, 1976.

18 Deleu, 'A Task for Contemporary Architecture', p. 239. This project to shoot nuclear waste to the sun also appears in the collage book.

waste.'[18] Here Deleu wryly pointed to two interrelated moves of powerful nations such as the US: shipping waste to developing countries while searching for virgin territory into which to expand, including that of outer space.

It is from within this complicated nexus of environment, population, communication, and architectural modernism that I want to investigate Deleu's work as it relates to the figure of mobility, concentrating on his earliest works and, in turn, his revisiting of them decades later. Deleu's work, as we shall see, manifests some of the most critically ambitious and conceptually fascinating architectural responses to this period of great historical change.[19] Le Corbusier and Mies had indeed passed away.

19 Critical to Deleu's response to his time was an engagement with the ageing ideals, or what he termed the 'social attitude' of architectural modernists who, as he put it, 'were convinced that it was the architect's conceptual duty to design ways to provide decent housing to everyone and the government's duty to realize this.' 'Those objectives,' he continued, pointing to CIAM's formulation of Existenzminimum, 'were strongly corrupted during the fifties and sixties,' their ideal standards becoming normative, means to extract maximum profit. Deleu, *The Ethics of Architecture*, s.p.

Mobile Medium University

In 1972, T.O.P. office undertook its first major project: a competition entry for the Universitaire Instelling Antwerpen (University Institute Antwerp, or U.I.A.) entitled *Mobile Medium University*.[20] The competition was launched in the wake of a decision to decentralize the Belgian university system, a move Deleu read as yet another threat posed to agricultural land by development, one that called for a 'visionary policy' to 'protect as patrimony free space, open terrain, pristine or virgin ground.' It was in this context that he first pointed to the 'explosive growth of population on "Spaceship Earth",' a condition to which he responded via a proposal to situate the U.I.A. at sea, to produce an institution literally travelling the globe upon three recycled aircraft carriers—U.I.A 1, 2, and 3—supplemented by no less than 33 helicopters and 'communication media'. 'A progressive policy,' the architect's project statement read, would attempt 'to burden the earth with as little ballast as possible.'

20 *Mobile Medium University*, 1972.

In addition to the environmental claims associated with the U.I.A. project, pedagogical ambitions were articulated as geopolitical ones. (In this sense it is rather uncanny that the institution shares its name with the Union Internationale des Architectes, founded in 1948 as a non-governmental organization to act as a liaison between architects and the United Nations.)[21] Deleu described his response to the program as a 'contemporary translation of the notion "University".' 'It seems to me,' he remarked, 'that a university that sails around the world with its pupils, connected via electronic media, "diplomatizes" real world citizens, with an expanded view of the world.'[22] In another drawing for the project, one ironically referencing posters associated with the occupation of the Parisian Ecole des Beaux-Arts in May 1968, we find the exclamation: 'During my studies at the U.I.A. I was all over the world... I am a real international, not a consumers' diploma!' Deleu returned to an implied cosmopolitanism in 'A Task for Contemporary Architecture', arguing that his reconceptualization of the institution of higher education meant 'students would thus become universal world citizens with a broad vision during their studies.'[23] Yet if appealing to dreams of cosmopolitan citizenship, the project was not, strictly speaking, post-national in character. If perhaps haunted by Fuller's dream of a global humanity recast as nomadic 'citizens of the world', *Mobile Medium University* did not subscribe to Fuller's universalizing paradigm, as evident not only in the invocation of patrimony cited above but also in the naming of each ship.[24] As indicated in another stunning depiction of the three ships sailing in unison, U.I.A. 1 was named 'eddy merx' [sic], troping on the name of the legendary Belgian cyclist Eddy Merckx; U.I.A. 2 was named 'gaston roelands' [sic] after the famous Belgian Olympic steeplechase champion and long-distance runner Gaston Roelants, the alteration serving to insert the word 'land', and; U.I.A. 3 was named 'raymond ceulemens' [sic] playing on the name of world champion three-cushion billiards player Raymond Ceulemans by changing 'mans' to 'mens', the Dutch word for man or human.[25] Here we find a more complex topology at work: the project did not assume the eradication of geopolitical boundaries associated with the Nation-State system, but a traveling national institution would certainly challenge their traditional demarcations.

It was, importantly, a specific genre of ship that Deleu proposed to use in his recycling program. As Anna Meseure notes in 'The Remanence of the Everyday', the project entailed 'a kind of pacifist recycling of the surplus stock of warships,' putting them

21 *Mobile Medium University*, 1972.

22 Project text for *Mobile Medium University*, 1972. I want to thank Stefaan Vervoort for translating this for me.

23 Luc Deleu, 'A Task for Contemporary Architecture', unpublished manuscript version of the text, 1994, T.O.P. office archives, p. 2.

24 See R. Buckminster Fuller, 'The World Game: How to Make the World Work', in *Utopia or Oblivion: The Prospects for Humanity* (New York: Bantam Books, 1969), pp. 157–161.

25 I want to thank Wouter Davidts for unpacking the references at work in these alterations.

26 Anna Meseure, 'The Remanence of the Everyday', in: *Luc Deleu, Luc Deleu & T.O.P. office 1967–1991* (Antwerp: Museum voor Hedendaagse Kunst, 1991), pp. 12–13. Phrases inverted.

'to peaceful and meaningful use.'[26] Here too, of course, we find the legacy of Fuller's long-standing ambition to turn 'weaponry arts' to 'livingry arts'. Deleu's choice of warships at this moment could not have failed to resonate with their use in the Vietnam War as it spread into Cambodia, both countries then experiencing not only massive violence against their populations but also unprecedented environmental damage. And, as noted above, it was a particular type of warship that appeared in the first version of *Mobile Medium University*; aircraft carriers from which were being launched a stream of fighter-bomber planes whose packages included not only incendiary bombs but the defoliants and other chemical weapons responsible for the 'ecocide' in Indochina. That is, the ships were key components of a US military strategy bent on flattening villages and destroying forests in the attempt to counter rural insurgencies and force the displaced populations to move to urban concentrations where, it was believed, they could be more easily monitored and controlled.[27] Warships, if certainly abundant, were not exactly surplus at this moment and Deleu's ironic suggestion that they be treated as such was a powerful provocation. Indeed, as his project implies, once considered obsolescent they could be appropriated for artistic (and in this case peaceful) purposes. Deleu pointed out that the artistic, or the aesthetic dimension was important here. In the process of their appropriation the ships' appearances too had been détourned: U.I.A. 1 was colored black and white; U.I.A. 2 was painted fluorescent blue and fluorescent yellow; U.I.A. 3 was colored brilliant green and brilliant red. 'By means of these colours,' the architect posited, 'the university will have the most monumental impact in the visited ports.'[28]

27 See Barry Weisberg, *Ecocide in Indochina: The Ecology of War* (San Francisco: Canfield Press, 1970).

28 Project text printed on poster.

Deleu reiterated this tactic of appropriating newly (or potentially) obsolescent transportation technologies when *Mobile Medium University* appeared in slightly different form as the *Proposal for a Mobile University in Antwerp*, the first of his remarkable series of manifesto-like proposals dating from 1972–1980.[29] In this instance we find a civilian vessel, the S.S. *France*, selected for recycling. Constructed in 1962 as the largest cruise ship in the world, by the early 1970s its efficacy as a mode of luxury transportation between Europe and the US was coming under significant pressure by air travel. Furthermore, in June 1978, almost half a decade after the Arab countries' oil embargo and subsequent oil crisis of 1973, Deleu drafted a related proposal for recycling supertankers, *Unit for (Mobil) Sea Cities*.[30] This, we are told, had the

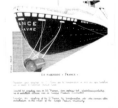

29 Proposition for the Recycling of the SS France, 1972.

30 *Unit for (Mobil) Sea Cities*, 1978.

capacity 'to fuel energy on the spot.' Depicting a supertanker as a giant, mobile, seafaring piece of ground upon which to host greenhouses for growing vegetables and fruit, and behind which floats a fish breeding tank, the sketch describes 'Semi-self supporting vessels for x inhabitants by recycling supertankers.' Supertankers to transport oil were far from obsolete. The largest in history, *Seawise Giant* (which at 458 meters long exceeded the height of the Empire State Building), was constructed the following year. But the vehicle's actual obsolescence was not the point. It was the ability of architects to communicate an image of another world that was at stake. As Deleu understood all too well, and as indicated by 'mobile medium' in the title of his project, architecture is a medium, a medium of communication, one that is conceived and produced, and circulates within the sphere of media; it is a discipline constituted as a media object and that produces media objects.

Mobile Medium Architecture

The constellation of historical forces informing *Mobile Medium University* and the media through which these forces become legible symptoms of their time might be best unpacked through Deleu's remarkable collage book *Tribune* (1972–75). Primarily taking the form of a scrap-book, on the pages of which he accumulates provocative juxtapositions of media images of American militarism, expanding communications technologies, environmental concerns, and the infrastructure and component parts of global (even interplanetary) transportation systems, among other images, it also served at times as a working notebook within which *Mobile Medium University* appears as part of a larger architectural endeavor.[31] The cover features an article from the front page of the *International Herald Tribune* reporting on a general strike in Britain. Onto the lead image of police grappling with protesters is collaged an early video recorder. Following SONY's release of the Portapak in 1967, portable video technology was widely hailed at the time among the counterculture and underground video community as providing an accessible, tactical, and decentralized means for producing

31 *Tribune*, 1972–75 (cover).

alternative channels of information and feedback into (hence interrupting the information monopoly of) the one-way distribution channel of broadcast television.[32] As evident in two important films made by the architect during this period—*Situations* (1970–73) and *Police* (1972–73)—Deleu's invocation of portable video technology spoke to the fact that it did not function simply as a mechanism of liberation of information but remained a product of, and operated within, what Gilles Deleuze would later theorize as a control society.[33] In the former

32 See, for instance, Michael Shamberg, and Raindance Corporation, *Guerrilla Television* (New York: Holt, Reinhart and Winston, 1971).

33 See Gilles Deleuze, 'Postscript on Control Societies', in: *Negotiations: 1972–1990* (New York: Columbia University Press, 1995), pp. 177–183 and Gilles Deleuze and Toni Negri, 'Control and Becoming', in: *Negotiations*, pp. 169–176.

we find a recursive structure of filming within the space of the city, in the latter a remarkable sequence of tracking and surveillance of police and police vehicles as they simultaneously circulated within the city and controlled or regulated circulation.[34] Opening the collage book one finds tucked inside the slipcover an IBM 96 column punch card, an input device introduced in the early 1970s in association with IBM System/3 computers. On the opposite page is an advertisement for another portable media tool, a Kodak XL Super8 movie camera. Released in May 1972, this was an

34 *Tribune*, 1972–75 (inside front cover).

amateur hand-held camera notable for the capacity to film in ambient light conditions, as might be necessary for surveillance operations. Immediately below the image of this portable device is the stamp 'T.O.P. office'—an acronym for Turn on Planning—featuring the inverted image of Earth. The stamp is reiterated at strategic points throughout the book, marking that an image has been appropriated into his project for alternative ends. Indicating, we might say, that an image has been 'turned on'.

35 *Tribune*, 1972–75 (spread 3).

Turn the page again and we encounter a manifesto about mobility, architecture, and communication that reminds us that it is not just physical transportation that is at stake in Deleu's images of mobility, or in his architecture.[35] It reads,

MOBILE
ARCHITECTURE
MEDIUM
MEDIUM-MAN
energy : → energy belt → energy clothing.
MAN + ENERGY
can be plugged in to all media
minimize transport by maximizing communication
communication = transportation x K
communication/transportation = K

On the next page we find *Mobile Medium University* for Antwerp situated as a component of the T.O.P. office project: *Mobile Medium Architecture* or *M.M.A.*[36] In addition to further collaged material—including a newspaper classified listing for a video recorder and a color image of the dramatic rock formations of the American Southwest, a key icon of the vanished American frontier—are two enigmatic comments regarding the communication matrix within which the new mobility, and the new 'medium-man', necessarily operates. The first reads,

36 *Tribune*, 1972–75 (spread 4).

'your friend has no address
always changing coordinates
to find your friend
you will have to communicate intensely
address book → CoordinatoPhone, CoordinatoVideo.'

Stressing that such apparent liberty to move about is suspended within a regulatory system and an information environment geared towards increasing control, the second comment, inscribed immediately below, reads, 'If the administration keeps track of your coordinates the system is ever again worn out.'[37] It was, I want to argue, through this articulation of an apparently increased freedom to move about or gain access to multiple media channels coupled with the recognition of the apparatus of control within which one performed that mobility that Deleu conceived of architecture as a mobile medium. He had recognized, that is, the manner in which the system facilitating mobility, and even eliciting an increasing deracination from place, simultaneously drove the need for ever-more advanced forms of communication and control and with it an expanding security apparatus. This system had become the milieu in which architecture now operated. The question was 'how' and 'to what ends?'

37 I want to thank Wouter Davidts for his kind translation.

The collage book *Tribune* offers further clues: on the page opposite the announcement of *Mobile Medium University* we find a photograph of New York's financial district skyline with the launch of a NASA rocket superimposed. It is entitled T.O.P. office *M.M.A.* Beneath is an array of print media, including; a postage stamp bearing an image of Belgium's King Baudouin, a woman lasciviously licking her right breast, heavy equipment for earth moving, police motorcycles, the insignia of the United States' Central Intelligence Agency, and the typed words 'suppose they gave a war and nobody came.' (The latter was a slogan from the Vietnam War that was adopted as the title of a 1970 feature film.) In large orange text are the hand-written words 'Turn on Promotion'.[38] Among the vast collection collaged into this 300 page document are repeated images of: film and video cameras and playback equipment, audio equipment, boats and ships (opening with aircraft carriers but also including cruise ships, tankers, yachts, and other vessels, many on fire or sinking), docks and shipping containers, airplanes (from biplanes and passenger jets to fighter planes), zeppelins, helicopters, motorcycles, cars, vans, trucks, tanks, trams, trains,

38 *Tribune*, 1972–75 (spread 6).

Tribune, 1972–75 (spread 13).

Tribune, 1972–75 (spread 14).

39 *Tribune*, 1972–75 (spread 30).

40 *Tribune*, 1972–75 (spread 52).

Tribune, 1972–75 (spread 74).

42 Regarding the container works Meseure writes, 'Luc Deleu was even more explicit in 1986 when he erected a *Small Triumphal Arch* in Tielt in 1986 over an armored car. His aim was to criticize the technical constructions and function of a highly industrialized transport and communication society. At the same time he attacked the aggressiveness of the industrialized countries and their interests, often defended by force of arms, by framing and surrounding a symbol of this aggression—an armored car—with containers. Containers symbolize the market economy which can function, if not solely, then certainly better in peacetime. The relationship between military vehicle and container is, however, also evident. Arms dealers from the industrialized countries ship their weapons in dismantled and packaged forms in containers to the Third World: merchants of death. The triumphal arch at Tielt is also an eloquent monument to, or rather against, this.' She notes that triumphal arches and obelisks are 'always an ode to power.' Meseure, 'The Remanence of the Everyday', pp. 18–19.

railway infrastructure, space vessels and rocket ships, transit tickets, maps, globes, mission control rooms, television, computer systems and interfaces, beaches, currencies (both coins and notes), cigarette packets, oil refineries, vernacular and historic buildings, suburban developments, office towers including the World Trade Center in New York and the Sears Tower in Chicago, interspersed with soft- and not-so-soft pornographic images of women.[39] One page includes a *Time* magazine cover featuring a NASA image of Earth with the caption 'Time brings you the world'.[40] On another we find U.S. President Richard Nixon shaking hands with Elvis Presley, and later an image of Henry Kissinger on the phone while reading a newspaper captioned, 'Be a TOP Office Multi Mixed Media Man!' Margaret Thatcher appears with the text bubble 'We Cann't [sic] affort [sic] socialism'.

Within this complex field of references appear images signaling that a number have been appropriated as T.O.P. office projects: trucks bearing the stamp of the firm, rail freight containers re-functioned as dwellings, with captions such as 'A T.O.P. office container home is good for you!'[41] Aircraft and shipping containers too are cast as harboring the prospect of functional redirection for dwelling, appropriating a key icon of the global circulation of commodities (including weapons) to other ends.[42] Here we find the infrastructure and components servicing the usual flow of goods—a flow driven by a neo-liberal, neo-imperial economic system perpetuating structural inequities, exploitation, violence, and greed—and redirected for other forms of mobility. Deleu's proposals, to reiterate, put its components to other, more

41 *Tribune*, 1972–75 (spread 5).

Tribune, 1972–75 (spread 21).

43 Deleu, 'A Task for Contemporary Architecture', (unpublished), p. 3.

44 Luc Deleu in 'Trans-location: Interview by Marc Mer, Thomas Feuerstein with Luc Deleu', typescript dated summer 1993, p. 3.

peaceful, uses. The containers notably return at a later date, when, as Deleu wrote, 'I myself realized the *Proposal for Mobile Monuments with containers*.'[43] Expanding on this in 'Trans-location', an interview conducted by Marc Mer and Thomas Feuerstein, Deleu noted of his use of containers to produce monuments, 'By the choice of universal archetypes (triumphal arches, gates, obelisks, towers, bridges), built with universally known objects that can be found everywhere on earth, I thought to have complied with the requirements of a mobile monument.'[44] Far from neutral architectural forms, those triumphal arches, obelisks, etc., were, as Feuerstein stressed, evident 'symbols of imperial self-presentation,' here ironically asserting 'a liberation from architectonic statements of power and identity.'[45]

45 Thomas Feuerstein in 'Trans-location': Interview by Marc Mer, Thomas Feuerstein with Luc Deleu', p. 3.

Later in the collage book an image of Earth from outer space is captioned 'Peace-City, T.O.P. 73', above which the words 'We (all) live in an infinitely small space' emanate from a text bubble.[46] The facing page announces 'Mobile World Exhibition, A TOP Office Project.'[47] Five spreads later we find a design for an exhibition structure or 'stand', including a drawing of a simple box-like space annotated with a list of requisite electronic equipment. In two of the four upper corners are to be installed Super8 and color television cameras, respectively, with projectors, speakers and other sound equipment located at various heights to transmit information to a wall-sized screen. Here viewers would be quite literally suspended within an information environment as exhibit, their movement symptomatically tracked and projected within the infinitely small space of a Mobile World Exhibition.

46 *Tribune*, 1972–75 (spread 61).

47 *Tribune*, 1972–75 (spread 66).

Perhaps the most potent crystallization of the architect's response to this nexus of historical forces is the repeated appearance of a project titled *Mobile Medium Architecture* of 1973.[48] Popping up throughout *Tribune* are images of Deleu's own customized Opel Blitz, a refunctioning of a German truck widely known for having been the Wehrmacht's vehicle of choice during WWII.[49] Painted a steel grey, with red trim on its wheels, fenders, and ladder-ac-

49 In 'The Loxodromic Course of an Architect', Guy Châtel notes that this particular truck had formerly been used as an ambulance. Unpublished manuscript, 1993, translated by L. Gillemot, T.O.P. office archives.

48 *Tribune*, 1972–75 (spread 27).

Tribune, 1972–75 (spread 35).

50 The Opel Blitz appears at other points in the collage book *Tribune* (1973–75), but not necessarily as this project. For instance, it appears in a doorway on spread 5, opposite images of Aircraft Carriers, connecting it directly to *Mobile Medium University* and on the following spread in association with a reel to reel player and bomber plane.

cessed roof rack, it bore the words 'Mobile Medium Architecture Promotion' along one side, with the T.O.P. office logo appearing on the door. The project's first main appearance is rather discrete; we find it situated among commercial vans, a peculiar bubble car by French industrial designer Paul Arzens, and an ad for a 'house on wheels'.[50] Later we come across a drawing depicting it in psychedelic colors with a skyscraper cast as a hood ornament, a gesture wryly inverting Hans Hollein's *Rolls Royce Grille on Wall Street* of 1966.[51] (Hollein's best-known photo collage, his 1964 *Aircraft Carrier City in the Landscape*,

had preempted Deleu's use of this military vessel, a detail not incidental here.

51 Hans Hollein, *Rolls Royce Grille on Wall Street,* 1966.

That Deleu was in dialog with Hollein was even more evident when he appropriated the title of Hollein's famous 1968 manifesto in an account of his own work. 'Alles ist Architektur', that is, was recast as an article outlining his conceptually brilliant intervention into the Belgian laws of February 20, 1939 and June 26, 1963 ensuring the monopoly of the Order of Architects. To this day Deleu retains a copy of the January 1968 double issue of *Bau*, in which Hollein's manifesto initially appeared.) In turn we encounter a photograph of *Mobile Medium Architecture Promotion* accompanied by an image of a sun-oven,

52 *Tribune,* 1972–75 (spread 65);

Tribune, 1972–75 (spread 114).

supertanker, and petroleum refinery, superimposed with the words 'Power Research Promotion'. Yet another appearance, a color snapshot, shows the Deleu family in front of the van during a year-long road trip to Macedonia. Here it shares the page with an image of a ship cruising off the lower shore of Manhattan.[52] Finally, making connections to protests against the war in Vietnam, it appears opposite a photograph of John Lennon and Yoko Ono's legendary March 1969 week-long 'bed-in' in Amsterdam, with the words 'Bed Peace, Hair Peace' appearing behind them.[53]

53 *Tribune,* 1972–75 (spread 128).

Deleu provided further clues to the disciplinary stakes motivating *Mobile Medium Architecture* in the project text.[54] If, as he put it, comfortable transportation was a potential emerging within contemporary technocratic society, the

54 *Mobile Medium Architecture Promotion,* 1973.

conception of automobiles nevertheless continued to operate within an opposition—'immobiles' versus 'mobiles'—within which cars were often cast negatively as the counterpart of fixed modes of dwelling or real estate. It was in this sense that *Mobile Medium Architecture Promotion* was launched as a conceptual correction or revaluation of the status of 'mobile' architecture, one departing not only from immobility but also from forces driving real estate speculation. Acknowledging the ubiquity of cars, and the degree to which they had irreversibly altered forms of living, he continued: 'Architects and urban planners only see immobile architecture. Through this model, T.O.P. office wants to make a first step towards a promotional campaign for mobile medium architecture. As such, this is a conceptual project, one that is constantly present in reality. It attempts to oppose mobile living, furnished with media, to cities and towns.'[55] Deleu is once again taking seriously the power of architectural images to produce and disseminate conceptions of alternative modes of living and of the architectures that might be affiliated with them.

55 I want to thank Stefaan Vervoort for translating this for me.

Within such images of alternative modes of dwelling, and in particular in the association of mobility and media, we can identity precedents from the experimental architectural work of the 1960s and early 1970s. We need think only of famous Archigram projects such as David Greene's *Living Pod* (1966) or Mike Webb's *Cushicle* (1966) and *Suitaloon* (1968) to recall that related ideas were circulating.[56] But it is perhaps in the work of the American counter-cultural collective Ant Farm, particularly in projects such as *Truckstop Network* of 1971, a project which extended their practice of customizing cars to propose a dispersed mobile self-governed community connected via both transportation and communication networks, that we find a closer affiliation.[57] Customized and other 'funk' vehicles had by this time become a chosen mode of dwelling among the American counter-culture, their very mobility and distinctly alternative aesthetic speaking to the refusal to participate in the 'American Way of Life'.[58] They spoke of the refusal, that is, of normative modes of life affiliated with a wasteful consumer society and its dominant structures of power. Their entry into architecture aimed to amplify this critique. In *Spaceship Earth*, with which we began, Deleu attended quite precisely to the importance of this conjunction, explaining, 'Urban planning and architecture are always a structural and three-dimensional packaging of socially dominant attitudes, and in this way

56 David Greene (Archigram), *Living Pod*, 1966.

57 Ant Farm, *Truckstop Network Placemat*, c. 1971.

58 On Ant Farm and the counter-cultural practice of customizing cars, see for instance Felicity Scott, *Living Archive 7: Ant Farm* (Barcelona: ACTAR Editorial, 2008), and William Chaitkin, 'The Alternatives', in: *Architecture Today*, ed. Charles Jencks (New York: Harry N. Abrams, Inc., 1982), pp, 220–299.

the contemporary urbanization of the world (orbanization) emanates from the hegemony of capitalism, with its high consumption and low use of space.'

59 *Tribune*, 1972–75 (spread 91).

60 Luc Deleu, *Tribune*, 1972–75 (spread 94).

Tribune also includes a project titled simply 'Mobile Architecture: Proposal'.[59] Announced under the distinctly psychedelic caption 'For your trips!', and forming something like a domestic-version of *Unit for (Mobil) Sea Cities*, the proposal was offered as a 'First step to selfgenerating house.' Depicting a truck built-out to support a greenhouse and 'Filled up with ground for biological system,' it reinforces the connection not only to customized vehicles but also to their affiliation with exodus from what was widely referred to at the time as 'the system'.[60] Immediately below it is a photograph of police in riot gear beating protestors. A bad trip indeed in the rhetoric of the moment.[61]

61 Related proposals such as *Self-Power Man* of 1978 also resonate with this search of a means of exodus from the system that, while deploying communication and other prosthetic technologies, remains in alignment with the ethos of dropping out.

Turn on, Tune in, Drop out

I want to return to the caption 'Turn on Promotion' appearing in the opening pages of the collage book in association with *Mobile Medium Architecture*. It offered another rendering of the office's acronym T.O.P., more typically read, as mentioned earlier, as short for 'Turn on Planning'. If we take seriously the implied reference to Timothy Leary' catchy phrase 'Turn on, tune in, drop out', then we might speculate that Deleu was proposing that once a practice (whether planning, promotion, or architecture) had been turned on to a new consciousness which, whether aided by psychedelic drugs or not, aimed to achieve a departure from conventional modes of perception and understanding, it could in turn tune in to the world around it and even drop out. Dropping out entailed relinquishing connections to the capitalist system and its hierarchies and techniques of power and control, a refusal to participate within its institutions and normative modes of life including, we might say, those invested within fixed architecture. To some degree I think this is what is going on in the work of Deleu that I have been tracing here, but there are further complications to Leary's implied narrative when it encounters architecture here. First is the question of whether the addition of the word 'office' is to be understood ironically or paradoxically, as marking the limits of any experimental architectural practice. Can an architectural or planning office drop out? Is this not a contradiction in terms or even a category mistake? That is, if it succeeded in disarticulating its practice from longstanding roles of environmental control in the service of capital, would it remain architecture? Deleu, as we have seen, remained cognizant of the normalizing role the discipline plays, referring, as cited above, to architecture as 'always a structural and three-dimensional packaging of socially dominant attitudes.' But his work also implies that experimental practice can launch images of a counter-logic, even images of counter-conducts by architects.

Deleu indicated on a couple of occasions that his work neither sought to negate or strictly oppose the system nor to operate entirely outside of it, but rather that he attempted to operate *otherwise* with architectural expertise, to different ends. For instance, in the interview 'Trans-location' he repeatedly qualified that his work was not entirely anarchistic in nature. Pointing to Deleu's *Proposal to Classify Public Transport as a Monument*, Feuerstein had read a 'certain criticism of the obsession with mobility' within the project, asking the architect, 'Where does the paradox of mobility lie?' Deleu responded, 'In my urban design concept, the contrast between mobiles and real estate does no longer exist (mobiles are an essential part of the world and the town, and consequently belong to the field of urban design and architectural theory). For the first time in history, we could live in a mobile society, still,' he continued, pointing to the structural violence of the current system, 'our contemporary society is very static (nomads, gypsies, bargemen are repressed and a fixed home address is obligatory).' The proposal, he wryly went on, was in fact a 'functional' one. It was addressed not to restricting or stilling movement as such but rather to removing the appeal to novelty that drove consumer society from the realm of public transit.[62]

62 'Trans-location', p. 2.

Feuerstein then turned to *Mobile Medium University*, suggesting that Deleu had 'equate[d] mobility with universality,' that the concept of mobility had undergone 'a redefinition away from locomotion' and towards a 're-assignment of function' in which the warship had become a 'pacifist university.' To Feuerstein this indicated an 'anarchist conviction.' Deleu disagreed, offering a clarification:

'to link mobility to anarchy does not seem right to me. Anarchy means absence of government, lack of organized rule, disorder and chaos. However, *anarchism* in the sense of the pursuit of individual freedom at the expense of central authority, the banning of all authority for authority's sake, has always been the motive behind my thinking. However, I prefer *total decentralization* to the word anarchism, a concept that is not possible thanks to various systems like, for instance, G.P.S. (Globel [sic] Positioning System), wireless phone and fax, radio, (...)'

After reiterating the idea that the traveling university would facilitate 'an intellectually broad-minded society of the future,' he added somewhat cryptically, perhaps pointing to the other prospects for global thinking, 'What is possible for the army *must* also be possible for universities.'[63]

63 'Trans-location', p. 3.

In both responses to Feuerstein we find Deleu moving the conversation away from a oppositional paradigm towards an account of his search for a manner of critically operating within the dominant system, appropriating the infrastructural, transportation, and communication technologies of capitalist development, even its military vessels, to other (more equitable and less violent) ends. Indeed, as he made clear in *Spaceship Earth*, he was not an anarchist but believed in the value of government and in the practice of instituting new policies as a means to counter the destruction of public space. 'The policy-makers could completely rethink a lot of open space, which cannot serve private purposes, in its entirety,' he noted, continuing,

'If there is one thing that might easily be placed under the almost exclusive authority of administrative powers, it is indeed open space, so as to safeguard and optimize it for today's generation, but chiefly for future generations and their society. Authority is backed up by policy (why should there be authority without policy?) and a policy is of necessity based on the evaluation of research and the proposals and creations that ensue from it. It seems to me that the (re)organization of the world is more than ever a contemporary policy topic. Increasing intolerance, refugee, starvation and race problems, and religious and other wars are obvious signs of this.'

If planning was to be turned on, that is, the ambition was certainly for it to operate within a new register of consciousness, one able to tune in to questions of displacement, social and economic inequity, environmental problems, violence, racism, and war. Deleu was not, however, proposing that architects drop out but rather that they work in a conceptual register to reveal the discipline's relation to such contemporary forces, and that they do so in a strategic manner that promoted structural transformations from within.

In *Spaceship Earth* Deleu also turned to the critical vocation pertaining to architecture's status as a medium of communication, reiterating the connection of this status to the terms outlined in his *Orban Planning Manifesto* of 1980. Alluding to geopolitical transformations that had complicated Cold War oppositions, he argued:

'Architects can also create an image of a new world and, after the collapse of communism, the policy-makers could well ask the urban planners to represent the ultimate ideal of the capitalist society: capitalism for everyone. It is precisely infrastructure, public space and open space that belong to everyone and could in the sense be the domain, and theme, of the art of contemporary capitalist building. In this way urban planning would be given an orban framework and would become a part of a larger whole, global planning.'

Hence it is not surprising to find Deleu returning to *Mobile Medium University* in 1989, right after the fall of the Berlin Wall, when the model of the three brightly colored aircraft carries appeared (we might even say was re-appropriated) in

64 *Mobile Medium University revisited (floating U.I.A.),* 1989. See Deleu, 'A Task for Contemporary Architecture' (unpublished).

65 *The Museum of Architecture,* collage 1983.

67 *Self-Power Man,* 1978.

the context of new maps of the planet, and again in 2006 as part of the ongoing project *Orban Space.*[64]

In *Orban Planning Manifesto* Deleu stressed the fact that in an age characterized by massive environmental pressures, the task of the town planner-architect—what he called the orban planner—had radically transformed, likening this change to the impact of photography on the pictorial function of Western painting.[65] His role, the architect posited, had translated into the dissemination of 'information': 'he is a medium, a trendsetter and/or town fool, etc… He designs, publishes, performs, shows, realizes or plays, etc.' The orban planner, he added in concluding, 'has become primarily a theoretician, who in rare cases realizes his visionary views on spaces of the planet earth.'[66] At stake for Deleu and T.O.P. office, and dating to early work such as *Mobile Medium University*, was the necessity to articulate a theory, and a medium, that accounted for the impact of the forces of modernity driving increased mobility. Remaining a central concern through to his current work on orbanism, this theorization involved demonstrating connections between physical mobility, environmental security, and the global circulation of commodities.[67] Freedom to circulate, he recognized, was not only a sign of emancipation but also, simultaneously, a symptom of neo-liberal economics and of the rising territorial insecurity that was a necessary counterpart to its drive to globalization. To put it simply (and as suggested by the complex articulation of mobility with information and surveillance technologies on the opening pages of *Tribune*) with increased liberty to move about, and with increased flow of images, resources, and goods, comes increased regulation and control. It is for having recognized the contours of these emergent techniques of power that Deleu's work stands as a remarkable critique of architecture's imbrication within this globalizing milieu, at once symptomatizing, conceptualizing, and even embodying (as a medium) the forces of modernity driving that increased mobility. The work of T.O.P. office not only spoke (and still speaks) to the increasingly global nature of environmental systems but also to the capitalist economics and liberal ideologies, electronic technologies, media circulation, transportation infrastructures and their component

66 Luc Deleu, 'Orbanistisch Manifest/ Manifeste d'orbanisme/ Orban Planning Manifesto', in: *Vrije Ruimte—Espace Libre— Open Space* (Antwerp: Internationaal Cultureel Centrum [I.C.C.], 1980), pp. 20–26. In 'A Task for Contemporary Architecture' he stressed this point again, noting 'with the T.O.P. office I wanted to develop an urbanistic theory, because I was convinced that a theory of urbanism and architecture in itself can be more important than realized urbanism or built architecture. Theory always comes first and realizations of urbanism and architecture are always founded on a theoretical basis.' (p. 237)

parts (such as containers and aircraft carriers), warfare, and violent forms of displacement and fixing that inform and drive the regulation of those environmental systems. At the historical moment when architecture was ceasing to operate in terms of fixed or finite objects and began to participate in the construction of this global milieu, these distributed elements, he demonstrates, had become critical to the medium of architecture recast as the more planetary conception of orbanism.

Plug-in-mens.
~~De mens zelf in de energie~~ (draagt de energie) van zijn apparatuur

MOBIELE
MEDIUM **UNIVERSITEIT** TE
ANTWERPEN

BY   T.O.P. OFFICE
MOBIL MEDIUM ARCHITECTURE
M.M.A.

UW VRIEND HEEFT GEEN ADRES
STEEDS VERANDERENDE COÖRDINATEN
OM UW VRIEND TE VINDEN
ZUL JE STERK MOETEN COMMUNICEREN
ADRESSENBOEKJE ⟶ COÖRDINATENFOON
VIDEO

telefunken bandopn. inl. tel. na 19 u.
38.93.34.   (20446-A)

Splintern. **videorecorder** Philips
(2 mnd. oud, waarborg) wgs om-
stand. 27.500 F + 3 videoband. à
3.400 F. Event. ook adaptor à
4.250 F. Tel. 37.71.70.   (20440-A)

Bidet splinter. T. 52.60.22

Gust en Jan, beiden 9 jaar, komen uit
school en praten nog wat over de
voorbije godsdienstles. Jan zegt:
— Geloof jij dat de duivel werkelijk
zou bestaan?
Waarop Gust antwoordt:
— Maar nee, zie eens wat ze ons
hebben wijsgemaakt over Sinterklaas.
Wees gerust, 't zal ook wel vader zijn.

ALS
DE
ADMINISTRATIE
UW
COÖRDINATEN
BIJHOUDT
IS
HET
SYSTEEM
WEER
AL
MAAR
VERSLETEN

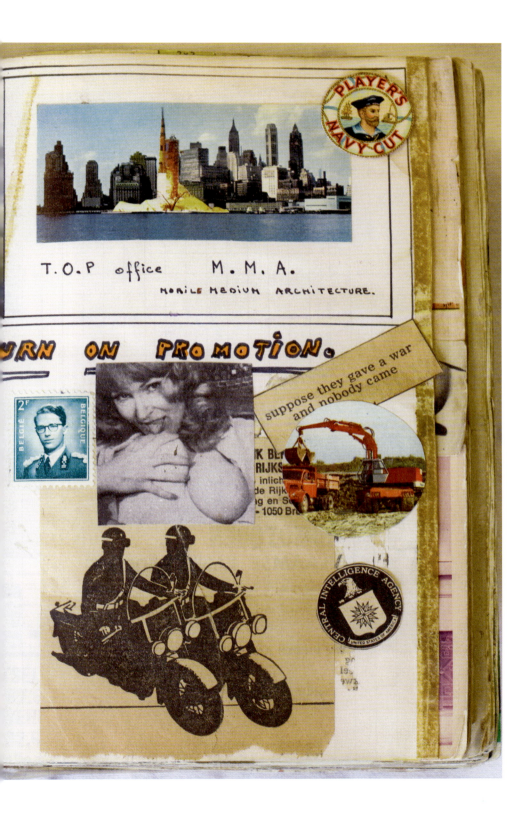

T.O.P office   M.M.A.

MOBILE MEDIUM ARCHITECTURE.

URN ON PROMOTION.

suppose they gave a war
and nobody came

WIJ LEVEN IN EEN ONEINAIG KLEINE RUIMTE L.D.

PEACE-CITY   T.O.P. 73

Het dynamiet werd in 1866 uitgevonden doo_
Nobel. Hier kleine patronen voor geofysisc_
onderzoek en grotere staven voor het late_
springen van gesteenten.   (Foto B.P.D_

Tigris

Flying on Sunshine

The prospects for a solar mega-industry were highlighted by the flight of the Solar Challenger—the first plane powered entirely by sunshine to fly the English Channel. *Page 40*

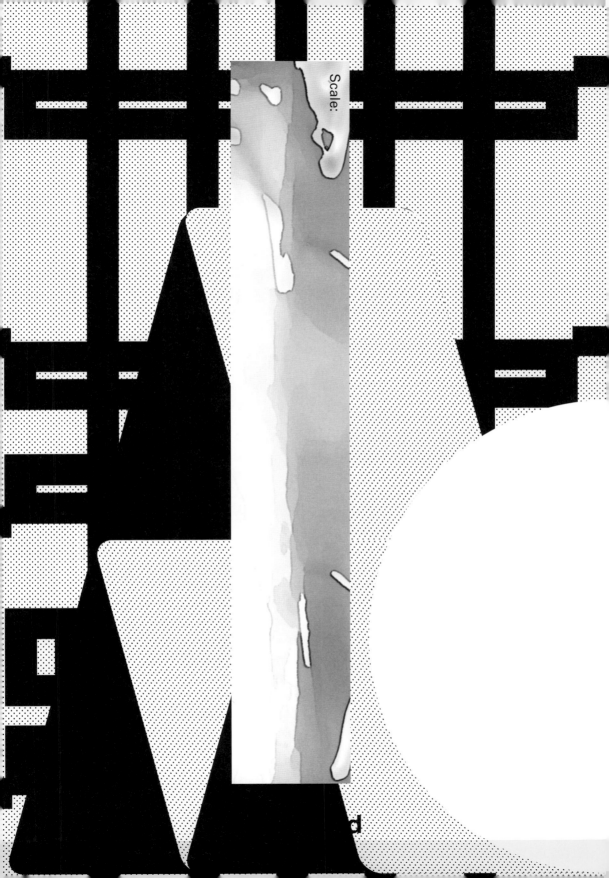

Scale:

Scale:

Luc Deleu — *Gouden Driehoek* (setsquare golden section), 1983

T.O.P. office — *Housing (&) the City*, Barcelona, 1989 (scale and perspective), section (as a plan)

Office Kersten Geers David Van Severen - Office Space — Keywan — painted Styrofoam, picture KG, 2011

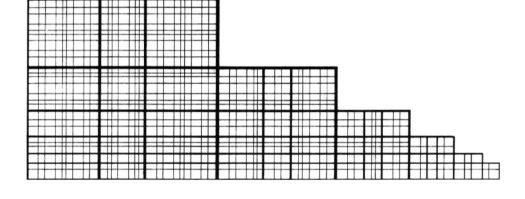

T.O.P. office — *Housing (&) the City,* Barcelona, 1989 (scale and perspective), section — turned (as an elevation)

Office Kersten Geers David Van Severen — Office Space — XPO —
painted Styrofoam, picture KG, 2011

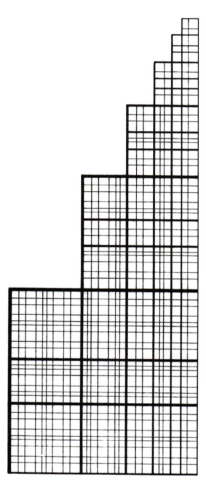

T.O.P. office — *Housing (&) the City*, Barcelona, 1989 (scale and perspective), section — turned (as a section)

Office Kersten Geers David Van Severen — Office Space —
Belvedere Walraevens — painted Styrofoam, picture KG, 2011

Peter Fischli David Weiss — *Raum unter der Treppe* — painted Styrofoam (Museum für Moderne Kunst, Frankfurt am Main/Stuttgart, Cantz Verlag, 1995, p.10)

ORBAN

SPACE

Wouter Davidts

Architecture Without Address
Orban Lessons in Scale and Perspective

'Size doesn't count. It's scale that
counts. It's human scale that counts,
and the only way you can achieve
human scale is by content.'
Barnett Newman, 1970[1]

I.
Scale models make great pictures. When photographed from a certain perspective and distance, the model's miniature world can be tran-
scended and the inherent promise of a built
reality turned into an appealing image—one
that becomes realistic in itself. Luc Deleu must
have known this when he graduated as an architect. In 1970
he captured *Church in the Dunes* (1968) and *Europakruispunt*

2 *Church in the Dunes,*
1968; Europakruispunt,
1969.

3 *Studio photograph of*
Container Construction,
1981.

(1969), two designs made during his last year
at the Higher Institute of Sint Lucas in Brussels,
in stunning photographic series.[2] The vast photographic archive of T.O.P. office reveals that
Deleu has continued to do so. During the past
four decades he has put scale models of nearly
all his projects in front of the camera.[3] To begin
this essay, I would like to single out one hitherto
unpublished photograph, made by Deleu and
his friend the artist Dominique Stroobandt during a playful afternoon in the crowded office
space at Cogels Osylei in Antwerp in December 1987.[4] The picture shows a plastic figurine
walking towards the photographer in a dark al-
ley between two parallel walls. The walls are
composed of stacked shipping containers from
model making kits and
bear the corporate name
and logo of the US-based
trading company Sea-
Land. Upon closer scrutiny,
the construction turns out
to be a scale model of *Por-*
te Ø, one of the many triumphal arches that Deleu
has made since 1981, with

1 Barnett Newman,
Interview with Emile de
Antonio (1970), in: John
O'Neill (ed.), *Barnett*
Newman: Selected
Writings and Interviews
(New York: Alfred Knopf,
1990), pp. 302–308 (307).

4 Studio Photograph of *Container*
Construction (Porte Ø), 1987 (with
Dominique Stroobandt).

5 *Big Triumphal Arch*, Barcelona, Spain, 1987.

6 *Porte Ø*, FIAC art fair, Grand Palais, Paris, France, 1991.

other notable examples of large arches in Neuchâtel (1983), Barcelona (1987) and Hamburg (1989) and smaller versions in Basel (1983), Tielt (1986) and Nîmes (1996).[5] The scheme for *Porte Ø* was devised in 1984, its name derived from the mathematical scheme of the golden ratio, which governs the opening of the arch. In 1991 the arch was installed in front of the Grand Palais in Paris on the occasion of the FIAC art fair.[6] However, any indication of the Parisian context is absent from the photo graph. The toy container construction has been put directly on the table-top, amidst the multiple objects, models and tools that populate it. A pencil and some other drawing devices that lie behind the protagonist's back disturb the deliberate 'reality' of the model.[7] They are too big to inhabit the same world as the figurine. They do not belong to the space of the model but to the realm of design: it looks as if they have been left behind by the Gulliver-like character, which turns out to be Deleu himself, squatting down in the back, with his eyes just above the tabletop and raising his right index finger in a warning gesture. The photograph represents one of the inevitable challenges of architectural design: how and when does a scheme obtain the appropriate size, that is, how and when does it enter into a balanced scalar relationship with the material world it is destined to inhabit, with its multitude of objects, bodies and buildings? But first and foremost, the photo graph depicts a familiar moment within the design process: the mustering of a model by taking up the perspective of an actual occupier of the space that is being devised and shaped. During a project's inception, one is continuously tempted to imagine oneself occupying that very space. Despite its accidental and playful nature, the photograph hints at a central predicament of architectural design for which the scale model is a primary mode of mediation: the pursuit of measurement.

7 Alfons Hoppenbrouwers has rightly pointed out the willful 'realistic' aspect of Deleu's scale models with containers: 'The containers are combined into triumphal arches, tower constructions, pyramidal piles, etc.; maquettes which suggest a reality. The suggestion of that reality is enhanced by putting scaled down human figures, cars and trees next to them'. Alfred Hoppenbrouwers, 'April 1984', in: Luc Deleu and Marc Hostettler, *Luc Deleu: Prototype d'un Monument Mobile* (Brussels: Sint-Lukasstichting/ Neuchâtel: Editions Media, 1984), s.p.

II.

Porte Ø and the container arches in general belong to an extensive body of work that Deleu started in the fall of 1980 and that he has consistently labeled as 'lessons in scale and perspective.' In the familiar narrative of Deleu's career, a key experience is assumed to have stirred these works: a 90-day-long road trip through the United States in the summer of 1980. Two particular visits during this 'first long voyage' were of decisive importance: the first to Manhattan, New York and the second to the Mariposa Grove of Yosemite

8 Luc Deleu in conversation with author at T.O.P. office, Cogels Osylei, Antwerp, 8 September 2011.

9 Luc Deleu, 'Luc Deleu: Postfuturismus? Interview met Katrien Vandermarliere', *Artefactum* 18 (1987), pp. 12–17 (12) (my translation).

National Park, California.[8] Standing in front of and on top of the skyscrapers and amidst the sequoia trees, respectively, Deleu found it impossible to personally fathom their size. He came to the conclusion, as he pointed out in an interview in 1987, that 'scale is a very questionable notion.'[9]

Soon after his return from the American journey, Deleu initiated a wide set of exercises in the relative or perceptually shifting dimensions of objects, bodies and buildings. He started with a schematic drawing, entitled *Principle of a Lesson in Scale with Two Buildings of Identical Volume Featuring the World's Tallest Tower* (1980).[10] In this drawing two towers are positioned on a crossroads in an empty urban grid, one standing and the other one lying down. Walking alongside the 'Fallen Monarch' in Yosemite and later finding an old postcard showing a complete cavalry regiment standing on the fallen colossal tree, had made Deleu realize that 'the experience of the difference between horizontal and vertical (...) al-

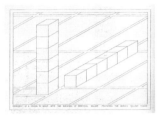

10 *Principle of a Lesson in Scale with Two Buildings of Identical Volume Featuring the World's Tallest Tower*, 1980.

11 Luc Deleu, *The Ethics of Architecture*, April 1988 (unpublished), T.O.P. office archives, s.p.

lows a better understanding of scale.'[11] The new perspective introduced by two identical, yet differently positioned elements, architectural or other, would provide a deeper comprehension of the differential perception of the (in essence) same size of both elements. Shortly afterwards, Deleu tested out the same principle with a fully-fledged scale model, entitled *Principle of a Lesson in Scale with Two Buildings of Identical Volume Featuring the World's Tallest Tower* (1981).[12] Whereas the drawing is marked by an overall diagrammatic disposition, the model shows an ambiguous balance between reality and abstraction. Here, the towers are devoid of architectural detail and thus remain stark shapes, the only light tone being provided by the colorful toy cars glued onto the streets in between the two elements. A similar tension marks a homonymous, all-white model from the same year.[13] Here, two detailed paper model versions

12 *Principle of a Lesson in Scale with Two Buildings of Identical Volume Featuring the World's Tallest Tower*, 1981.

of the ocean liners *Queen Elisabeth I* and *II* are juxtaposed with two identical schematic towers, one positioned vertically and the other horizontally on a quay. The model is displayed in a plexiglass box on a pedestal; a silver-colored slide projection screen provides the backdrop. Spatially contained yet frontally projected as a whole, the model thus ingeniously doubles the distinct regimes of the scale replica and the drawing.[14] It combines the

13 *Principle of a Lesson in Scale with Two Identical Buildings Featuring Queen Elizabeth I and II*, 1981.

14 This double nature is underscored by the fact that there exist two different photographs of the model, in which the slide projection screen is placed behind two sides of the plexi box.

16 The exhibition 'Perspective & Scale' at the Zeno X Gallery, Leopold De Waelplaats 16, ran from 14 November to 18 December, 1981. The installation *Scale & Perspective* opened on 18 December 1981 in Montevideo, Kattendijkdok–Westkaai, Magazijnen 3–4–5 and lasted until 31 December, 1981. I wish to thank Frank and Elianne Demaegd of Zeno X and for providing me access to their archives, and Annie Gentils for providing me with archival material on Montevideo.

spatial disposition of the former and the pictorial constitution of the latter, and in doing so exemplifies the coalescence of object and image that will continue to mark most, if not all, of Deleu's later work. This quality comes to full fruition in the astonishing installation *Scale & Perspective* in the alternative space Montevideo in Antwerp in December 1981.[15] Coinciding with the *finissage* of the exhibition *Perspective and Scale* in the domestic spaces of the private Zeno X Gallery at the other end of the city, showing aforementioned models and drawings, Deleu had a tower crane mounted horizontally in the vast warehouse of Montevideo.[16] The colossal lying crane was both contained by and in contrast with the architecture of the warehouse, providing visitors with a disturbing visual juxtaposition of two different types of objects, each displacing the other. Body, object and building were forced into a radically new scalar equation, within which it was no longer clear who provided the key measure. Any conventional understanding of the 'propriety' of the relational size defined by body, object and building was radically unhinged.[17]

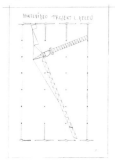

15 *Scale & Perspective with Tower Crane*, Montevideo, Antwerp, 1981 (drawing).

Looking back at the bulk of work that was produced in over little more than a year, it remains remarkable how swiftly Deleu managed to transpose his ideas from the drawing table into actual space, effectively coalescing, yet not aiming to resolve, the

17 *Scale & Perspective with Tower Crane*, Montevideo, Antwerp, 1981.

difficult separation between the imaginative realm of design and the crude reality of execution. The lessons in scale and perspective at once perform and stage the difficult exercise of translating ideas into practice. By doing so, they masterfully double their own subject matter: the intricate question of scale, or, the improbable task to find a proper measure for all objects imagined and devised by man.

III.

Subsequent to the installation of the crane in the space of Montevideo Deleu performed various manipulations of a wide range of ready-made objects, always against specific spatial backdrops. Electricity pylons were laid horizontally on an urban square, shipping containers piled in a warehouse, glass containers assembled in bulk in a vestibule, lampposts laid down in pairs in parking garages or school

18 *Glass Containers in Bulk*, Villa Arson, Nice, France, 1989.

buildings, a crash barrier was mounted on the walls of a gallery, etcetera.[18] Time and again, the displaced objects and their new context engaged in an exciting confrontation, or, as Geert Bekaert once noted, produced 'an exciting interaction (...) especially between the different semantic regimes within which objects and space maneuver.'[19] In tandem with these astute handlings of material objects, Deleu further explored the notions of scale and perspective in tangible architectural designs. Following the sketch of two buildings with an identical volume that were put in a different

20 *Scale & Perspective: Barcelona Towers* (Housing (&) the City), 1989.

position, Deleu eventually developed this principle in baffling yet fully functional schemes for tumbling apartments and plummeting housing towers.[20] His explorations of scale and perspective were, in other words, not limited to the domain of spectacular installations but were undertaken by default within the field of architectural practice as well.

Indeed, as Deleu explained in an interview in 1987, the decision made in 1980 to focus on scale and perspective did not solely rest upon his travel experiences in the United States. First and foremost, it was fuelled by his desire to work with 'two typical (...) and rather formal notions in architecture.' The turn to formalism was made consciously, he continued, since his work prior to 1980 was always termed 'political'.[21] In an unpublished essay of 1988, entitled *The Ethics of Architecture*, Deleu further complicated this assessment. Here he explained that the lessons in scale and perspective also found their motivation in the undeniable importance of history. '[W]hen I made a trip through the United States,' Deleu wrote, 'I learned to understand the importance of (the "European") patrimony.'[22] He acknowledged that the absence of a distinct history of urban development, architectural tradition and cultural heritage allowed the Americans to be rash and adventurous, but he understood on the rebound that these three assets were vital and indisputable to a high-quality living environment. Yet the ensuing aspiration is both surprising and puzzling: 'I have been trying to make my work more plastic and less pamphletary. I now concentrate more on the plastic and structural aspects of architecture, not to deny its essential, social and political aspects, but to make them evident.'[23]

Many of the earlier projects by Deleu indeed show an overtly political stance, as they take up position against the self-indulgent and hypocritical nature of the disciplines of architecture

19 Bekaert, 'Luc Deleu: A Self–Power Man', p. 28: '(...) overal ontstaat een spannende wisselwerking niet alleen tussen die objecten en de vreemde plek waar ze zich bevinden, maar vooral tussen de verschillende betekenisniveaus waarin objecten en ruimte bewegen' (my translation). Bekaert rightly points out that Deleu's strategy shows little kinship with Duchamp's ready-made, as the objects 'resist their metamorphosis'. Their power as installations is caused by the fact that they remain lamppost, crane, glass container, etc.

21 Deleu, 'Luc Deleu: Post-futurismus? Interview met Katrien Vandermarliere', p. 13.

22 Deleu, *The Ethics of Architecture*, s.p.

23 Deleu, *The Ethics of Architecture*, s.p.

24 This number of proposals and advices is not fixed, as Deleu continues to this day to edit, even delete, old ones and adding new ones—the most recent one being the proposal to reinstall 'informal economy', instigated by a voyage to Greece (Deleu in conversation with author at T.O.P. office, Cogels Osylei, Antwerp, 28 November, 2011).

and urban planning in general, and against the institutionalization and bureaucratic nature of the architectural profession in particular. Deleu thus has said goodbye to the profession, laid the last stone of Belgium, and willfully offended the professional league of Belgian architects by abusing their rules and regulations. The *Proposals and Advices* that he formulated since 1972—no less than 75 of the former and 8 of the latter in 1980—perhaps exemplify Deleu's radical attitude at its best.[24] Despite their often playful or even absurd intent, these proposals and advices can be understood as the guiding principles of the work and practice of Luc Deleu and his collaborators at T.O.P. office. They have provided, as it were, the political and ethical basis of all the future projects. All schemes are characterized by a radical appeal for freedom, open-mindedness, generosity, and imagination—qualities that were scarce in, if not totally absent from, the discipline of architecture yet vital to confront crucial problems and challenges within a broader societal context and in the world at large.

25 'Luc Deleu: 20 futuristieke voorstellen voor stedelijke agglomeraties (26.6.77)', *A+* no. 7–8 (1977), pp. 52–53: 'Ik beschouw het als de taak van de architect om mee te werken aan de vorming van een toekomstbeeld voor de aarde, waarin ieder, in elke willekeurige woonvorm, kan leven' (my translation).

26 Luc Deleu, 'Introduction', in: *Vrije Ruimte—Espace Libre—Open Space* (Antwerp: Internationaal Cultureel Centrum (I.C.C.)/Ministerie van Nationale Opvoeding en Nederlandse Cultuur, 1980), p. 3.

When Deleu published '20 futuristic proposals for urban agglomerations' in 1977 in the architecture journal *A+*, the official periodical of the Belgian league of architects, he stated that it was 'the task of the architect to contribute to shaping a future view on planet earth, within which one and all would be able to live in whatever type of dwelling.'[25] Indeed, if the proposals and advices served one goal, it was to find a new yardstick for the practices of architecture and urban planning in a world that was threatened by demographic explosion on the one hand and excessive land use on the other. The proposals and advices, Deleu writes in the introduction of the catalogue published on the occasion of his first retrospective, held at the I.C.C. in Antwerp in the spring of the pivotal year of 1980, helped him to develop a 'world view' and to examine 'the new meaning of the profession of town planner architect, who does not necessarily have to build.'[26] The

27 'Orbanistisch Manifest—Manifeste d'Orbanisme—Orban Planning Manifesto', in: *Vrije Ruimte – Espace Libre—Open Space (exh. cat. 22 maart– 20 april)*, Antwerpen, Internationaal Cultureel Centrum (ICC)/Ministerie van Nationale Opvoeding en Nederlandse Cultuur, 1980, pp. 20–26 (20–21). It is noteworthy that Deleu uses different neologisms to describe the new type of urban planning on the scale of the earth, depending on the language. While it is a differentiation of the adjective *urbanistisch* in Dutch (*orbanistisch*), it turns into a transformation of the noun *urbanisme* in French (*Orbanisme*), to become a noun in itself in English (*Orban Planning*). The first version of the *Orban Planning Manifesto* was rather clumsily translated and edited, witness the many changes that Deleu later made. An entire facsimile of the edited original catalogue of 'Vrije Ruimte – Espace Libre – Open Space' can be found in the catalogue of Deleus next solo exhibition in Antwerp: *Luc Deleu: Postfuturismus?* (Antwerp: deSingel/Wommelgem: Den Gulden Engel, 1987), pp. 40–50. This edit also contains a first revision of the list of *Proposals and Advices*.

fundamentals of this pioneering practice were to be found in the three-lingual *Orban Planning Manifesto*, published on the following pages of the same catalogue.[27] In this manifesto, which is heavily indebted to the ideas of Buckminster Fuller, Deleu made a radical plea for— besides imagination and nerve—concrete exercise to work on the scale of the earth. '[I]f we don't know how big "big" is,' R. Buckminster Fuller alerted in his *Operating Manual for Spaceship Earth* of 1969, 'we may not start big enough (...).'[28]

28 Buckminster R. Fuller, *Operating Manual for Spaceship Earth* (1969) (Baden: Lars Müller Publishers, 2008), p. 67.

In this respect the lessons in scale and perspective constitute less of a break within the work of Deleu than it may look at first. They can be put on a direct par with the so-called pamphletary works of the previous decade, as they institute a different level of *practice*. The lessons in scale and perspective may not wear a political and social agenda on their sleeve, yet they allow that very agenda to attain a new degree of experimentation as well as gain a new scale of operationality, both literally and figuratively speaking. The turn to formalist exercises, then, is not one that abdicates political and social awareness, quite the contrary. It allows the scalar concerns that were already fully present in the earlier work to obtain a new level of accomplishment; the exercises masterfully blend the inventive with the practical, the diagrammatic with the tangible, the conceptual with the plastic—in both the installation works as well as in the architectural schemes.

IV.

When it dawned on Deleu that scale was a dubious issue, there was little that he could turn to. Architecture wallows in treatises on proportion, from Vitruvius' *De architectura* to Le Corbusier's *Le Modulor*, but it lacks a theory of scale.

29 It is remarkable that the term scale is absent as term in the indexes of major works on architectural theory published in the last decades. Adrian Forty, who dedicates a book to the vocabularium of architectural practice (*Words and Buildings: A Vocabulary of Modern Architecture* [New York: Thames & Hudson, 2000]), doesn't even discuss it, let alone include it in the index.

Even though scale happens to be one of the most common terms in both daily and theoretical discourse on architecture and buildings, it has not met with substantial critical, theoretical or historical attention yet.[29] Scale, not to be confused with size, which is absolute and the result of numerical convention, is relative and dependent on perception. Architecture lacks a theory that opens up the relative nature of scale and elucidates the ambiguous dynamics that transpire between human beings, objects, architecture and the environment at large. To overcome this, Deleu embarked on a private study of scale. However, to pursue this goal, as he soon came to understand, the existing parameters and the conventional understanding of the size of things (that is, of objects, bodies and buildings) had to be radically revised—a venture the architect shared with a generation of the most radical of postwar artists, of whom Mel Bochner once wrote that they gave '"new dimensions"

30 Mel Bochner, 'Review: New Dimensions' (1966), in: *Solar System & Rest Rooms: Writings and Interviews, 1965–2007* (Cambridge, MA: MIT Press, 2008), p. 34. Bochner mentions a.o. Donald Judd, Sol LeWitt and Robert Smithson. Indeed, when looking at the lessons in scale and perspective by Deleu, inevitably the work of the aforementioned and other canonical artists of the 1960s and 1970s comes to mind. In many respects the sculptural works but also the architectural schemes are reminiscent of postwar art, in particular those of certain neo-dada, minimalist and postminimalist strategies. The lessons in scale and perspective comprise of found, appropriated and displaced objects, singular shapes, stacked volumes grid-like structures, and serial systems. Yet Deleu himself is wary of explicit references to postwar American art, as he claims to have little or no kinship with the work of American artists such as Mel Bochner, Judd, LeWitt or Smithson—especially since his first visit to the US only happened in 1980 and he knew very little of these artists' work. Despite Deleu's antagonism to the comparison, I nevertheless contend that, if there are no direct references to be discerned, there are many affinities, if only in terms of conceptual approach, at play. While the art and artists of the 1960s and 1970s did not immediately develop a clear-cut notion of scale, let alone produce a theory of scale, a notion of the relative size of an artwork nevertheless emerged that is not directly dependent on either contextual conditions or on phenomenological circumstances, but emerges as a product of the issues that are being addressed '[T]the scale of a work of art', Douglas Davis asserted in 1976, 'can be measured by its effect upon the whole culture, in terms of its predestined arc of action—where it attempts to go, the issues it tries to confront, and its chosen audience'. See: Douglas Davis, 'The Size of Non-Size', *Artforum* XV no. 4 (December 1976), pp. 45–51 (45).

33 Luc Deleu, 'A Task for Contemporary Architecture', in: *Sites & Stations: Provisional Utopias* (Lusitania 7), ed. by Stan Allen with Kyong Park (New York: Lusitania Press, 1995), pp. 234–242 (236).

not to finite experience of objects, but to the categorical understanding of art.'[30]

Still, as he has never failed to stress, Deleu's ambitions have always been situated manifestly in the realm of architecture and urban planning. 'With my work,' he ends a short unpublished statement on scale and perspective in 1986, 'On the one hand I wish to comment upon (contemporary) architectural thought, and on the other hand provide examples and suggestions for a future organization of our "Spaceship Earth", by using object from the past.'[31] The lessons in scale and perspective are, in other words, plain architectural drill.[32] They are aimed at broadening architectural thought and discourse and hence they resonate squarely within the broader realm of architectural culture. It is within that precise realm, I would like to argue, that these lessons target a crucial lack—one they uncover first to then develop the proper tools and strategies to overcome it.

In the polemical essay 'A Task for Contemporary Architecture' from 1995, Deleu recalls how the effects of the 'unprecedented expansion of the built environment' since World War II affected his idea of an architectural practice.[33] The dramatic rise of consumer capitalism and commodity culture, coupled with the steady increase of population figures on planet Earth, defied the established theoretical premises and the conventional design strategies of modernism:

'It (…) became obvious that the pressure of human space on earth had increased enormously on account of population growth and, chiefly, consumption patterns, with all its consequences for the environment. The consumer society requires a different approach than the production society of the beginning of this century.'[34]

31 Luc Deleu, 'Schaal & Perspectief', [Switzerland], 1986 (unpublished), T.O.P. office archives, s.p.: 'Met mijn werk wil ik enerzijds commentaar leveren op het (hedendaagse) architecturale denken en anderzijds voorbeelden en voorstellen geven voor een toekomstige organisatie van ons "Ruimteschip Aarde", door objecten uit het verleden te herbruiken' (my translation).

32 Bekaert, 'Luc Deleu: A Self-Power Man', p. 28.

34 Deleu, 'A Task for Contemporary Architecture', p. 236.

The spectacular developments in technology and media further complicated the task: 'The first communication satellites, were launched, enabling us to see events from all over the world in "real time" on our home TV screen.'[35] One of those televised events that made a lasting impression on Deleu was the Apollo 11 voyage to the moon in 1969. It fundamentally changed his understanding of life on Earth and made him realize that architectural thought and practice urgently needed to expand the frame of reference. The modernist's focus on 'human scale' of the built environment had become insufficient. The human body no longer served as the primary yardstick for an architectural design and turned out to be but one of the terms in the scalar equation. A new gauge had imposed itself, Deleu recollected, which forced architects to come up with a new understanding of the scale of their operational framework, territory, tools and products:

35 Deleu, 'A Task for Contemporary Architecture', p. 240.

'Modernism was no longer good enough, thinking on an urban scale was no longer sufficient—it was essential to start thinking on an earth scale, with world planning. It is impossible to develop a city as an autonomous unit when in reality it lives off the whole earth.'[36]

Architecture had to transform into what the architect idiosyncratically termed *Orban Planning*, a praxis that would know two basic scales: 'man and the earth.'[37] Yet key to Deleu's approach is that from the very start both man and earth are reduced to mere numbers. *Orban Planning* takes its cue from a dry calculation of land on the surface of the earth available for the present-day world population. Throughout the past 40 years, Deleu has regularly updated his calculations, following the advent of new data through different media and inventories made by his T.O.P. office collaborators, all the while continuously mapping the loss of available space per world inhabitant. 'When I started my A[rchitecture] career in 1970,' he scribbled down in 1994 on a scrap of paper, there were '4.1 ha or 5.6 soccer fields' per 'earthling.' Dryly he observed that in 24 years the numbers had decreased to '2.66 ha or 3.6 soccer fields.'[38]

37 Luc Deleu, 'Aarde, passagiers en gebouwen/Earth, passengers and buildings', in: *Drijvende vliegvelden en andere infrastructuren/Floating Airports and Other Infrastructures*, special issue of *Forum* 34, no. 1 (March 1990), pp. 5–14 (8).

36 Deleu, 'A Task for Contemporary Architecture', p. 237. In Deleu, *The Ethics of Architecture* (1988), Deleu already formulated a similar viewpoint: 'Instead of extending architecture to the town, as did the "modernists" because they realized that housing problems could only be solved through a town concept, architecture would now have to be treated on a global scale. This does not mean that the whole world must be designed, must be comprised in one plan, that is clearly far too complex [sic]. But the earth will be an indication of the scale of your work as an architect.'

38 *Calculation of surface per world inhabitant*, T.O.P. office archives, dated 24 March, 1994.

V.

The candid coupling of data (world population), surface (land availability) and facility (soccer field) would later act as the guiding principle of what is undeniably Deleu's magnum opus and, first and foremost, that of T.O.P. office: *De Onaangepaste*

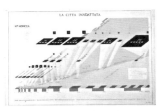

39 *The Unadapted City: Ten Plates (Plate I Horeca)*, 1995–99. The project of *The Unadapted City* would also mark a new phase within the daily constitution of T.O.P. office, as it redefined the authorial position of the work significantly. With *The Unadapted City*, Deleu and his collaborators developed a new model of collaborative practice, partly based on aleatory procedures and the matrix of a (musical) score. Isabel De Smet and Steven Van den Bergh, collaborators from the early stages of *The Unadapted City*, played a major role in this new development and became associates of T.O.P. office.

Stad (D.O.S.) or *The Unadapted City*.[39] The immediate reason for this decade-long urban study goes back to the project *Usiebenpole* of 1994, a design for a new city quarter for 120,000 inhabitants on a small, long island in the Donau River in Vienna.[40] The task of determining what size the new section of the city had to

40 *Usiebenpole*, 1994–96.

be, turned out to be a difficult one. Especially the question what dimensions would be best for the necessary facilities for 120,000 inhabitants seemed hard to answer. To Deleu's surprise T.O.P. office discovered that a manual, let alone a calculation model, for conceiving and subsequently designing the dimensions of the urban infrastructure and equipment complementing the living quarters did not exist. To remedy this, they recycled the design for the HST-infrastructure for Brussels as the backbone of the scheme for the linear city and used the score of Johan Strauss' *An der schönen blauen Donau* as a ready-made yet arbitrary matrix for the arrangement of functions along that spine.[41]

The goal of the ensuing project of *The Unadapted City*, began by T.O.P. office in summer of 1995, was the study and implementation of models for the development and organization of urban infrastructure and equipment. Both of these, Deleu has consistently argued, are not only vital to the organizational comfort of dwelling, they are quintessential in constituting our present-day and future society's patrimony. As public space is ever more colonized by private corporations, 21st-century architecture and urban planning should see it as their social and political task to develop schemes that protect and redevelop public space for the common interest. To this end, the disciplines are in need of an ingenious and adamant rethinking of the infrastructure and the utilities of cities and require a framework that transcends local concerns and negotiates planetary developments.

The Unadapted City, Deleu explains in the essay 'Urbi et Orbi (D.O.S. XXI)' of 2002, entails an 'urbanistic, spatial and theoretical research into the establishment of a possible interplay between urban facilities that is related in an unadapted fashion to numbers of inhabitants.'[42]

41 Whomever has listened to Strauss' *An der schönen blauen Donau* and in the meanwhile checked the designs for *Usiebenpole*, must have come to the conclusion that it is rather difficult to reconcile the smarmy melody of the waltz with the stark lay-out of the urban scheme. Thanks to Stefaan Vervoort for urging me to indulge this exercise.

42 Luc Deleu, 'Urbi et Orbi (D.O.S. XXI)', in: Luc Deleu and Hans Theys, *Urbi et Orbi: De Onaangepaste Stad Urbi et Orbi: De Onaangepaste Stad* (Ghent: Ludion, 2002), pp. 21–138 (55): '(...) De Onaangepaste Stad: een voortdurend, over verschillende jaren gespreid, stedenbouwkundig, ruimtelijk en theoretisch onderzoek naar de mogelijkheid een samenspel van stedelijke voorzieningen te creëren dat op zijn onaangepaste manier gerelateerd is aan inwonersaantallen.' (my translation).

The instruments of this enterprise are 'a mathematics of the anonymous number' and 'a geometry of space.' One of the most intriguing aspects of *The Unadapted City* is indeed the uncompromising way in which numbers are transposed into primary spatial design decisions.[43] The database and the spreadsheets that result from an ongoing calculation of required infrastructure, equipment and living space serve as the key devices that members of the T.O.P. office team 'unconditionally accept and never question'; they deliver 'the program that needs to be spatially translated.'[44] The design is based upon the paradoxical premise that the inherent inaccuracy of a universally valid urban program and the sheer impossibility to base it on mere population figures allows for an absolute acceptance of that program. While Deleu is very aware of the potentially disturbing nature of this approach, he wholeheartedly advocates it:

43 *The Unadapted City: Ten Plates (Plate V Sports)*, 1995–99.

44 Deleu, 'Urbi et Orbi (D.O.S. XXI)', p. 35.

'Numbers related to population size deliver complex dimensions. Geometric dimensions of a city are precise, utilizable, comprehensive and relatively stable. Mathematics with anonymous city dwellers on the contrary is ambiguous, fleeting, confusing and very volatile, hence it plays a different role in the design procedure. Even though such a mathematical research cries for tolerance, it calls up associations—even though only at first sight—with programming and standardization.'[45]

Treating future dwellers as mere anonymous units throughout the development of *The Unadapted City* might indeed at first appear technocratic, if not inhuman. Yet it is the radical adherence to mathematics of the anonymous number in defining the size of cities, I would like to argue, that constitutes the true social and political nature of the project. It brings Deleu's career-long ambition to develop a model for architectural and urban planning practice on the scale of the earth in the era of late-capitalist globalization to its beneficial next step. Deleu's plea for a 'planetary concern' comes with a set of responsibilities that disallow the architect to be 'an obedient tailor of neoliberalism.'[46] *The Unadapted City* willfully suspends those multiple figures that are customarily addressed: commissioners, clients, even either social or demographic target groups are left out of the loop. *The Unadapted City* withdraws itself from the obligation to fulfill, accommodate or please whatever desire, dream or wish one would project onto

45 Deleu, 'Urbi et Orbi (D.O.S. XXI)', pp. 35–37: 'Aan bevolkingsaantallen gerelateerde cijfers zijn echter zeer complexe dimensies. De meetkundige dimensies van een stad zijn precies, hanteerbaar, overzichtelijk en relatief stabiel. De rekenkunde met anonieme stadsbewoners daarentegen is meerduidig, ongrijpbaar, verward en zeer wispelturig waardoor zij in de ontwerpprocedure een andere rol speelt. Hoewel zo'n cijfermatig onderzoek schreeuwt om tolerantie, roept het—maar dan enkel op het eerste gezicht—associaties met programmering en normering op.'

46 Deleu, 'Urbi et Orbi (D.O.S. XXI)', p. 26: 'een lijdzaam confectioneur van het neoliberalisme' (my translation).

47 To imagine oneself living, walking, let alone cycling through *The Unadapted City* would in this respect testify of a grave misunderstanding of the actual proposition of the project. For an instance of this voluntary identification, see Hans Theys, 'De Ligusters op de Sagittarius-Promenade. Inleiding tot een handboek voor stedenbouwers', in: Luc Deleu and Hans Theys, *Urbi et Orbi: De Onaangepaste Stad* (Ghent: Ludion, 2002), pp. 5–19.

it.[47] The question of how big a 'big' city has to be is candidly disconnected from both anthropomorphic criteria and human concerns. *The Unadapted City* no longer regards scale as matter of bodies and subjects; it reduces scale to sheer statistics, the epitome of a fully administrated world. Paradoxically enough, by doing so, it radically works against the grain of the irreversible process of globalization. The planetary development in the second half of the 20th century, as masterfully described by Peter Sloterdijk, has not resulted in the global village that McLuhan (and Deleu to some degree as well)

48 Luc Deleu, 'Alles ist Architektur', in: *Das letze Haus im Steir* (Graz: Haus der Architektur, 1995), pp. 36–48 (44).

once predicted.[48] Rather, it has led to a global dissipation of increasingly calculating private individuals: a rapidly growing terrestrial legion of restless yet anxious consumers.[49] In order to focus precisely on those very urban elements that are at risk of falling victim to the rash forces of privatization yet are vital to the future formation of the public space of the city, *The Unadapted City* does

49 See the chapters 'De synchrone wereld', 'De tweede oecumene' en 'De immunologische transformatie: op weg naar "samenlevingen" van de dunne muren', in: Peter Sloterdijk, *Het kristalpaleis: Een filosofie van de globalisering* (2004), trans. Hans Driessen (Amsterdam: SUN, 2006).

not deny but momentarily suspends their existence. There is no you or me that *The Unadapted City* speaks to. The very ethical force of the project, I contend, resides in its radical refusal to address.

In the past *The Unadapted City* has often, in particular by Deleu himself, been described as a theoretical project, benefiting from a self-instituted freedom. This contention, however, as Guy Châtel has rightfully pointed out, fails to acknowledge certain critical aspects of the work. The underlying postulates of the project were rarely, if ever, verified during its decade-long genesis, as the design forged ahead by superimposing the insights of previous stages. While it is '[u]ndeniably spec-

50 Guy Châtel, 'Plan Obus and Vipcity, as from father to son', *Interstices—Journal of Architecture and Related Art* 7 (September 2006), pp. 21–33.

ulative in character,' Châtel argues, 'its desire to be exemplary predisposes it towards representation.' *The Unadapted City* is marked by an intriguingly dual ambition to at once show and tell. As '[r]epresentation is constructed in the course of its enunciation,' Châtel concludes, 'the work is much more a discursive than a theoretical undertaking.'[50] *The Unadapted City* does not aim to provide a clear-cut model of future city planning that can be implemented. The impressive array of tables, diagrams, drawings and models that T.O.P. office has produced over the years tackle the manifold issues that are at stake within the respective practices of architecture and city planning.[51] One of those primary *subjects* of *The Unadapted City* is scale.

51 *The Unadapted City: Ten Plates (Plate VIII: Culture & Entertainment)*, 1995–99.

Guided by the principles of *Orban Planning*, it applies a *dispositif* that is neither local nor private, but global and civic. In *The Unadapted City* human scale is achieved by addressing scale no longer as a formal problem to solve, but as a conceptual issue to engage with: a topic that is defined by neither contextual nor phenomenological conditions, but grounded in demographic and geographical data. Not unlike the lessons in scale and perspective, it does not produce new theorems. *The Unadapted City* performs and stages, time and again,

the relentless exercise of finding sizeable urban forms and structures. In chorus it delivers a story as well as an image of an urban project: it demands to be 'read' as one long visual and material essay on the dimensions of the city.[52]

52 *The Unadapted City: Nautical Mile*, 2004.

53 *Orban Space: Passage to the Antipodes (La Malu II: Voyage Palermo – Richards Bay (espace orbain) (12/07/2007–22/11/2010))*, 2006–09.

VI.

In 2007, Luc Deleu embarked on a new adventure. Upon the invitation of Bernard Blondeel, an Antwerp-based art dealer with whom Deleu has had a decade long professional and personal relation, he became one of the crewmen on Blondeel's yacht *La Malu II*. Over the course of 4 years and in 8 stages, Deleu made a journey around the world.[53] The voyage was not merely an old dream coming true, but once again a consistent pursuit within Deleu's four decade long career. World travel, whether around or away from the earth, had always fascinated the architect. *Tribune*, the collage book made in between 1972–75, abounds with scrap images of all kinds of travel vessels, combined with figures of commodity culture and global transport.[54] On spread 63 it reads that 'we live in an infinitely small world,' paraphrasing Phileas Phogg's notorious statement that 'the world has become smaller'.[55] Not unlike Jules Verne's protagonist, it ultimately led Deleu to undertake a journey around the world in eighty days. The adventure was first developed as

54 *Tribune*, 1972–75 (spread 63).

55 Jules Verne, *Around the World in Eighty Days* (1873) (London, Harper Press, 2011), p. 16.

56 *Around the World in 80 Days 'Weber–Madrid–Weber'*, 1993.

a cartographical study between 1991–93, resulting in a wide array of works that investigate different modes and calculate diverse trajectories upon paradigmatic maps of the world, drawn by among others Mercator, Van der Grinten and Buckminster Fuller.[56] In a newspaper interview of 1994, Deleu however announced that a study would not suffice. The miscellaneous calculations, drawings and models required practical assessment that was grounded in actual perception: 'I want to make the journey to get a grip on and a real feeling for the scale of the world. An

57 Inge Ghijs, 'De reorganizatie van de wereld. Urbain Mulkers en Luc Deleu in het Mercatormuseum', *De Standaard Magazine* no. 24 (June 1994), pp. 11–13: 'Ik wil de reis doen om de schaal van de aarde in mijn vingers te krijgen. Als orbanist moet je dat kunnen. Ik wil niet de hele wereld ontwerpen, dat zou belachelijk zijn. Maar ik wil weten hoe alles in elkaar zit op onze aarde. Hoe het er reilt en zeilt. (...) Tijdens al die voorbereidingen ben ik ook al een stuk op reis. Ik ken de aarde nu beter, en dat is toch waar het een orbanist om te doen is.' (my translation).

59 *40° 24' 904S 176° 17' 551E over its antipode 40° 24' 904N 3° 24' 449W (ERNSLAW ONE TTD, WEBER, NEW ZEALAND over its antipode PLAZA MAYOR, MADRID, SPAIN)*, 1999 (detail).

61 Sloterdijk, *Het kristalpaleis*, p. 16.

62 Johann Wolfgang von Goethe, Palermo, 3 April 1787. *Italienische Reise* (1817) (Munich: C. H. Beck, 1981), pp. 230–231: 'Hat man sich nicht ringsum vom Meere umgeben gesehen, so hat man keinen Begriff von Welt und von seinem Verhältnis zur Welt'. Translation from J.W. Goethe *Italian Journey*, trans. W.H. Auden and E. Mayer, London: Collins, 1962. Not unlike Goethe, Deleu was deeply affected by the particular sensation of being surrounded entirely by water with no reference point other than the horizon; witness the many photographs of sea horizons Deleu took during this journey to be found in the photographic archives of T.O.P. office.

orbanist should have that. (...) In preparing for the journey I am traveling already. I know the planet better now, and for the orbanist that's what it's all about.'[57] In 1999 Deleu and his wife Laurette Gillemot embarked on their first trip around the world, yet in 72 days, primarily on board of the cargo ship Speybank and partly by airplane.[58] The resulting superimposed photograph of Madrid and Weber, each other's earthly antipodes and respectively the start and middle stage of the journey, presents an improbable perspective on the sphere: bottom and top, top and bottom are united in a single panoramic picture.[59] In 2002–03 Deleu traveled once more from Spain to New Zealand, now resulting in an equally spectacular doubled photomontage.[60]

58 Equator. Photograph made during journey around the world aboard cargoship *Speybank*, 1999.

60 *Journey Around the World (Academical Upgrade 2&3 Setenil over Auckland)* 5,6 km north–west of SETENIL, SPAIN, N 36° 52. 683' W 5° 14. 126' 2003 June 19, 18H 47' 54'' to 18H 50' 16'' UNIVERSAL TIME OVER MOUNT EDEN, AUCKLAND, NEW ZEALAND, S 36° 52. 683' E 174° 45. 874' 2002 DECEMBER 20, 6H 47' 54'' to 6H 50' 16'' UNIVERSAL TIME, 2002–03.

The sailing trip around the globe definitely provided the climax of Deleu's investigations of the earthly surface, yet it was also the quintessential act that the orban planner still had to perform and experience. Globalization, Sloterdijk has argued, is not merely the result of the rapid technological progress made during the second half of the 20th century. The latter is only the third phase in a process that started with the morphological understanding of the world as a sphere in classical times, yet came to fruition during the radical phase of unearthing that was practically executed by Christian-capitalist seamanship and politically implanted by the colonialism of Old-European nation states since the end of the 15th century.[61] Globalization did not commence on land then, but over sea. Furthermore, as Johann Wolfgang von Goethe found out after a sea voyage from Naples to Sicily undertaken at the end of March 1787, an extensive stay on the sea decisively alters one's world view. 'No-one who has never seen himself surrounded on all sides by nothing but the sea,' he penned down in his diary, 'can have a true perception of the world and his own relation to it.'[62]

Although started as a personal adventure, the sailing trip turned into an essential part of the last and larger project that Luc Deleu and his collaborators of T.O.P. office started in the spring of 2006 and are at present still working on: *Orban Space.* The aspirations are manifestly ambitious: to develop a new paradigm for public space on an 'orban' scale, that is, a paradigm that encompasses the wide spectrum of public space from the scale of the local street to that of the planet. The first major result of this project is the voluminous, quadrilingual *Terminology.* On a 600-odd pages and in 7 chapters,

63 The respective chapters are: 1. Scale; 2. From Virginity to Hyper–Urbanization; 3. Water, Mother of Infrastructural Space; 4. Wake Up and Dream, The City; 4. Fora; 5. Setting & Location; 6. Artificial & Cultured Landscapes; 7. Public Space, from Wild to Domesticated.

Deleu and his long-term associates Isabelle De Smet and Steven Van den Bergh attempted to gather all available terms to describe public space(s) on earth, on all possible scale levels and to map out the connections, hierarchies and priorities.[63] They data-mined such diverging media as dictionaries, encyclopedia and various Internet resources (predictably, wikipedia, the free, collaborative, multilingual Internet encyclopedia, served as the prime site). The resulting terms do not only stem from the standard vocabularium of architecture and urban planning, but also from other 'jargons' that steer the discourse on space: popular, legal, administrative, political or other. The Borgesian end result is a book that can serve as a dictionary, atlas, thesaurus, encyclopedia, catalogue and a manual for architecture and urban planning practice all at once. Not unlike *The Unadapted City, Orban Space* is founded on abstract base material. A nomenclature of abstract terms however has taken over from the mathematics of the anonymous number.

In a continuous feedback loop with the laborious fine-tuning of *Terminology*, T.O.P. office is developing a complex graphical scheme, entitled *Orban Space Analytics.*[64] Akin to the way in which T.O.P. office reworked the ten plates of *The Unadapted City* over time, it now gradually charts distinctive registers of public space—

64 *Orban Space: Panels,* 2006– (studio photograph dated 19 December, 2008).

from universal, worldwide to local, within networks, transport or fora—in seven diagrams (as for now still presented

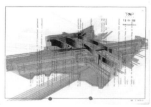

65 *Orban Space: Sector X,* 2010.

against a backdrop of an astronomic map of signs of the zodiac) that correspond to the seven chapters in *Terminology.* Sector X, an exhibition at the gallery Rossi Contemporary in Brussels in 2010, so far presented the most material outcome of *Orban Space.*[65] To provide the taxonomic efforts with a tangible counterpart, T.O.P. office embarked upon a study of the use of public space within the immediate urban surroundings of its headquarters—a 'sector' of Antwerp that is marked by a dense web of infrastructures, as it lies in between the highway ring, the Singel outer city ring and two main lines for passenger and freight trains (e.g. the HST-line from Paris to Amsterdam). Mapping out the assorted traffic flows (from pedestrian and motorized to public) that traverse this local context, T.O.P. office produced a set of seven scale-less, colorful objects in cardboard and plexiglass. Frontally attached to the wall, these astounding works emerge as an ambiguous blend of relief, model and painting and are inadvertently reminiscent of the *Prouns* by El Lissitzky.[66] The *Sector X* works however are not the product of the abstract aim to transpose a pictorial scheme into space but rather of a threefold reverse procedure. They are

66 El Lissitzky, *Prounenraum*, 1923 (reconstruction 1965, Van Abbemuseum, Eindhoven).

driven by the aim to map, visualize and overlay the various regimes of traffic that colonize and utilize public space—from the corporeal to the virtual—and their respective degrees of intensity, distribution and intermingling. The superposition of the different traffic flows generated an intriguing architecture in and of itself, detached from the objects, bodies and buildings that populate the site to which the works correspond. The resulting objects hence no longer represent the public space(s) of the urban area of Berchem, Antwerp in particular.[67] The very attention to the most local of contexts allowed T.O.P. office

67 *Orban Space: Sector X*, 2010.

to deliver a speculative statement about public space in general. Beyond its material nature and visual characteristics, the scale-less *Sector X* objects tentatively convey public space as first and foremost a multilayered force field.

VII.

Over the past four decades Deleu and T.O.P. office have used many different types of objects and a wide range of media to convey their work. One item that stands out, yet remained hidden in the vast archives, is a souvenir for visitors to an exhibition at the Maritime Museum in Amsterdam in 1988. In the gift shop eager consumers could buy a DIY model of *Porte Ø*.[68] To construct one's own paper arch on a scale of 1/200, it sufficed to cut out the shape of the arch along the dotted lines, ply the different facades and glue the flysheets together. Two barely noticeable lines indicate the golden section within the main opening of the arch. Even though *Ø Poort '84–'88* is undeniably a curious object, it can be regarded as an exemplary

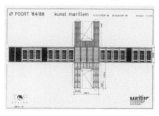

68 *Ø Poort '84–'88*, 1988.

outcome of the practice of Luc Deleu and T.O.P. office. If only because of the fact the shop's customers did not obtain toy containers that had to be stacked, but rather a pictorial shape on paper that required precise manual labor to be modeled into a spatial structure. The resulting gadget is, once again, an ambiguous admixture of object and drawing, of model and diagram; but first and foremost, it is design scheme turned merchandise. Playful and serious at once, this odd 'widget' nevertheless provides a lesson in scale and perspective that is simple and radical: to give new dimensions to the categorical understanding of architecture, one needs exercises of both conceptual and corporeal nature.

XXVIII

Principle of a Lesson in Scale with Two Buildings of Identical Volume Featuring the World's Tallest Tower, 1981

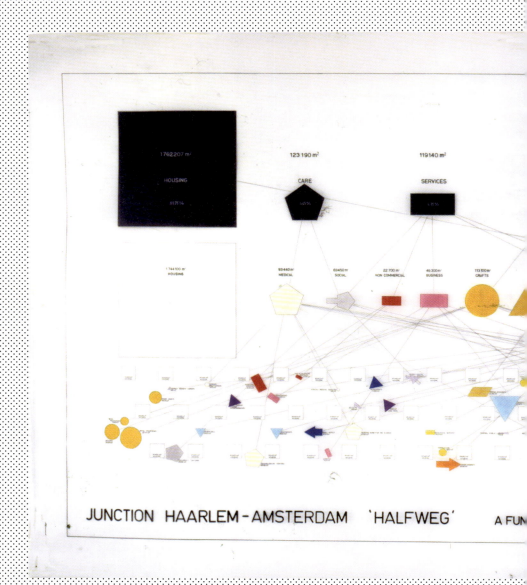

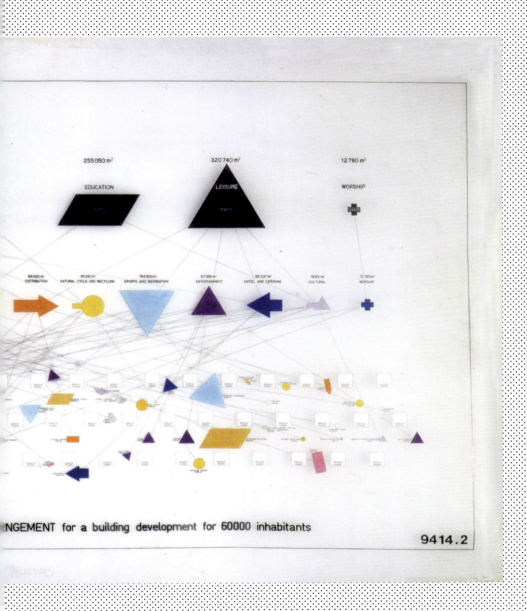

255 050 m²

EDUCATION

320 740 m²

LEISURE

12 780 m²

WORSHIP

NGEMENT for a building development for 60000 inhabitants

9414.2

XXX

Works XXVII-XXXIII

Luc Deleu – T.O.P. office

236

40° 24' 904S 176° 17' 551E over its antipode 40° 24' 904N 3° 24' 449W (ERNSLAW ONE TTD, WEBER, NEW ZEALAND over its antipode PLAZA MAYOR, MADRID, SPAIN), 1999

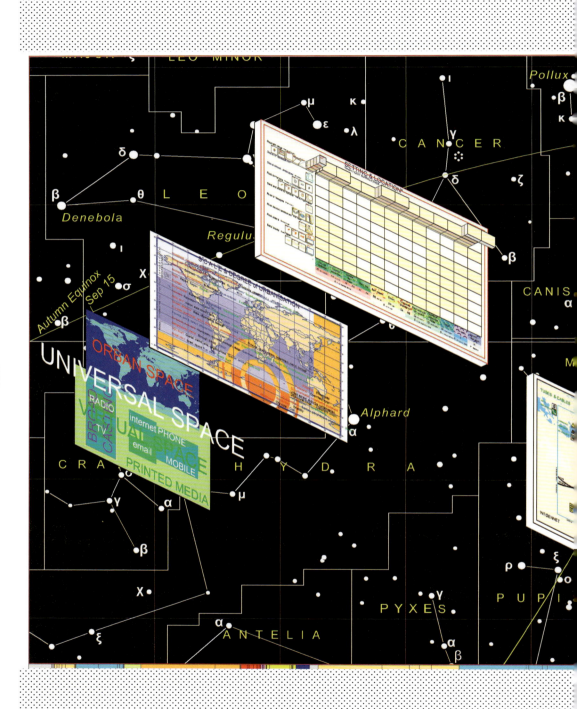

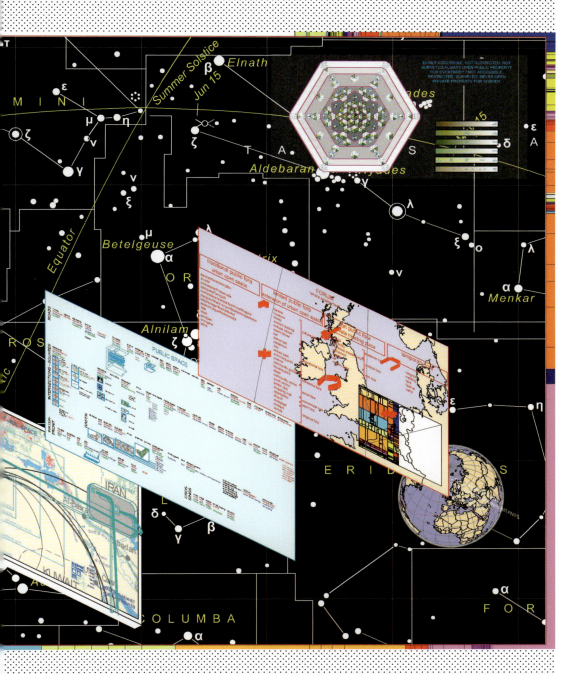

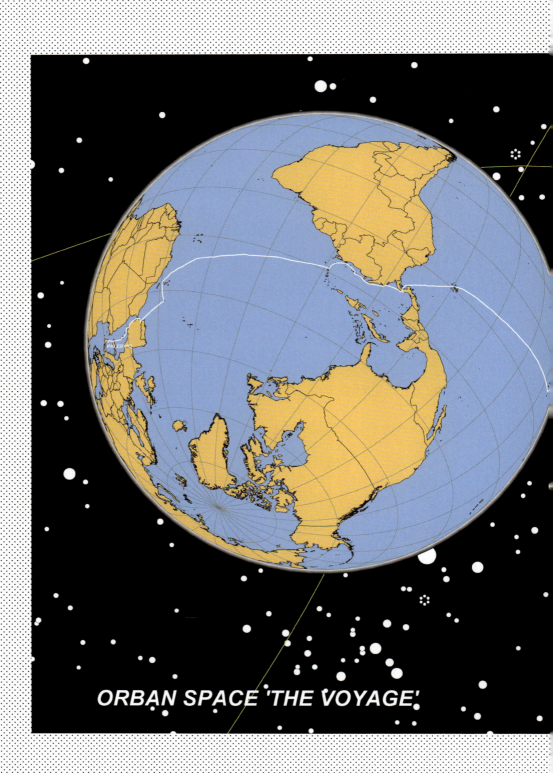

XXXI

ORBAN SPACE 'THE VOYAGE'

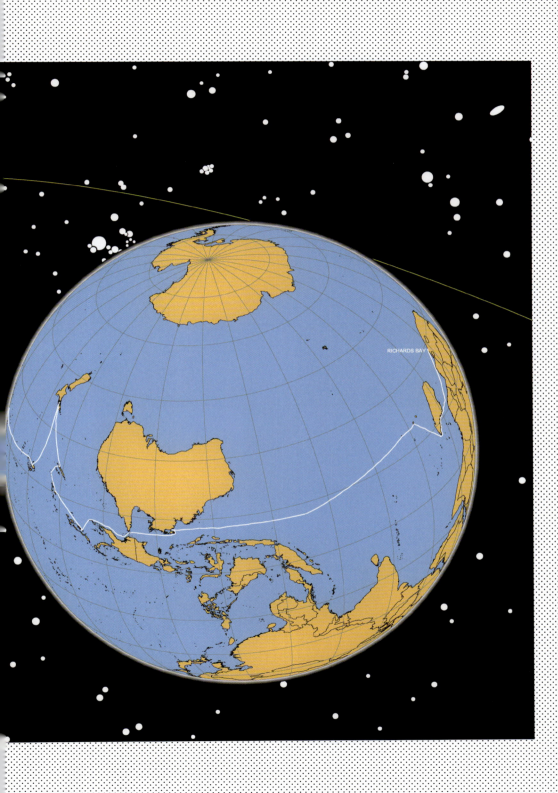

RICHARDS BAY

Depiction:

Hapag Lloyd

Depiction:

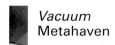 *Vacuum*
Metahaven

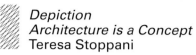 *Depiction*
Architecture is a Concept
Teresa Stoppani

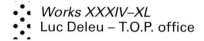 *Works XXXIV–XL*
Luc Deleu – T.O.P. office

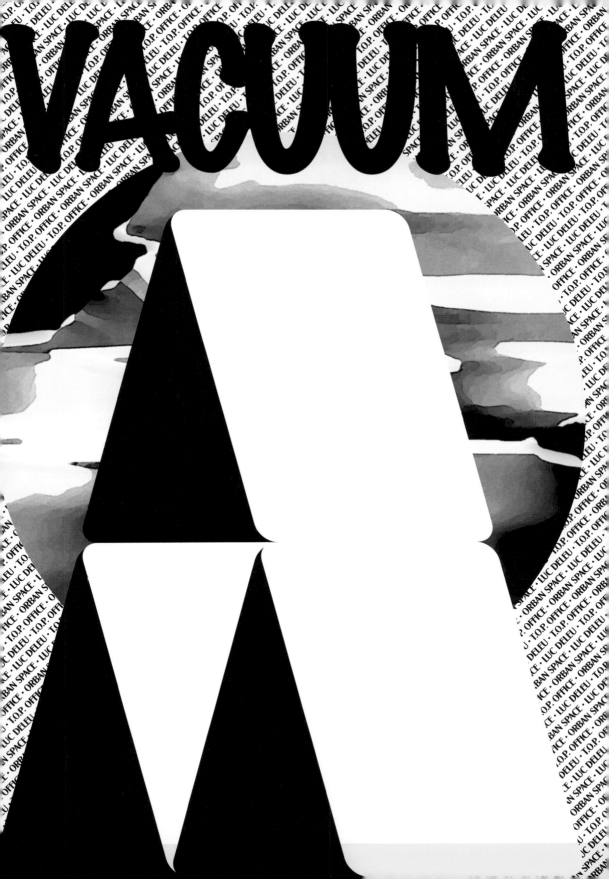

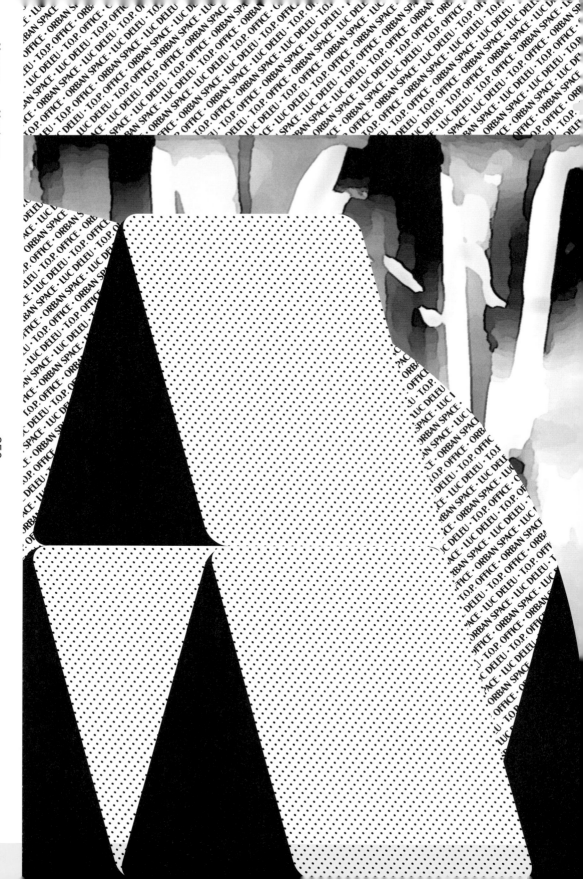

Promotional Pattern, Aircraft Carrier, Ice Rivers, House of Cards, Globe Grid, and Horizon

Globe Grid, Containers, Ice Rivers,
Globes, and Horizon

Containers, Globe Grid, House of
Cards, and Horizon

Globe Grid, House of Cards, Aircraft Carriers, Orb,
and Ice Rivers

Teresa Stoppani

Depiction
Architecture is a Concept

'Architecture will always be elusive and volatile,
malleable and changeable. But it will certainly be
so that architecture is beyond stone, concrete, steel,
glass and insulation and belongs to the realm of
the mind. Architecture is a concept, not an object.'
Luc Deleu[1]

1 Luc Deleu, '31 overpeinzingen omtrent architectuur (Academical Upgrade 05, Deel I)'/'31 reflections on architecture (Academical Upgrade 05, Part I)', in: Bart Bulter and Arjen Oosterman (eds.), *A/S/L Architectuur/ Stedenbouw/Land- schapsarchitectuur: Jaarboek Academie van Bouwkunst Amsterdam 2004–2005/A/U/L: Architecture/Urbanism/ Landscape Architecture: Yearbook Academy of Architecture 2004–2005* (Rotterdam: 010 Publishers, 2005), pp. 269–279.

Depiction conventionally indicates the repre- sentation of a concept or an object by means of a picture. Yet how does architecture relate to depiction? Can architecture depict? To address what architecture 'does' in terms of depiction, it is necessary to move away from the phe- nomenology of perception and from art his- tory. Whereas painting presents a view of the world on canvas, architecture involves a vision that makes a world within that very world. The question to explore here is not so much the rela- tionship between architecture as an object and its visual representation before and after con- struction, but rather the very instance of depic- tion performed by architecture itself. Depiction in architecture, far from being the two- or three-dimensional representation of architecture itself, is the framing of reality by architecture: how architecture interprets and 'depicts' a reality that may be physical or imagined but is always embodied in architecture itself. Conceived in this way, architecture does never merely entail building: it is in itself a depiction—of the world, of an idea, of itself. Architecture in itself re-presents, and it therefore both interprets and con- structs a reality.

In the case of Luc Deleu and T.O.P. office, depiction amounts to a complex practice. Since Deleu doesn't consider architec- ture strictly as an act of designing and building but rather as a crucial social and political environmental intervention, his work no longer strictly coincides with architectural objects, built or unbuilt. As architecture becomes a critical agent, a polemical provocation, the expression of a socio-political con- science and much more, the narrow definitions of depiction are unbefitting, reductive and ultimately dispensable. Con- ventional modes of representation are constantly challenged and redefined while they are used. Even though Deleu makes use of the drawing—the conventional triad of plan, section, and elevation—as a basic tool of architectural expression, just as much as he uses the scale model—the prime device for the study of formal compositions as well as for public presentation—both media are never sufficient, nor are they the most effective ways to 'depict' projects and ideas. Deleu's architecture conveys a mode of 'depiction' that is radically different.

There are three tools that best represent Deleu's engagement with architecture: the statement, the installation, and the map. The statement usually takes the form of a manifesto-like declaration or a written proposal accompanied by sketches or cartoon-like illustrations; or, more systematically, it may take the form of a dictionary, suggesting the terminological redefinition of the discipline. The installation, crucially framed by the performance of its making, is mostly urban and site specific; it addresses the universals of space making, such as thresholds, boundaries, place marking, monumentality. The map, always large-scale, encompasses the whole earth or even ventures in outer space; it refrains from the figurative and manipulates the conventions of modern cartography to return it to a complex compendium of information and critical agendas.

Statements, installations and maps are for Deleu much more than architectural media. As critical tools, they pull and stretch architecture beyond its conventional domains, addressing an environment that is as big as our planet and beyond, and charging the discipline with the uneasy consciousness of space and with the responsibility toward the environment (as architects and as human beings). Selectively used, statements, installations, and maps emphasize those components that are essential to the performance of architecture as a critical practice: communication (the statements), located practice (the installations) and networked relations (the maps). Finally, they are brought together, completed and enacted with another exemplary mode within Deleu's practice: the journey.

From Statement to Photo Sequence:
Depicting Architect(ure)

Architecture is never innocent: it chooses and takes responsibility, in whatever form it may be expressed. Deleu's works since the early 1970s manifest a sense of unease for the role of the architectural profession in society. This is expressed through a series of positions presented in the form of 'proposals' and 'advices', brief and provocative design statements, accompanied by collages, vignettes and sketched ideas that are meant to be circulated in the public realm: for Deleu, public space is the true realm of architecture, addressed not always and not necessarily by building. The long list of *Proposals* and advices (developed from 1972 to 1980 and revisited in 2000 and 2002) ranges from the *Proposal for complete disuse of public lighting*, to the *Proposal of an international dunghill in the Sahara*, to the *Proposal to classify the public transport*

2 *Proposals,* 1972–80.

5 *Museum for Broken Art,* 1978 (postcard).

7 *Ready-made Housing Architecture (Luc Deleu Manifesto to the Board),* 1979–85.

as monument, the *Proposal for urban agriculture*, all the way to the *Proposal for urban game*.[2] All public, supra-urban and supra-national—even if some of the proposals originate from specific local issues, such as the state of the architectural profession in Belgium—these statements are informed by Deleu's *Farewell to Architecture* exhibition at the art space Vacuum voor nieuwe dimensies (Vacuum for New Dimensions) in Antwerp in 1970 and his subsequent *Proposal for the abolition of the law of 20.02.1939* exhibition at Spectrum Gallery in 1978.[3] From then on, Deleu's lifetime architectural project will engage in the critical redefinition of architectural practice and in its widening onto a global ambit of material intervention within the world. Many of Deleu's photographic series—ranging from the catalogue of *Situations Trouvées* (1977–)[4] to the *Museum for Broken Art* (1978)[5]—but also the physical installations—such as the superposition of the proportional construction lines (*tracés regulateurs*) over the façade of Le Corbusier's Villa Schwob in La-Chaux-de-Fonds (1987)[6]—exemplify the contention that, divorced from building, architecture first and foremost re-frames reality. This approach is exemplified by *Ready-made Housing Architecture (Luc Deleu Manifesto to the Board)* (1979–85),[7] a groundbreaking project aimed at subverting the regulations defining the code of practice and legitimizing the architectural profession. The series of single family homes, designed and built by their owners yet legitimized by the Deleu's signature on the projects' drawings and documentation, are presented in several pages of contact prints. The seriality and self-similarity of these houses is once again documented and denounced by the seriality of the photographic documentation.

Deleu's project, I would argue, is therefore the depiction of reality within reality. The architect observes reality as it is and comments on it; often this work consists in the framing of the world, and the

3 'Voorstel tot afschaffing van de wet van 20 februari 1939', Spectrum Gallery, Antwerp, Belgium, 1978.

4 *Situations Trouvées,* 1977–.

6 *Tracés Régulateurs on Villa Schwob (Le Corbusier),* La-Chaux-de-Fonds, Switzerland, 1987.

subsequent exposition and redefinition of the existing as new, anew. But reality is never neutral or passive; it responds in turn and questions and challenges the architect. Again the photo sequence best documents these uncertainties and doubts, which always introduce and implicitly anticipate future developments in the architect's work. A series of photographs from the T.O.P. office archives, some of which were gathered in 1984 in the small publication *Urbild eines beweglichen Denkmales*, documents the installation of *Two Small Triumphal Arches* in Basel, Switzerland in 1983.[8] The shipping containers that will make up the new temporary monument reach the site on a large lorry, and are readied to be placed near the stone statue of a saint.[9] The following image shows one of the containers placed on two mechanical lifts and ready to be installed, but in a further photo the three containers, about to be assembled in the temporary and precarious monument, are still lying on the ground in disarray— until the very end we don't know how they will come together, and what new order they will find.[10] The next image, which surprisingly is not included in the aforementioned publication, however provides a view on a horizontal container devoid of doors.[11] Suddenly, if not for once, we are granted a view into the interior of a container.[12] What is really opened up here is a question on the limits of architecture, the curiosity to possibly reconsider an element that will soon be used in many of Deleu's projects as an instrumental given and as a tool for the marking of public space, rather than rediscover it, instead, as a space and as an interior. The open container presents us, as it were, with an open question on the role of the architect and the boundaries of authorship.

8 Luc Deleu and Marc Hostettler, *Luc Deleu: Urbild eines beweglichen Denkmales* (Brussels: Sint–Lukasstichting/ Neuchâtel: Editions Media, 1984). Simultaneously, a French edition documenting the *Large Triumphal Arch* for Neuchâtel was published: Luc Deleu and Marc Hostettler, *Luc Deleu: Prototype d'un Monument Mobile* (Brussels: Sint-Lukasstichting/Neuchâtel: Editions Media, 1984).

9 *Small Triumphal Arch*, Basel, Switzerland, 1983 (installation photo).

10 *Small Triumphal Arch*, Basel, Switzerland, 1983; *Small Triumphal Arch*, Basel, Switzerland, 1983 (installation photos).

11 *Small Triumphal Arch*, Basel, Switzerland, 1983 (installation photo).

12 Other photographs in the publication show how concrete blocks are loaded into a vertical container for stability, yet another horizontal view into a container is lacking.

Containers: The Immanent Index

Deleu's 1977 *Lego Constructions* inaugurate a long series of modular projects in which the architect moves from modeling with standard Lego blocks to the use of large scale shipping containers.[13] While the projects have in common the use of predefined modular units, they differ, beyond their scale, in the shift from a largely polemical project to a critical redefinition of relations and formal arrangements. If

13 *Lego Constructions: Obelisk*, 1983.

the given unit is accepted as such (Lego blocks or shipping containers), what is exposed is the power of architecture to reinvent articulations, and to newly arrange and place. This is the crucial difference between these latter projects: while the *Lego Constructions* combine units according to their pre-defined interlocking possibilities and produce site-less prototypical abstractions, the numerous container installations always become 'architecturally' specific. Disregarding or challenging their stacking and space-saving modularity, Deleu uses the containers as self-supporting materials for the invention of architectural 'markers'. The container installations are precarious and unlikely structures in threshold spaces, which always manifest or underline an awareness of space. They demand a mode of attention that architecture perceived 'in distraction' (Walter Benjamin)[14] is never granted, and therefore become both relational and site specific. Marking threshold spaces or attaching themselves to (and attacking) given constructions or urban spaces, these compositions challenge the order of urban sites and locations. They are evocative of the way in which Kazimir Malevich's *Architektons*[15] or El Lissitzky's *Prouns*[16] define relational systems of volumes and forms in space. Yet while the context of operation of the latter is, most often, the interrelation of several such arrangements within the boundary of the pictorial space or of the exhibition gallery, Deleu's containers attack the city and, metaphorically and with a certain irony, the very global commerce system that generated them as modules of a standardized market economy. *Architektons* and *Prouns* operate on the threshold between painting and architecture, or, as El Lissitzky said of the Prouns, they are 'the station where one changes from painting to architecture.'[17] What Deleu's container projects do instead is to move from architecture to representation: repeated in its variants, the series of container projects as a whole 'represents' architecture, distilling it to its most essential role of critical spatial practice. The form of the container unit is taken as ready-made and appropriated by architecture: it serves as the 'pixel' of a new form of drawing in space. The original function is disregarded and voided, yet a new alternative functional program is not assigned. If architecture's primary mode of depiction consists of the framing of reality, then a container installation, placed in different arrangements and interacting with different situations in the world, not only produces a ubiquitous and recognizable universal sign, but also a 'placer' and a 'marker' of architecture.

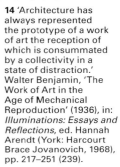

14 'Architecture has always represented the prototype of a work of art the reception of which is consummated by a collectivity in a state of distraction.' Walter Benjamin, 'The Work of Art in the Age of Mechanical Reproduction' (1936), in: *Illuminations: Essays and Reflections*, ed. Hannah Arendt (York: Harcourt Brace Jovanovich, 1968), pp. 217–251 (239).

15 Kasimir Malevich, *Gota*, 1923.

16 El Lissitzky, *Proun Portfolio. Proun 3A*, 1920.

17 Jan Debbaut et al. (eds.), *El Lissitzky 1890–1941, Architect, Schilder, Fotograaf, Typograaf* (Eindhoven: Stedelijk Van Abbemuseum, 1990), p. 32.

Deleu uses the container, as it were, as a pencil to draw the world on the world. The idea of architecture, its image, and its construction are collapsed in these disconcerting objects, whose obstinate presence performs again and again the act of placing.

18 *Project for a Monument*, collage, November 1980.

Project for a Monument, a collage of four Polaroid pictures glued in a grid-like composition onto a paper with the letterhead of T.O.P. office, dated November 1980, shows how Deleu prepared for subsequent projects.[18] A set of toy containers, which he had bought by chance in a model shop some time earlier that year, served as the building elements for a multicolored, massive square volume. Only a few years later Deleu would start to realize a family of temporary yet monumental constructions that range from the more conventional projects for triumphal arches (1981–82, realized in Neuchâtel in 1983, in Basel in 1983, in Barcelona in 1987, and so on) and for obelisks (realized in Antwerp in 1987 and in 2003), to a series of more complex, experimental and precariously balanced arrangements.[19] For the 'Tower of Babel' exhibition in Montevideo in Antwerp (1984), for example, Deleu for once liberated the containers from their orthogonal space-saving stacking systems and literally scattered and disorderly amassed them in the vast exhibition space.[20]

19 *Untitled*, 1986 (drawing).

20 *Containers in Bulk*, Montevideo, Antwerp, Belgium, 1984.

The *Big Triumphal Arch* installed in Neuchâtel in 1983 is a celebration of the very act of framing.[21] The design of the arch is not as relevant as is the positioning and arrangement of the elements, whose individual differences are not only tolerated but embraced and documented: standard and modular, each piece becomes unique, marked by graffiti or bruised by use. Placed like a monument, rather than becoming focus of attention or spatial organization, it 'locates' a temporary frame to look both at the lake and the Alpes and back at the city. The 1985 master plan for the *Pantacom Container Depot* in Antwerp on the contrary exempts the containers from the construction of single monuments and subjects them to an at once graphical and spatial organizing system

21 *Big Triumphal Arch*, Neuchatel, Switzerland, 1983 (drawing).

22 *Pantacom Container Depot*, Antwerp, Belgium, 1984.

of vast scale combination.[22] While the container is a self-same standardized tool to measure the word, it is also a receptacle of mysteries that Deleu never exposed or explored until the *ORBINO* project (1988, then realized in various sites in the Netherlands and Belgium)

23 *ORBINO*, Alkmaar, the Netherlands, 2007.

enters inside its volume and inhabits it.[23] Here the container is designed and used as an exhibition gallery or a radio station. Probably the most powerful manifestation happens with the installation of several container installations for the Middelheim exhibition in Antwerp (2003).[24] Here a population of different container constructions establishes a landscape of relations, suggesting the possibility of repetitions, adaptations, transformations and punctual but networked interventions that map the ground in situ, like a gigantic one-to-one drawing by points and lines.

24 'Luc Deleu', Middelheimmuseum, Antwerp, Belgium, 2003 (North East view of exhibition lay-out).

The early projects with shipping containers are marked by a certain randomness: the containers are graffitied, dirty, used and reused, at random. No matter what they are, they have their own determination, which is not part of the project. While they serve as elements of the composition, they are not objects of design. Surprisingly, in the more recent projects the containers, bar a few exceptions, have become neat, polished, clean, monochromatic and identical: they have become pixels of a digital drawing and design. Also gone is the idea of precariousness, weathering and instability, both chronological and structural, even when they compose an apparently unstable arch of four components (*Speybank* project [1999], realized in Antwerp [2003],[25] Yokohama [2005], and Ghent [2007]) or further play on the triumphal arch trope (*New Big Triumphal Arch*, Middelheim Open Air Museum, 2003[26]). It is the *MACBA Piece* in Barcelona (1997) that exemplifies the containers' original role of marking and framing public space, in this case by affixing a cruciform composition of containers to an existing blind building façade.[27] At once a transformer and an attacker

25 *Speybank*, Middelheimmuseum, Antwerp, Belgium, 2003.

27 *MACBA Piece*, Museum of Contemporary Art (MACBA), Barcelona, Spain, 1997.

26 *Big New Triumphal Arch*, Middelheimmuseum, Antwerp, Belgium, 2003.

that stitches across the public space of the square and inflicts upon the bare volume of the building, *MACBA Piece* evokes the critical stance of the 1970s containers proposals, which look like monuments but instead confuse and displace.

Point to Line to Globe: Mapping the World

'Architecture has two basic scales: man and the earth. Architecture as ORBAN PLANNING (the world scale as context) can, in a modest way, contribute to a substantial improvement of the general climate of life on earth. (...) There is a great need for new visionary models for the "earthly space".'
Luc Deleu[28]

28 Luc Deleu, 'Aarde, passagiers en gebouwen/Earth, passengers and buildings', in: *Drijvende vliegvelden en andere infrastructuren/Floating Airports and Other Infrastructures,* special issue of *Forum* 34, no. 1 (1990), pp. 5–14 (8–9).

29 *Journey Around the World in 80 Days (Madrid–Weber–Madrid),* 1992–93.

For Deleu it is the responsibility of the architect to consider the whole world as his working context. While he continues to operate punctually with local interventions and installations, their seriality, their repetition, their variation, and the corresponding documentation suggest a planetary dimension of his *opus*. As the container monuments continue to dot the world, Deleu begins to plot and reveal the true scale of his project. The installations, photos and collages of *Journey Around the World in 80 Days* (Madrid–Weber–Madrid) (1992–93)[29] present the tools of depiction for this endeavor: instead of floor plans, Deleu uses world maps in Mercator, Van Grinten and Fuller projections and drafting tables set up for the calculation, planning and tracing of routes; and instead of architectural models, he repeatedly employs earth globes as maquettes of his journey. The 1999 revision of the project, *Journey Around the World in 72 Days,*[30] further specifies both its ambitions and its representations: from New Zealand to Spain, as if continuing the previous project with the return journey, the route here measures the antipodes of the world, embracing its maximum extension. Its corresponding

30 *Journey Around the World in 72 Days* 40° 24' 904S 176° 17' 551E over its antipode 40° 24' 904N 3° 24' 449W (ERNSLAW ONE TTD, WEBER, NEW ZEALAND over its antipode PLAZA MAYOR, MADRID, SPAIN), 1999 (detail).

visualization by means of a doubled photograph is an infinite horizon, a travelling line that concentrates, overlaps and fades in the similarities and differences of the world: in one strip photomontage the superimposed panoramas expand their views to different horizons, from Spain to New Zealand to Spain, constructing a trans-continental site that reveals the true dimensions and the assignment of architecture in a linear way.

In parallel to the theoretical journey around the world, more conventional architectural tools are used to striate the world, with open and linear city projects. *The Unadapted*

31 Constant, *New Babylon*, 1963.

City—De Onaangepaste Stad (D.O.S.) (1995–2006) proposes a linear development organized along an elevated spine of public transport, which incorporates also the most important urban spaces. Reminiscent of Le Corbusier's *Plan Obus* for Algiers (1930–33), but light on the ground, and raised above the existing developments like Constant's *New Babylon*,[31] Deleu's linear city remains as open and as expandable as his horizon photomontages. The potentially endlessly long spine becomes the line for the juxtaposition and interaction of differences—not a planned order, but a facilitated chaos that promotes difference and freedom. The urban district of *The Unadapted City: Brikabrak* (1998) proposes its prototypical urban fragment, that can later be curved or fragmented, cut and reassembled, while *The Unadapted City: Dinkytown* (1998) produces a complexity of spatial arrangements within the rectilinear spine, articulating it and intersecting it with sinusoidal lines and a mixture of different spaces. The arrangements suggested by *The Unadapted City: Octopus* (1999) break down the continuous linearity of the project in fragments and sub-organizations, introducing perhaps a possible surface development (and maybe the ambition to digress from linearity and blanket the globe?).

While these different iterations of *The Unadapted City* are represented and exhibited with large-scale linear models, they remain only fragments of the true intention, which is to address the Earth as the site of architecture, and to do it through a series of linear traces—literally leaving traces, as it were, on the world's surface. It is finally *The Unadapted City: Vipcity:* (2001–04) that fully addresses the systematic linearity of the project. Here linear drawings, diagrams, 'decks scores' and notated time sequences systematically address the intention of conquering the world with a project of smooth striation that organizes infrastructures for life while enabling the arbitrary along its 'scores'.[32]

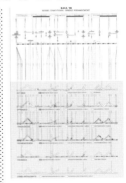

32 *The Unadapted City: Dinkytown (Bridge arrangement),* 1998.

In 2006 the mappings of *Orban Space* return architecture to the systematic representation of the world. Moving away again from the figurative and from the forms of architecture, the panels of the project are in fact the beautiful arrangement of charts and quantitative diagrams that inform us on the state of the globe, defining possible categories for classification and analysis. The concerns of architecture are classified, systematically catalogued, and colorfully depicted: 'Infrastructural space (tubes and cables)', with great emphasis on oil network and piping; 'Setting and location', diagrammed in climatic zones; 'Networks and nodes', ranging from street to urban, national, regional and transcontinental to worldwide level; a visual definition of 'Urbanized public space', inclusive of infrastructural spaces and forums; and a catalogue of 'Scales and degrees of urbanization'. As anticipated in Deleu's 1970s proposals for architecture, the true concerns of this architecture are not to be found in buildings or objects, but in the systems of infrastructures and their expanding networks, a global architectural project. A gigantic map of the skies provides the fitting background for the synoptic montage of the plates, free floating in space (literally) to be modified in time, replaced and layered with transformations and updates. This is a constantly changing map of visualized world data, whose configuration and depiction change as dynamically as their object of concern.

Journey: Like a Comet's Tail

In 2006 Deleu embarks on an actual sailboat tour around the world, putting to practice his contention that the concern of the architect can only be planetary or beyond, and following up on the 1972 project for a peripatetic *Mobile Medium University* aboard aircraft carriers and the 1990s installations of *Journey Around the World.* This 'project' is much more than a journey of exploration or reconnaissance in preparation for a design intervention: the journey is in fact the project itself. Like any architectural work, it is a work of planning and tracing lines, making marks, and leaving tracks in the world. There does not need to be a building as the envisioned

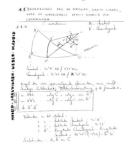

33 *Berekening van de reisweg, grote circkel, voor de wereldreis vanuit Madrid via Chandigarh,* 2005 (map with calculations for a journey around the world, T.O.P. office archives).

end result: the architecture is in fact the journey that the architect plans and realizes. The true representation of this travel project then is not its travel log, nor its photo or video documentation, but the set of calculations, diagrams, annotations, and traced routes that first prepare and then accompany the journey.[33] The ideal lines of travel, the translation of an ideal geometry of exploration from the plan of the sea charts to their nautical translation in great circle lines on the globe; the adjustments to physical conditions, land masses, sea currents, weather, winds and all the other accidents that must be taken into account to make the journey 'real': this itinerary is indeed a project.

The 1972 project for a traveling university had found its mobile housing on decommissioned aircraft carriers—undoubtedly playing on architecture's long love affair with the ship, that ideal space of survival, miniature world in a vessel, but also heterotopical container of redefined social relations. Its representations nevertheless, even in the form of the provocation leaflet, continued to be figurative and to use the conventions of 'architectural' plans and sections and suggestive renderings. With the realization of the journey around the world, Deleu returns architecture to its essentials of space making. He no longer appropriates predefined forms as such, nor uses given elements as re-combinable modular units—even though these turn into 3D pixels more than building blocks

34 Gilles Deleuze and Félix Guattari, 'The Smooth and the Striated', in: *A Thousand Plateaus: Capitalism and Schizophrenia* (London: Athlone, 1996 [1988]), pp. 474–500.

in the later projects. Instead the project here is the journey, its itinerary a Deleuzian line of flight, a light form of striation implemented on the oceans, the smooth space par excellence.[34] If smooth space, as per the Deleuzian definition, is never free from striation, then Deleu's journey is an epitome of pure architectural striation—a project of unstable knowledge and of reinterpretation of the world. Again, a map provides the primary mode of the project—even if in this case conventional geographic cartography is used only as a basis for an invisible architecture of movement—and serves as a diagram of the world. Deleu's project does not produce 'building'; it produces knowledge of the world. His notebooks of calculations, annotations, instructions, coordinates, tracings of rhumb lines, and travel plans define a use-less journey. The end result is a pure architecture divested of utilitarian purpose. The aesthetic dimension of this project (in his writings Deleu often ventures into discussing the beauty of architecture and its fundamentally aesthetic task in the world) is thus redefined as a production of freedom from both the form and the function that conventionally define architecture. And therefore its 'depiction' can no longer be a drawing.

35 Bas Jan Ader, *In Search of the Miraculous, Art & Project Bulletin* 89 (August 1975). Jan Verwoert, *Bas Jan Ader: In Search of the Miraculous* (London: Afterall Books, 2006).

Deleu's personal journey on a sail boat invariably brings to mind Bas Jan Ader's 1975 tragic attempted crossing of the Atlantic, part of his project In *Search of the Miraculous*.[35] There is nothing tragic, solitary or mysterious to Deleu's journey though. What fundamentally distinguishes his project from Ader's is the meticulous planning of the architectural journey, the extensive calculations and tracings, and their systematic documentation. Deleu's *Journey Around the World* is not an existential journey of artistic self-introspection, but an architectural project that maintains its public dimension. He does not flee reality in search for the miraculous, but deeply engages with the real. The lines of flight that his journeys trace across the globe are ways of engaging with it, by measuring, mapping, framing, and leaving scattered traces—like a comet. *The Container*,[36] a 2009 proposal for a public art project entitled *Comeet*, indeed leaves one of these fragments to mark the world: ironically yellow, solitary, fallen on earth but belonging to the universe, precariously balanced on one sole point of contact with the ground, a free standing (or, more likely, hovering) shipping container is no longer part of an obelisk or a triumphal arch or any other monumental arrangement, but just itself: a trace in the world.

36 *The Container*, 2009.

Deleu's overall project, then, is constituted by the many traces that this unusual and provocative architect has been leaving in the world throughout his career. The only fitting 'depiction' of his opus are the works themselves, the words, the maps and the many different ways in which Deleu has 'installed' his provocation in the world, again and again, in scattered fragments, but with unfaltering integrity and consistence.

PROPOSALS 1972-1980 REVISITED 2011

Proposal for total decentralization (of Antwerp).
Proposal for complete abolishment of traffic rules (in Antwerp).
Proposal for complete disuse of public lighting.
Proposal to plant fruit avenues.
Proposal to switch to 12 volts.
Proposall for the implantation of urban dunghills.
Proposal to introduce plastic money (in Brussels).
Proposal for long lawns.
Proposal for an open sewerage (in Bruges).
Proposal for mobile monuments.
Proposal for an international dunghill in the Sahara.
Proposal for naked Olympic Games (in Montreal).
Proposal for urban wood production.
Proposal to shoot nuclear waste to the sun.
Proposal for car-free noons.
Proposal for non-programmed TV-broadcasts.
Advice for vegetable-boxes instead of flower-boxes.
Advice for consumption strikes.
Proposal for an irrigation system using rain water.
Proposal for visible telephone wiring and electricity cables.
Proposal to classify the public transport as monument.
Proposal to recycle monuments into social housing.
Proposal for free masonry.
Proposal for protection of weeds.
Proposal for city beehives.
Advice to close the Zoo (in Antwerp).
Proposal for the abolishment of the law on the protection of the title and the profession of architect.
Proposal for roof horticulture.
Proposal to switch to biological power.
Proposal to stop leisure activities.
Proposal for the restoration of the public transport.
Proposal for road softening.
Proposal for roof pavements.
Proposal for urban agriculture, urban horticulture and urban forestry.
Proposal for city orchards, city pastures and urban cattle.
Proposal for urban fishing ponds.
Proposal for urban game.

www.topoffice.to

luc deleu
stedebouwkundige - architect
cogels-osylei 42
2600   berchem-antwerpen
tel.   031/30 40 67
bank : brussel lambert nr. 320-0295854-74
b.t.w. 509.535.753

VOORSTEL TOT KLAS-
SERING, ALS MONUMENT,
VAN HET OPENBAAR VERVOER
(TE ANTWERPEN)
'76-'78

Voorstel tot klassering, als monument, van het openbaar vervoer (te Antwerpen), 1976-78

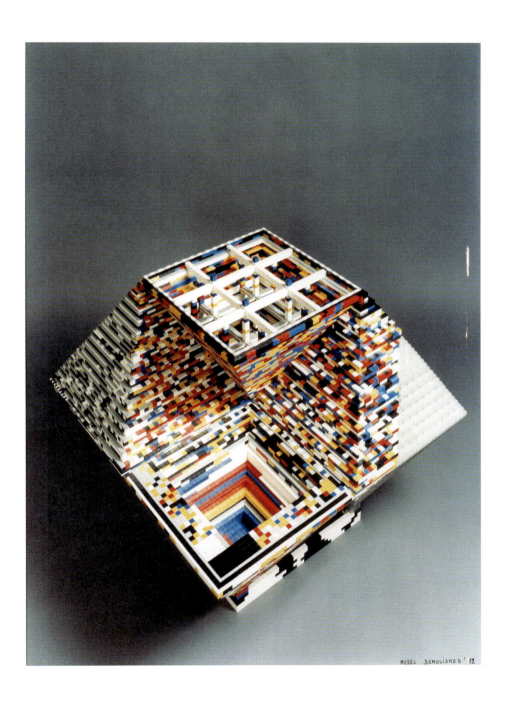

MODEL DEMOLISHED '82

Works XXXIII–XXXIX   Luc Deleu – T.O.P. office

Journey Around the World in 80 Days (Madrid–Weber–Madrid), 1992-93

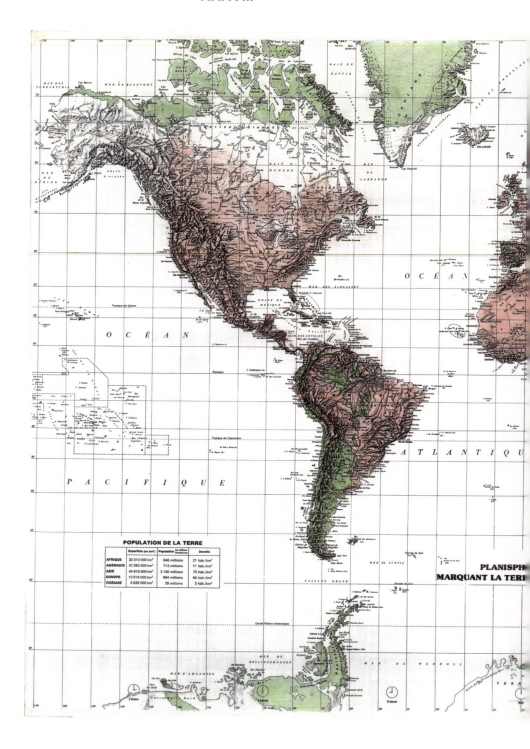

POPULATION DE LA TERRE			
	Superficie (en km²)	Population (en millions d'habitants)	Densité
AFRIQUE	30 310 000 km²	646 millions	21 hab./km²
AMÉRIQUE	42 083 000 km²	713 millions	17 hab./km²
ASIE	44 519 000 km²	3 100 millions	70 hab./km²
EUROPE	10 519 000 km²	694 millions	66 hab./km²
OCÉANIE	8 935 000 km²	28 millions	3 hab./km²

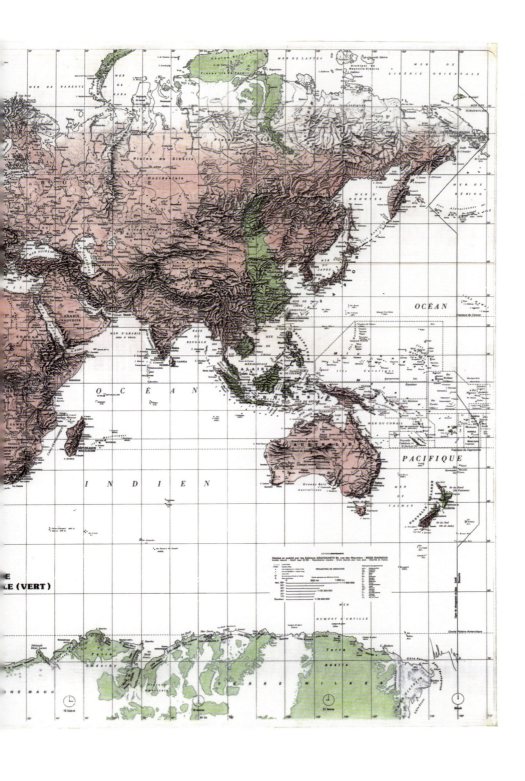

LE (VERT)

New Small Triumphal Arch, École de Beaux-Arts, Nîmes, France, 1996 (photocollage)

Small Triumphal Arch, Basel, Switzerland, 1983. (installation photo)

Manifesto:

Hapag Lloyd

Manifesto:

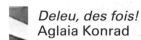
Deleu, des fois!
Aglaia Konrad

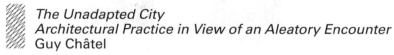
The Unadapted City
Architectural Practice in View of an Aleatory Encounter
Guy Châtel

Works XLI–XLVII
Luc Deleu – T.O.P. office

Deleu, des fois!

Aglaia Konrad

candidate city

Ho Chi Minh City   tropical city
shopping city   matrix city

temporal city   spacial city   unrelised city
                                              dim city   ocean city

opian city   outer city
          readable city   nearest city   sonic city

union city   garden city   commuter city
                                              his city
al ity   future city   alphabet city

pact city   emblematic linea city   Mexico City

personal city instant city   walled city   underground city
                                                    true city   old city
              visible city   huge city   surrogate city

vast city

open city   fun city rhizome city   next city
                                         vulnerable city
          no city   No Stop City   transit city   silent city

ue ci Bab el-oued City   non stop city moving city   utopian city   concrete city
                                                                        african city
          underwater city   unrealised city
sa city
ourban city   marine city   automobile city
      semiotic city
                    Unadapted City
her city   xenophobic city   triton city   rumor city
www. city   plug-in city

neon city   zionist city   ocean city
nowhere city   postmodern city   agglomeration city
                              a city
          Functional City.   slow city
                                  prefab city   major city
          inner city   airport city comprehensive city   your city

parallel city   tomorrow city   broadacre city
urred city
UNO City   toy city   skywaft city

nkytown   surrogate city   polder city   twenty century city
              pleasure city   mobile city
              pilot city

ficional city   multiple city   new city   heterotopian city

ss city tower city   pirate city   one city   compressed city
      fast city   nuclear city
              quick city   asian city

                          additive city   generic city   any city
naked city   circular city
ltural city   vip city

      omega city   compact city floating city   evolutionary city   dual city
dd city
      container city

          factory city
      alfa city bamboo city
eternal city   sea city   data city   habor city
                              continious city

During collecting
the illustrations
for this lecture
I became fascinated by
Japanese architecture
and a
wide
acquaintance
seems
highly interesting
to me.

On the importance and non-importance of architecture.
Luc Deleu, unpublished lecture, feb. 1985, p.12

the power of the visionary

Urban structures become more and more complex.
Open space becomes rare.

'Housing & the City'

It is clear that "re-use, insertion and (re)integration" should be a means for the architects and urban designers to tell an architectural story with the aim to evoke (architectural)emotions and to visualize an architectural and urban concept

architecture has to be utopian

Our actual concrete sk

More

for me the essential in architecture is the spacial organisation,
in which
every individual can develop himself and think on different levels

How do I create more and better public space in the future?

The new buildings too will once have to be re-used.

en ask for more re-use, because they are hard to demolish

structures have to be re-used

and the material itself cannot be recuperated.

Although the Modernists and CIAM are accused of having ravaged the city and messed up public space, it is only during the last couple of decades that the city, the periphery, the country and the environment have really been ruined - in splendor - by buildings, architecture and urban design that preserve a status quo. The result of this non-critical realization of every given program will force us back to the early Modernist' approach that was based on meaning and program.

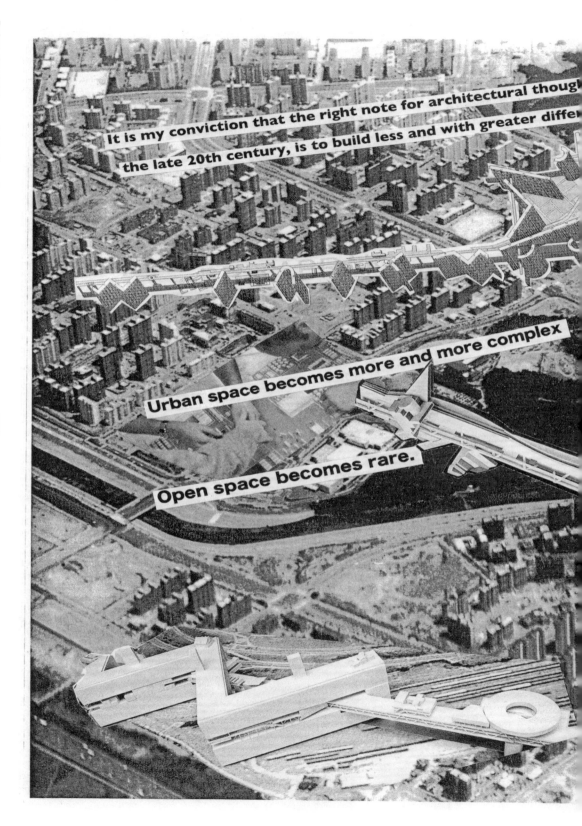

It is my conviction that the right note for architectural though the late 20th century, is to build less and with greater diffe

Urban space becomes more and more complex

Open space becomes rare.

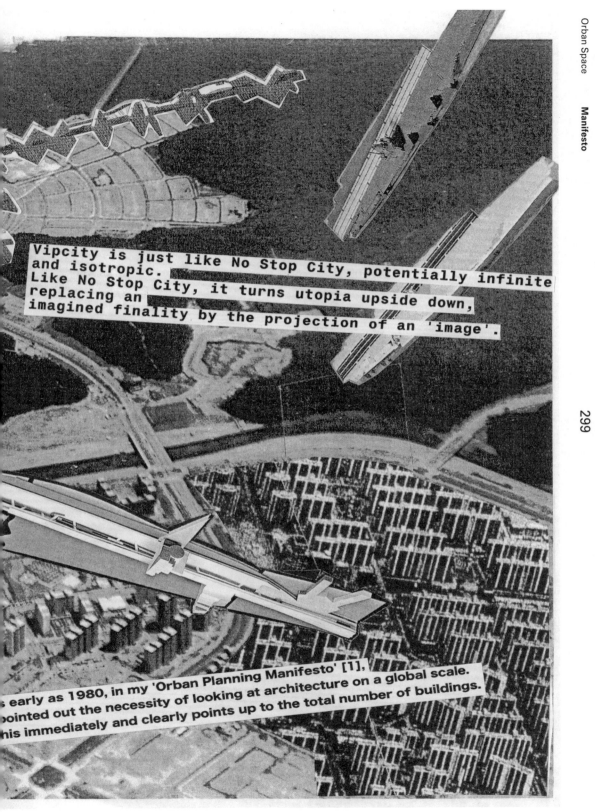

Vipcity is just like No Stop City, potentially infinite and isotropic. Like No Stop City, it turns utopia upside down, replacing an imagined finality by the projection of an 'image'.

early as 1980, in my 'Orban Planning Manifesto' [1], pointed out the necessity of looking at architecture on a global scale. his immediately and clearly points up to the total number of buildings.

Apart from its material function, architecture has a spiritual function and task.
The imaginative power of architecture
must create examples fot the future perspectives,
and it must stimulate the imagination;
architecture as medium,
as data carrier
for future generations.

search for
nonomous architecture
wide social context'
d be a contribution to the
ual discussion on architecture
in other words
ltiplicity of language
thin unity of concept.

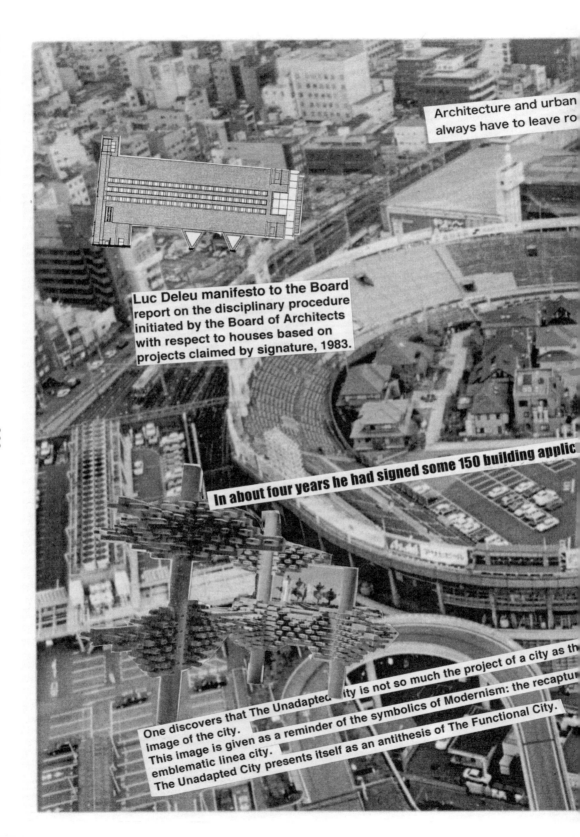

Architecture and urban
always have to leave ro

Luc Deleu manifesto to the Board
report on the disciplinary procedure
initiated by the Board of Architects
with respect to houses based on
projects claimed by signature, 1983.

In about four years he had signed some 150 building applic

One discovers that The Unadapted ity is not so much the project of a city as th
image of the city.
This image is given as a reminder of the symbolics of Modernism: the recaptur
emblematic linea city.
The Unadapted City presents itself as an antithesis of The Functional City.

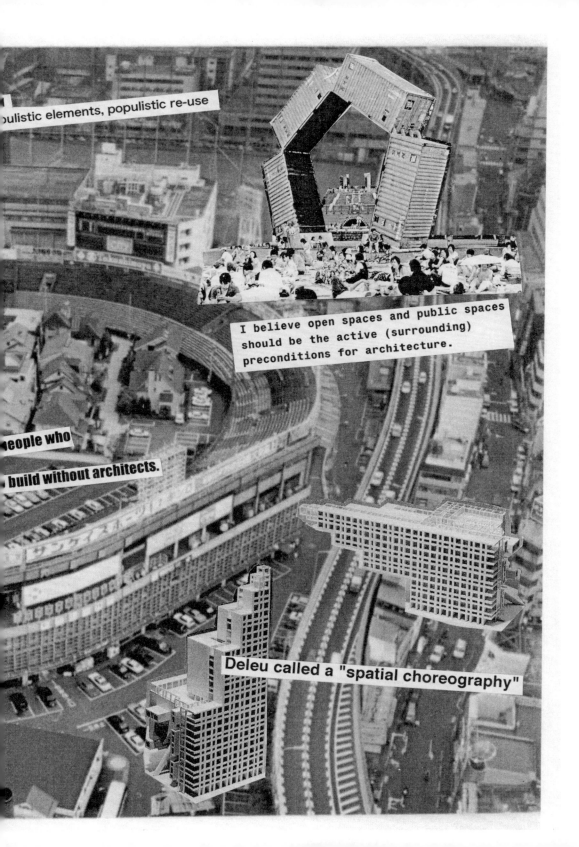

pulistic elements, populistic re-use

I believe open spaces and public spaces should be the active (surrounding) preconditions for architecture.

eople who

build without architects.

Deleu called a "spatial choreography"

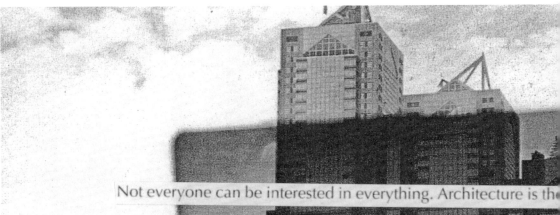

Not everyone can be interested in everything. Architecture is the

Built-up environment is increasing daily.

is not a dogma, and only obtains its significance next to other building
architecture
approaches

t every body's thing !

"Scale & Perspective"

back
large to small is scheduled
future.

candidate city

Ho Chi Minh City   tropical city

shopping city

matrix c

unrelised city

temporal city   spacial city   ocean city

dim city

utopian city   outer cit

readable city   nearest city   sonic

commuter city

union city   garden city

his city

future city   alphabet city

compact city   emblematic linea city   Mexico City

underground

personal city instant city   walled city   old c

true city

visible city   surrogate cit

huge city

vast city

open city   fun city rhizome city   next city

vulnerable city

no city   transit city   silent c

No Stop City

true city Bab el-oued City   non stop city moving city   utopian city   concrete city

africa

underwater city   unrealised city

mesa city

suburban city   marine city

semiotic city   automobile city   rumor city

her city   xenophobic city   Unadapted City   triton city   plug-in city

www. city

zionist city   ocean city   agglomeration city

neon city   postmodern city

nowhere city   a city   slow c

Functional City.   major c

comprehensive city   your city

prefab city

inner city   airport city   broadacre city

parallel city   tomorrow city

blurred city

UNO City   toy city   skywaft city

surrogate city

Dinkytown   pleasure city   polder city   twenty century city

pilot city   mobile cit

ficional city   multiple city   new city   heterotopian city

endless city   tower city   one city   compressed city

pirate city

fast city   nuclear

asian city

quick city   additive city   generic city   any c

naked city   circular city

agricultural city   vip city

floating city

omega city   compact city   evolutionary city   dual c

odd city   container city

factory city

bamboo city

alfa city   sea city   data city   habor city

eternal city   continious city

ORBAN

SPACE

Guy Châtel

The Unadapted City
Architectural Practice in View of an Aleatory Encounter

'A work of Architecture is invariably an advertisement of a point of view. It is never either pure form or pure function; nor can it simply be a mixture of both; but always it involves an act of judgement. It is an attitude taken up with regard to society, history, change, the nature of pleasure, and other matters quite extraneous to either technique or taste. Thus, a work of architecture, while always an index to state of mind, may quite often be construed as an illicit manifesto.'
Colin Rowe[1]

1 Colin Rowe, 'The Blenheim of the Welfare State', in: *As I was saying: Vol. 1: Texas, Pre-Texas*, ed. Alexander Caragonne (Cambridge, MA/London: MIT Press, 1996), p. 143; originally published in *The Cambridge Review* 31 October 1959.

A Plan
Vipcity, the provisional outcome of the long-term project for *The Unadapted City*, conducted by T.O.P. office under the leadership of Luc Deleu over some ten years (1995—2006), can be described as an extreme low-density regional town. With 76,000 inhabitants it occupies a ground surface of about 120 km². While half its population is housed in high-rise apartment slabs, the remainder is settled in an extensive allotment. The outline of the town coincides with the contour of this allotment: a somewhat warped rectangle with indented boundaries of 8.7 km by 14 km, quite simply resulting from the continuous layout of 15,140 identical plots within a grid of local access roads. The whole of it is apparently spread out on flat terrain. Absolute uniformity is only countered by some traversing highways and railways, and a fork of built-on infrastructure lines.

Vipcity merely exists in documents, drawings and models. Its most comprehensive representation is an overall plan with an insert showing an enlargement of a standard plot in serried ranks with its identical neighbors, and a legend dedicated to the calculation of the plot's apposite dimensions: the fraction of the earth surface available for dwelling is equally divided among the world population. For *Vipcity* this share is redistributed according to an average family size of 2.51 members. After deduction of the necessary utilities and access roads,

2 Cfr. T.O.P. office and Hans Theys, 'La Ville Inadaptée', in: Luc Deleu and Hans Theys, *La Ville Inadaptée* (Toulouse: Éditions Ecocart, 2003), p. 97, and Luc Deleu, 'Urbi et Orbi (D.O.S. XXI)', in: Luc Deleu and Hans Theys, *Urbi et Orbi: De Onaangepaste Stad* (Ghent: Ludion, 2002), pp. 72–73. Further on, the former book will be referred to as LVI, the latter as U&O.

3 The calculation was established in 1999. Since then, the world population has increased with a full billion people.

the size of the parcels is fixed at 0.5787 ha. The typical plot has a staggered delineation, resulting from a slanted arrangement in three equivalent rectangular parts. The shape of the lots, and through repetition of the city itself, appears to hint at future partitioning. The global ratio adopted for the land apportionment (an 'orbanistic' calculation) holds the prospect of a full occupation of terrestrial building ground. Even though in T.O.P. office's parlance the *Vipcity* plot is labeled a 'decent lot',[2] it is obvious that the seemingly fair principle of the ground's equal share-out is immediately outstripped by the relentless growth of the world population.[3] The reckoning thus infers that the plot is straightaway facing the preclusion of its decency. The fact that others settle for less ample living conditions atones for its availability. The *Vipcity* plot is evidently set aside for the privileged.

The plan of *Vipcity* exists in different versions, distinguished by a serial number, often complemented by a dangling participle. In *D.O.S. XXI — VIPCITY # 7* and *D.O.S. XXI — VIPCITY # 7 revisited* the acres are faintly revived by the drab colors of an underlain, blown-up roadmap.[4] In the upper left corner of the plan the characteristic pentagon delineating Brussels' inner city is recognizable. The *Vipcity* area covers the territory south-east of Brussels, encompassing the greater part of the Sonian Forest and the Wood of the Capuchins, reaching toward Hoeilaart, Overijse and Tervuren. *D.O.S. XXI — VIPCITY # 9 dislocated* is entirely similar, apart from the map on which it is superimposed, in this case featuring the northern area of Antwerp.[5] *D.O.S. XXI — VIPCITY # 9 adapted*, by contrast, situates the city somewhere on a coiling coastline, with its linear structures extending into the sea as jetties.[6] Here the allotment is reduced to accommodate a marina that provides anchorage for 3,106 yachts and (with an average occupation of four people per boat) lodgings for more than 12,000 sailors. Apart from this rather coincidental, entirely graphical and arithmetical revision of the settlement formula, the different versions of the plan make clear that the specification of a location has no influence on the city's overall scheme. In this respect the scheme's uniformity in *D.O.S. XXI — VIPCITY # 7 revisited* and *D.O.S. XXI — VIPCITY # 9 dislocated* is quite demonstrative. As explicitly stated by T.O.P. office, the suggestion of location is arbitrary and merely serves (through the recollection of a territory) as a scale indicator.[7] It is solely a marker for the city's expanse and the thinning of its substance.

4 D.O.S. stands for 'De Onaangepaste Stad': the Dutch name of *The Unadapted City*. Plan #7 is reproduced in: *LVI*, p. 99; Plan #7 *revisited* in: *U&O*, p. 67.

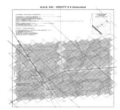

5 *The Unadapted City: Vipcity (# 9 dislocated)*, 2002.

6 *The Unadapted City: Vipcity (# 9 adapted)*, 2004.

7 Cfr. *LVI*, p. 98 and *U&O*, p. 72.

An Intention

Vipcity is a template for the settlement of the aforementioned 76,000 people. Being the spatial model of *The Unadapted City*, it has no factual existence outside the framework of this self-proclaimed 'theoretical' project. As it considers the formative potential of a city's equipment and services, the project at first consisted in gathering and ordering data. It gave way to an impressive series of graphic panels and an elaborate arithmetic model relating ten sorts of services to the number of people they sustain.[8] It thereby anticipated effective implementation by regrouping them according to their posited occurrence (structural, zoned or occasional) in a spatial system. The processing led to the unfolding of an extensive schedule for urban equipment set in parallel (and in proportion) to the corresponding dwelling surface. It is epitomized as a kind of flag (*DOS standard*), where colored bands represent services and a blank field stands for housing. Instead of being inferred from inhabitation, the complex of urban services is outlined as its nurturing agent: a 'housing generator.' Equipment is thus presented as the prime instrument to make the city. Its 'master program' is set at the disposal of town planners and the public agencies of a welfare system, perhaps enabling them to reconsider urban 'master form' at last.[9] This primacy of an organic and enduring program for human establishment, consistent with the functions and technology that support contemporary communal life, is a frequently repeated urging in Deleu's discourse, as is the ascendency of (what the Metabolist architect Fumihiko Maki called) 'collective form' or 'group form' over discrete form (especially that of the individual dwelling).[10] Deleu argues that the acknowledgement of those priorities is a necessary condition for a 'revival' (i.e. a return to the basics and ethics) of city planning, urban design and architecture. To this end *The Unadapted City* focused on the compounding of urban equipment, services and collective amenities. Therefore the housing issue had to be taken back to the schematic level where it strictly counts as mass and extent.

8 *The Unadapted City: Ten Plates,* 1995–99. The ten panels form a set shown for the first time in May 1996 at the Netherlands Architecture Institute (NAI) in Rotterdam. These documents were published in: Luc Deleu, *De Onaangepaste Stad: Werkdocumenten NAi96/ The Unadapted City: Work in Progress NAi96* (Rotterdam: NAi Publishers, 1996).

9 I borrow these notions of 'master program' and 'master form' from Fumihiko Maki, *Investigations in Collective Form* (St Louis: Washington University Press, 1964) as reprinted in Fumihiko Maki, *Nurturing Dreams: Collected Essays on Architecture and the City*, ed. Mark Mulligan (Cambridge, MA and London: MIT Press, 2008), pp. 44–56, esp. p. 45.

10 'Toward Group Form' is the title of Fumihiko Maki and Masato Ohtaka's contribution to *Metabolism: The Proposals for New Urbanism,* a publication issued in 1960 for the World Design Conference in Tokyo. 'Toward Group Form' is also included in Joan Ockman, *Architecture Culture 1943–1968* (New York: Rizzoli, 1993), pp. 321–324. Othaka was not involved in Maki's further elaboration on the same theme in 'Investigations in Collective Form'. It is in this latter essay that Maki launched the term 'megastructure' (in two words at the time). Deleu doesn't make a direct use of Maki's terminology, but there exists an obvious correspondence in their range of ideas. For Deleu's discourse about the city and the task of architecture, see for example Luc Deleu, 'Een andere taak voor de architect', in: *Architectuur in de Provincie: Realisaties in Oost–Vlaanderen 1963– 1993* (Ghent: Provincie Oost–Vlaanderen, 1993), pp. 11–14, and, idem, 'A Task for Contemporary Architecture', in: *Sites & Stations: Provisional Utopias* (Lusitania 7), ed. Stan Allen with Kyong Park (New York: Lusitania Press, 1995), pp. 234–242.

11 *The Unadapted City: Bing-Bong*, 1996.

At the time, *Bingbong* (1996) was designed to exemplify this necessity.[11] This first spatial arrangement for *The Unadapted City* was a mock-up of an urban district for 6,800 inhabitants, displayed on a ping-pong table. It brought Le Corbusier's *Unité d'Habitation* into play, not only as a housing standard but also as an effective yardstick for city planning: a one meter stretch of the *Unité* profile being considered to provide housing for about six people.[12] Hence the buildings were contrived as extrusions of its cross-section, to be bent and folded, and deployed on the pitch. The slabs were elevated above ground. They were threaded by a multi-story bridge providing public space and transportation, ad-

12 Le Corbusier, *Unité d'Habitation*, Marseille, France, 1947–52. Unité in Marseille seen from the north, its blind façade suggesting the possibility of extrusion.

13 Le Corbusier, *Unité d'Habitation*, Marseille, France, 1947–52. Referred to as 'la rue marchande du ravitaillement (services communs)', in: Le Corbusier, *Œuvre complète: Vol. 5: 1946–52* (Basel: Birkhäuser, 1995, 1953[1]), p. 194.

14 *Usiebenpole*, 1994. About *Usiebenpole*, see Guy Châtel, 'Le projet d'une ville inadaptée', in: *LVI*, pp. 43–56.

justed in height to the seventh and eighth floor of the *Unités,* thus interconnecting their 'commercial streets of provisioning (common services)'.[13] Apart from the putative extrusion of the *Unités*, *Bingbong* matched the formula of *Usiebenpole* (1994–1996), T.O.P. office's earlier project for the urban development of the Donau-Insel in Vienna. This proposal for a linear city consisted of an infrastructure line of 26 km with 110 clipped-on *Unités d'Habitation*.[14] The ground level was basically kept free from building in order to preserve the leisure activities to which the island is devoted. All the new makings were thus set out in overhead constructions supported by parking silos and linked by a bridge and a tunnel. The project, bluntly assembled out of historical shards (the traits of drastic 'first-machine-age' urban design effected in some kind of 'mega structure'), ran straight into the question of its apposite equipment. The plate called 'eigenmächtiges Funktionsarrangement' renders the development of the city's linear plan in parallel with the score of Johann Strauss's *An der schönen blauen Donau*, setting the whole functional scheme on the staves. Attuning the urban apparatus to the airs of a waltz offers an image of the city's composite order. Just as Stanley Kubrick's use of the musical piece in *2001: A Space Odyssey* suggests that the coupling of spaceships remains a flighty event, Deleu's transcription depicts a city that is basically constituted by aleatory encounter. Obviously, the document points to the fact that, since the planning discipline fails to provide suitable knowledge of the intricate order resulting from contingency, it leaves its object in disregard, in other words debarred from dependable concern and thus prey to willful abuse. Since *Usiebenpole* was based on an overtly whimsical pick, T.O.P. office brought it up as 'The Unsuited City'. Its consecutive project would concentrate on the issue of the city's formation; in this, first and foremost, on the entanglement of contingency and deliberate act.

A Sequence

The Unadapted City was set up as a progressive inquiry into this obscured question. The project would proceed from small to big, in other words be developed by means of addition and multiplication toward greater numbers and grander complexity. In order to achieve the gradual investigation, different thresholds were defined in the population numbers: 878 for the basic level, that is the proper present-day occupation of the *Unité d'Habitation* in Marseille, calculated on the basis of 2.51 people per residential unit; 1,600 for a street (corresponding with the original occupation of the *Unité*); 9,500 for a district; 22,000 for a little town; 72,000 for a regional town; 192,000 as the requisite size for a larger city. The project set forth with a spatial model simply derived from the *Usiebenpole* formula as amended by *Bingbong*. *Brikabrak* (1998, the second spatial iteration of *The Unadapted City* but in fact the first one retained for further use and development), was just that: an urban district for 9,500 inhabitants corresponding to a fraction of *Usiebenpole* featuring remodeled *Unités*, or, to *Bingbong* with a straightened-out infrastructure line of 2.65 km. The modular construction of the three-level bridge was geared to the ratio of the project's computation: 24 modules set to correspond to the bridge segment supportive of equipment for 878 inhabitants, or accordingly 43 modules for 1,600 people.[15] Hence the bridge segment could operate as a switchboard for the project, allowing for recounting its extent in different sequences: structure, equipment and population. In this first phase, the model was thus exerted to elaborate the multi-storied bridge as a 'slide rule' for city planning. In this procedure the mutual indivisibility of the different figures was the decisive factor, for it released a gamut of diverging rhythms within the 'score'.[16] Accordingly, it produced an array of coincidences, hence true complexity. This in the sense that, even though all appearing situations and configurations were in fact determined by the primal choice made for the admitted ratios, they remained concealed, largely unforeseen until they were effectively encountered. These coincidences thus presented themselves as just as many occasions for the planner to get to work and play his part. In fact, this appears to be the key feature in respect to the whole formal structure of *The Unadapted City*. The conflation of incongruous orders represents its elemental procreant principle. The project's countless odds are rushed on by the play of this one principle over the increasing numbers.

15 *The Unadapted City: Brikabrak (Bridge Basic Unit), 1998.*

16 Cfr. for T.O.P. office's statement about this in: *LVI*, p. 92.

In the register of composition it was the same sort of merger that shaped the elegantly complicated basement and ground figure of *Dinkytown* (1998), the following step in the advance of the project's spatial model. In its overhead structures, and apart from a shortening of the infrastructure line, this model was a straightforward replica of *Brikabrak,* once again a district for 9,500 people.[17] Within the further elaboration of the spatial distribution following the increase of the programmatic corpus, much care was taken with the tunnel where all motor traffic was dispatched alongside the services and amenities that are usually consigned to suburbia. The tunnel track was set out as a sinusoid and the whole adjacent arrangement obtained by transposition and mutation of this swerving line within the interval drawn by rallying ellipsoids.[18]

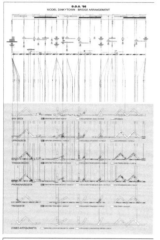

17 *The Unadapted City: Dinkytown,* 1998–99.

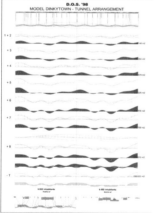

18 *The Unadapted City: Dinky Town (Bridge Arrangement),* 1998; *(Tunnel Arrangement),* 1998.

Octopus (1999) was conceived as a connecting piece for up to eight infrastructure lines.[19] It was introduced to append both original (and till then detached) linear quarters. Its superstructure was designed as a fibula, pinned on the crossing. The *Unité* extrusions were bent as to outline a huge star adorned with some florid curls. They provided living space for no less than 19,000 people, thus redoubling the population totals of *Brika-brak* and *Dinkytown.* Accordingly, the whole compound counting 38,000 dwellers, *Octopus* surpassed the T.O.P. office's minimal norm for a genuine town to a large degree. *Vipcity* (Fall 1999) would again double this number and transgress the threshold for a regional city. But as this last undertaking disposed of dwelling within the city's body, it caused a rift in the project's hitherto systemic formation.

19 *The Unadapted City: Octopus,* 1999.

A Rift

Vipcity's additional dwelling for 38,000 people was spread out over a gigantic allotment set in a flat area. The complex of equipment required by the up-scaling of the settlement was, for its part, deployed over a novel linear structure, a supplemental branch appended to the *Octopus* node. Since with *Vipcity, The Unadapted City* took up an expanse beside a linear extent, it finally supposed an environment. The *Vipcity* plan bears this out by clinching *Octopus* to the ground, representing it as girdled with the Zandvoort grand-prix

20 The *Unadapted City: Vipcity (# 7 revisited)*, *Octopus* anchor point, 2000; Zandvoort Circuit, Zandvoort, the Netherlands; Watersportbaan Ghent, Belgium.

21 *The Unadapted City: Vipcity (Decks Score)*, 2002; *(Amenities Maindeck)*, 2003.

circuit and tacked on by something like a slightly remodeled Ghent Water Sports Trail.[20] Apart from those arrangements of the *Vipcity* moorage, the larger part of the work was devoted to what was left of the city's body after it was stripped of its housing function.[21] The line bundling traffic and the whole increment of facilities was conceived as a full-blown 'megastructure', an uninterrupted linear apparatus 7.5 km long, with a discontinuous system of five decks caught in typical 'A'-frames, themselves standing on a plinth. The ground figure was based on the shape of the *Dinkytown* plinth, doubled in length by the addition of its mirror image. The frames were posted in zigzag as to suggest a waddling stride across the land.

The extent of the Vipcity spine can be measured according to a fixed correlation of the basic ratios: 1,000 inhabitants correspond to a 197 meter stretch of the megastructure, or, a length of 1 km structure corresponds to 5,066 people. Once again, it is an apparently limited set of preconceived spatial protocols and some additional programmatic subdivisions that generate the vast range of situational occurrences and coincidences, and a whole array of effective compositional occasions. A regular location of monorail stations superimposes a large-scale metric order upon the plait of the swerving decks. With the exception of the juncture with *Octopus* and the temporary end station *ZZZ*, all the emplacements are marked out by a pair of sizable, noticeably identical office buildings standing at either side of the structure, the one upright, the other level.[22] Then the pairs go to a dance. Every stance is a step in a full circumvolution: eight steps performing at every turn a shift in position by 36°.[23] The stepping duos chant the march of the megastructure.[24]

22 *The Unadapted City: Vipcity (The Core with Office Buildings)*, 2000.

23 *The Unadapted City: Vipcity (implantation MAS-Tower)*, 2000.

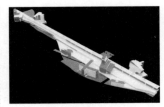

24 *The Unadapted City: Vipcity (model Unité & Powerpoint)*, 2001–02.

The insertion of this sequence of matching buildings set in pairs (decided upon shortly after May 2000), appears to be just as crucial as was the withdrawal of dwelling. Whereas in the former phases of *The Unadapted City* the role of architecture was merely denoted by mediation (through the name and reputation) of the *Unité d'Habitation,* architecture now literally comes on stage. The monumental edifices of *Vipcity* recapture the outline of T.O.P. office's competition project

for the *MAS* (*Museum aan de Stroom,* the City Museum of Antwerp, 1999), which was itself a revision of the remarkable building figure supporting a much earlier, similar contraposition of identical buildings planned for the crossing of the *Diagonal* and the *Carrer de Pere IV* in Barcelona (*Housing (&) The City,* 1989).[25] Those 'Barcelona Towers' were outlined as an assemblage of six cubes ordered on a straight edge, their sides diminishing in the proportion of the golden ratio. All their constituting parts were conceived to retain validity in both positions. But the buildings' sameness is merely formal. In fact it seems to contradict the specificity

25 *Scale & Perspective: Barcelona Towers (Housing (&) the City),* 1989. About this project, see Guy Châtel, 'Luc Deleu', in: Mil De Kooning (ed.), *Horta and After: 25 Masters of Modern Architecture in Belgium* (Ghent: Universiteit Gent, 1999), pp. 277–287, and 'Les Tours de Barcelone', in: *LVI,* p. 40.

of things that are (to be) built: the notion that they must be erected piece by piece, by means of construction. The configuration intimates that the placement and arrangement on site occurred after the buildings' assemblage. The stability of the stacking, typical of the upstanding edifice, somehow prevails on the stagy cantilevers of the prone version. It is the latter that was outwardly submitted to an additional operation: the horizontal building is a tower submitted to prostration.[26]

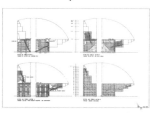

The *Vipcity* office buildings are more complicated, yet they keep this air of being shaped by some elementary doings: basically, (once more) an 'axillary' stacking of boxlike components, further straightened out by some clipping and flocked on one side by an unwinding cover. Answering a question from Marc Mer that probed the relevance of understanding the Barcelona project as an attempt to 'open' the location 'and hence to [comprehend it as] a renunciation of the static

26 *Scale & Perspective: Barcelona Towers (Housing (&) the City),* 1989.

concept of local identity aiming at permanence', an unruffled Deleu retorted that the proposition 'must indeed be seen as a celebration of the spot.'[27] The project basically actualizes the

27 Cfr. Marc Mer and Thomas Feuerstein, 'Trans–location. Interview with Luc Deleu', typescript dated summer 1993.

situational potential hitched to the crossing of the diagonals through the Cerdà Grid. Beyond being a composition of solids in open space, it reshuffles the urban situation as an articulated configuration of solids *and* void.

In Barcelona (and in *Vipcity*) the objective trait conferred to the buildings sustains the effectiveness of the configuration. It is obviously because the edifices bear visual evidence of their elementary conformation that their sameness can be assumed. Yet while this common root is revealed in unspecified, abstract terms, it is their difference that actually patterns the space, and that imposes itself on actual experience.[28] The postulated 'celebratory' quality of the whole placing (its monumental value) is thus to be situated in the unswerving ('uncultivated') acknowledgement of this converse: 'difference' and 'sameness'; an apposition of irreconcilable terms — 'to the point at which they surface into the public world of our experience.'[29]

28 *Scale & Perspective: Barcelona Towers (Housing (&) the City),* cylindrical swimming pool (model), 1989; tumbling apartment (drawing), 1989. In the Barcelona project an extraordinary effort was exerted towards an architectural specification of the ideal evenness of both buildings. The half-cylinder of the swimming pool embodies the hinge of the alleged rotation; the metric system applied to the fenestration of the residential parts, reasserts through proportional relation the formative operation of the stacking of cubes; the *Tumbling Apartments* avail astoundingly for inhabitation in both positions. Assuredly, the whole of this uncovers a poetics of making. But that is not to say that idealistic representations about architecture gain the upper hand. In this respect it is revealing that the 'secret' of the labyrinth situated on the second deck of the upright tower is disclosed through its exposition in the façade of the horizontal version. The whole effort of the making is engaged in a remorseless exposure of the riddles of architecture's 'scientology'.

The work on the megastructure and the meticulous elaboration of its response to the many situations instigated by the engagement of spatial and programmatic ordering went on until 2004. It culminated in the realization of the *Vipcity Nautical Mile,* a tectonically detailed model at a scale of 1:100 of one meridian minute length of the structure. No less monumental than breakable, this intricate 18.52m long object made of cardboard, foam, paper and wood, representing the megastructure standing on its plinth set at the *modulor* height of 113cm, gives a phenomenal, distinctly tangible presence to the *Vipcity* spine.[30] For their part however, the overall features of the *Vipcity* plan were definitively settled with *D.O.S. XXI — VIPCITY # 7 revisited* (2002) with the implementation of a plainly hierarchized system of roads and crossings upon the land expanse. In this respect, Deleu refers to the way Le Corbusier 'successfully' designed Chandigarh, at once 'structuring it, and leaving it free.'[31]

A Story

It will perhaps be clear that it is quite difficult to account for *The Unadapted City* without recounting its formation as a story. Obviously, this is due to the project's peculiar constitution, the fact that all its previous stages are fully (i.e. without any alteration) incorporated in the upshot. Deleu's understanding that no city possesses homogenous quality, and that in any case less remarkable quar-

29 Cfr. Rosalind E. Krauss, *Passages in Modern Sculpture* (Cambridge, MA and London, 1981, 1977¹), p. 267. For this discussion of the contraposition of identical objects I am largely indebted to Krauss' account of 'Untitled (L–beams)' by Robert Morris, this with the notable exception that in op. cit. 'sculptural meaning' seems to be only derived from experienced 'difference'.

30 The model was displayed for the first time on the occasion of the Luc Deleu – T.O.P. office exhibition Values in MUHKA, Antwerp, 2004.

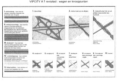

31 T*he Unadapted City: Vipcity (# 7 revisited),* roads and crossings, 2001–02. Le Corbusier, Chandigarh May 1952, plan with dwelling and facilities for 150,000 people.

32 Cfr. for this argument, *LVI*, p. 88.

ters take part in the townscape, supports this bias.[32] It underscores the particular procedure T.O.P. office adopted to elaborate the project. While projects often, in one way or another, proceed from the general to the particular, or are engineered 'from structure to event,'[33] and ultimately aim at completion through assimilation and synthesis of the yield of that process, *The Unadapted City* moves

33 Cfr. Claude Lévi-Strauss, *La pensée sauvage* (Paris: Plon, 1962), p. 37.

forward, by concatenation of decisions, and by lining up its successive products. Its strategy is mere conquest: conversance gained from exercise, acquaintance from advance in magnitude, improvement by recapture of interim result. Therefore the name given to a novel part is likewise given to the outcome. So, while *Octopus* is the connecting piece of *Brikabrak* and *Dinkytown,* it is also the name of the whole compound. Similarly, *Vipcity* is the superadded megastructure, plus the complete *Octopus* arrangement (i.e. including *Brikabrak* and *Dinkytown*) where it starts from, and the entire land expanse it draws in. The project's overall structure was not established beforehand, it was built up gradually by gathering its earnings. It was steered through an always renewed effort to make sense of what was on hand. Its outcome is thus necessarily provisional, as the same procedure can be carried out time and again, new dealings contrived from the encounter of the last occurring constellation with imagination and ingenuity. Thus, even though the perspective of an impending redoubling of population in *Not4you* is integral to *Vipcity,* the project can repose in its state of becoming.[34] In fact there is no need to conjecture on its future increase. Necessarily, this eventuality remains open.

There is of course still something to be said about the pervasive recycling of historical and other material that occurs in the project. The most apparent advantage of this phenomenon is that it enables a fast-forward progress. It allows

34 In *LVI*, the announced further development of the project is called 'Notforyou'; in: *U&O*, 'Not4you'.

for shortcuts in the elaboration of form. But, along with it, form drags subject matter. The renowned or referenced figures come down plainly bearing their features. They carry significant portions of structure and content, a whole apparatus of documentation, relations, associations, codes and images. Evidently, as a foundational reference, the *Unité d'Habitation* has a prominent presence in the project. It takes part in the play, not merely as a supernumerary, but as a genuine protagonist. The *Unités* stand for built structure and mass, and they introduce a concrete shape as well as a certain stratification in the posited use of space. But they also vouch for the presence of Architecture: they represent architecture's outstanding role in the formation of the city; they evoke history and invoke an ideology about communal life and the making of cities. The direct connection of their 'commercial streets of provisioning (common services)' to the multi-storied bridge (bearer of public space) seems to match the full width of Le Corbusier's intention (or

35 Corbusier, *Unité d'Habitation*, interior street, Marseille, France, 1947–52. Cfr. Manfredo Tafuri and Francesco Dal Co, *Modern Architecture* (New York: Rizzoli, 1976), pp. 344–345.

36 Cfr. Tafuri and Dal Co, *Modern Architecture*, p. 345: 'For their part, the *rues intérieures,* like the *rue commerçante,* speak just as clearly about the circumstances that constrain them to remain no more than broader corridors. (…) In this way the *Unité* communicates the irrationality of a hypothesis not brought to conclusion, a gigantic fragment of a global conception of the city destined to remain pure ideology.'

38 Le Corbusier, *Œuvre complète: Vol. 5*, p. 186.

39 As jotted in a sketch. Cfr. Le Corbusier, *Œuvre complète: Vol. 5*, p. 187.

longing).[35] Through the actualization of this pending quality of the *Unités* (the virtuality for those 'commercial streets' to become real streets in a radically 'other' city), *The Unadapted City* speaks of architecture's determination and urgings.[36] But if, through this act of appropriation, the project alludes to architecture's strength, it also enunciates its brittleness and setbacks. The introduction of the megastructure, which probably represents architecture's last and most striving attempt to escape this predicament (i.e. the unbreakable association of its resolve and vulnerability), and to seize the city, has the effect of articulating all this content along an argumentative line; a discursive braid in fact, as different codes entwine down this line.

Perhaps Le Corbusier's use of the image of the 'bottle-in-rack' best exemplifies this intertwinement of codes.[37] The *Unité d'Habitation* was originally conceived as a frame supporting independent dwelling containers, units 'completely unconcerned

37 Le Corbusier, *Unité d'Habitation*, 'bottle-and-rack' principle.

319

with the ground or with foundations,' apposite to prefabrication, as practicable as a 'savage's hut' and conveyable as a 'nomad's tent.'[38] Le Corbusier commended this device for practical advantages but immediately extended its bearings in a larger theoretical field: 'Henceforth dwelling has value of laboratory: social, technical, biologic, physical, etc.'[39] The same basic idea of a distinction between frame and cell was already constitutive of the *Plan Obus* for Algiers (project A, 1930) where housing for 180,000 people was foreseen in the substructure of the 'level 100m' highway trailed along the cliff line.[40] As witnessed by Le Corbusier's well-known perspective drawing, the whole apparatus was envisioned as 'a giant bookcase (…) on the shelves of which the inhabitants have built two-story houses to suit their own tastes

40 Le Corbusier & P. Jeanneret, *Plan Obus (Algiers)*, Project A, 1930. Le Corbusier, *Œuvre complète: Vol. 2: 1929–34* (Basel: Birkhäuser, 1995, 19341), p. 142.

41 Reyner Banham, *Megastructure: Urban Futures of the Recent Past* (London: Harper & Rowe, 1976), pp. 7–8.

42 Le Corbusier & Jeanneret, *Plan Obus (Algiers)*, 'dissipation' & 'creation'; 'highway at level 100m'.

(…).'[41] This new model for the city would come about with an amazing encounter of completely different but entirely corroborative rationalities: not only those relating to dwelling and mobility, but also those concerning the implementation of industrial building techniques, economy, organized use, civil good, hygiene, landscape and even beauty.[42] Thus, the appealing concept of 'frame-and-cell,' integral to this 'most general ancestor' of megastructures,[43] would spread and ramify, and ultimately become one of the ruling notions in the architecture and urban planning of the 1960s. Whether applied to linear or spatial extents, wielded in literal *fill-in, plug-in* or *clip-on* formulas, or used in more tempered variants, a major part of the proposals of that time were founded on the same basic idea of an enduring collective structure set at the disposal of transient individual accommodation and occupation.[44] As this whole filiation is so perceivably grafted onto *Vipcity*'s body (i.e. the ultimate embodiment of *The Unadapted City*), it becomes quite clear that it was summoned to elicit discourse, or at least to lay bare the discursive vein of the project.

43 Banham, *Mega-structure*, p. 7.

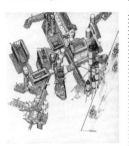

44 Peter Cook– Archigram, *Plug-In City*, 1963–64.

But this doesn't make it any easier to decide how T.O.P. office's practice ties in with this bequest, or how its undertaking exactly relates to the imported material. Anyway, it soon comes out that no hermeneutic construal of this sequel of 'subject matter' could successfully account for the drive of the project. In *S/Z*, Roland Barthes infers that the sheer impossibility to decide about the pre-eminence of either the symbolic or the operative code might be a definition of the narrative.[45] Both are 'subjected to the regime of the *and/or.*' In a comment or an explanation it would be 'im-pertinent' to decide for a hierarchy of codes, because this would 'crush the braid' of the pronouncement 'under a single voice.'[46] 'What is more, missing the plurality of the codes,' Barthes further argues, 'is censoring the working of discourse: the undecidability defines a making, the performance of the storyteller.'[47]

45 Roland Barthes, *S/Z* (Paris: Editions du Seuil, 1970), p. 84.

47 As I was so 'im-pertinent' to make a selective choice out of Barthes's argument, I quote it here at full length: 'Dans le récit (et cela en est peut-être une "définition"), le symbolique et l'opératoire sont indécidables, soumis au régime du *et/ou*. Aussi, choisir, décider d'une hiérarchie des codes, d'une pré-détermination des messages, comme le fait l'explication des textes, est *im-pertinent*, car c'est écraser la tresse de l'écriture sous une voix unique, ici psychanalytique, là poétique (au sens aristotélicien). Bien plus, manquer le pluriel des codes, c'est censurer le travail du discours: l'indécidabilité définit un faire, la performance du conteur (...).'

46 While I use the term 'pronouncement' Barthes speaks of course of 'l'écriture'.

A Mirror

Luc Deleu spins out a story. While it seems impractical to describe *The Unadapted City* without relating the sequence of its periods, this very sequence comes out to articulate a narrative. Yet, the tale seems ill-omened. If *Vipcity* were to be considered as a city, it would be the city of least resistance to the propensities of our time. It emerges as a venture of building industry and estate agencies, a city of total commodification where dwelling (once the city's very substance) is reduced to the availability of a mass produced unit, or 'just any old' piece of land. It is a city where collective equipment (designated by the very complexion of the project as the binder of communal life) is confined to a sanctuary where it is set on display, staged as a spectacle to the benefit of the wearied punters of bottled lodging and the dulled tenants of the residences. This city of 'broad acres' and packaged dwelling is 'unadapted' because, in its recounting of numbers and the depiction of a raked-over reality, the tale doesn't consider any appropriation or propriety.[48] Moreover, it is 'unsettled' in the sense that its reality never appears without disguise and can only be apprehended obliquely.

Vipcity is the representation of a place, yet to be found in no place. But as must be clear now, the fact that it is a 'nowhere-place' doesn't imply it is a 'good place.' At any rate, the staging of its self-cancelling 'decency' and hence the brazen irony of its name would have been sufficient to deter us from any temptation to scrutinize it for the spores of utopia. Nevertheless some revealing acquaintances impose themselves. Not unlike utopia (to use the terms of Frederic Jameson in describing it), *The Unadapted City* 'would seem to offer the spectacle of one of those rare phenomena whose concept is indistinguishable from its reality, [and] whose ontology coincides with its representation.'[49] Along with this, *Vipcity* rejoins utopia through the fact that it is 'non-fictional, even though' it is 'also non-existent.'[50] Manifestly, on behalf of the unpromising tale articulated in its construction and branded in its image, *Vipcity* can be construed as utopia in reverse.[51] It holds the image of a bad-dreamland, 'the radicalized image of a devious present, slyly hiding beneath the bubbling of the everyday.'[52] It is the specter that appears in the mirror the storyteller holds up to us.

At first, the asset of the whole undertaking thus might appear to be solely delivered in the field of critique. In the earlier stages of the project the critique seemed to be restricted to the purview of the city's formative disciplines: through the capture of an emblematic linear city and a 'choreography' of functional congestion, an antithesis to *The Functional City* as it emerged from the doctrine of the *Charte d'Athènes*, or a critique of Modernism by means of its own language; as it turned out, an iteration of the old story of the son killing the father.[53] From the introduction of *Vipcity* onwards the critique was more broadly addressed to the world: a representation of the city as mere facility and spectacle; *Vipcity*'s spinning rope-walk as the city's dancing skeleton in mutiny against the funeral march of the towers, and *The Unadapted City* as an allegory of the city's desperate struggle against its dissipation.[54]

48 For a more elaborate account of the project's name cfr. Guy Châtel, 'Le projet d'une ville inadaptée', in: *LVI*, pp. 52–53.

49 This is the opening remark in Frederic Jameson, 'The Politics of Utopia', *New Left Review* 25 (January–February 2004), p. 35.

50 This is part of the closing passage (not plainly the conclusion) in: Jameson, 'The Politics of Utopia', p. 54.

51 Not dystopia, rather utopia overturned, or a 'contra-utopia' as Dominique Rouillard worded it in qualifying the Italian *architettura radicale*, cfr. Guy Châtel, 'Plan Obus and Vipcity, as from Father to Son', *Interstices—Journal of Architecture and Related Arts, Gen-ius/Gen-ealogy* 7 (September 2006), p. 31: 'replacing and imagined finality by the projection of an image'. Jameson, 'The Politics of Utopia', p. 46, points to the fact that utopia is always 'somehow negative'. 'Its function lies not in helping us to imagine a better future but rather in demonstrating our utter incapacity to imagine such a future—our imprisonment in a non-utopian present without historicity or futurity—so as to reveal the ideological closure of the system in which we are somehow trapped and confined.'

52 Châtel, 'Plan Obus and Vipcity, as from Father to Son', p. 31.

53 That was basically the argument of my, 'Le projet d'une ville inadaptée', in: *LVI*. This text was written in 2001 when the whole impact of the rift brought about by the *Vipcity* development didn't yet occur to me.

54 Cfr. my jacket blurb for *U&O* and 'Plan Obus and Vipcity, as from Father to Son'. In the latter text I conjectured that the whole critique uncovered a revendication for 'independence' of the work of architecture.

But a reading halted at this point would miss the more beneficial proposals devised in the project. In addition, it would ignore the assenting, albeit undeceived position encrypted in it. There is a frankly positive proposition in T.O.P. office's efforts to get acquainted with the city as the quintessential 'form' of the collective. That all this was undertaken, not through theoretical conjecture, but through sustained practical exercise and elaborate design work clearly marks out a position. Yet, in order to point at this locus and to attempt to circumscribe it, it might be useful to summarize the activities taking place there.

A Praxis

As we have seen, T.O.P. office's exercises aim at mastering the effects of an increase in program, within a spatial structure. The multiplication of elemental combinations within the furrow of the program creates as many occasions to craft their equivalents in a spatial configuration. As far as architecture begins with that (the rendering of human needs in spatial terms), *The Unadapted City* is undoubtedly an investigation in architecture's capacities to grasp a great variety of situations and to operate suchlike translations without reducing them through routine. The intensity and prolificacy of this research by exercitation are demonstrated in the so-called 'scores' and other 'space arrangements'. These often magnificent graphics all stem from the aptitude of musical notation to deploy a gliding ordering, a discovery epitomized in the 'eigenmächtiges Funktionsarrangement' of *Usiebenpole*. In principle, this kind of experimental research can be wielded on whatever spatial model, as long as the model can be protracted far enough to keep up with the whole play. Linear systems, straight or bent, ramifications, grids, webs: all will do. But of course, as empirical research can only provide knowledge of the object considered, the entire exercise would wither to pure formal drill if it were not applied to a model 'pre-disposed' to embody this object (in our case, the city as communal scale and form). Self-evidently, this predisposition is not some objective quality the model would possess *per se*. The model is prompted by subjective thought, forged by imaginations of its purposiveness, selected because fantasy knows how to deal with it.

The complex of linear structures featuring (in) *The Unadapted City* was chosen for practical reasons (a line is the easiest to deal with),[55] but undoubtedly not before it had been recognized as a suitable support for the development of a city, and what is more, as the missing piece for the fulfillment of the bid for 'another' city entered by the *Unité d'Habitation*.[56] As made clear, the megastructure partakes in the same group of ideological preferences. In the setup of *Vipcity,* the rejection of earlier options for dwelling didn't break the ideological bond, since it was the proviso for the advent of this large-scale structure possessing the capability to unify the city's 'master program.' Moreover, as it demonstrates quite dramatically how much land expanse is to

55 Cfr. about the practical reason of the choice, *LVI*, p. 89.

56 Cfr. for the complex of Deleu — T.O.P. office's subjective motivations, *LVI*, pp. 94–95.

be engaged as counterpart of the superblocks, it was this turn given to the project that unlocked its critical stance. The split caused by the foregoing choice for another dwelling formula affected primarily the conditions of exercise. From then on, craft would be exerted on a piece of architectural form at the scale of the city, freed from any commitment to the delicate case of collective housing.

With this unconstrained pursuit, T.O.P. office resumes a thread dropped somewhere at the end of the 1960s. In *Mega-structure, Urban Futures of the Recent Past,* Reyner Banham recounts

57 Banham, *Megastructure,* p. 191.

that whereas, in only about one decade, 'megastructural' practice had known its rise and fall, it had found the time to degenerate into 'megaroutine', 'routinized design (...) unable to cope with two major problems: variation and scale.'[57] The design effort devoted to the development of the *Vipcity* megastructure precisely aims at getting to grips with those difficulties.[58] Under actual conjuncture this is markedly not to 'solve' the question of the city's formation, but to exemplify architecture's capacity to deal with 'group form.' At the same time however,

58 *The Unadapted City: Vipcity (Train Deck),* 2002; *(Bycicle Track),* 2002.

59 In this respect it would certainly be interesting to examine how the experience of *The Unadapted City* has empowered the work of T.O.P. office since 2004. However this couldn't be done within the scope of this essay.

this is true praxis: attending to this capacity arms T.O.P. office with corresponding capability.[59] Obviously, this could only be secured from practice on a workshop model of the city.

333

A (Specific) Form

The model was conceived as a support for replication (substitutive handling of provoked events with a dummy of the city). Learning and experience would ensue from rehearsal. The *Vipcity* megastructure that comes out as an utterly convincing piece of architectural craftsmanship, is in fact, and notwithstanding that, a prop on which a whole range of simulated contingent situations were fingered by design. The assumption that this could be something useful to do, and that it would be justified to bring it to the public (through exhibitions, publications, etc.) definitely points to an unconventional interpretation of the architect's task. However, this is entirely consistent with Deleu's account of the function of the 'town-planner-architect' (i.e. the 'orban planner') in his well-known *Orban Planning Manifesto* (1980): '*Information* (reduction of uncertainty) is now an important part of the *momental* orban planner's activities (...) He designs, publishes, performs, shows, realizes or plays, etc. *Free space* is his goal from now on.'[60]

60 Luc Deleu, *Orban Planning Manifesto,* originally published in Dutch, French and English in: *Vrije Ruimte—Espace Libre—*Open Space (Antwerp: Internationaal Cultureel Centrum [I.C.C.]/Ministerie van Nationale Opvoeding en Nederlandse Cultuur, 1980); reproduced in facsimile in: *Luc Deleu Postfuturismus?* (Antwerp: deSingel/ Wommelgem: Den Gulden Engel, 1987), pp. 40–50; republished in Dutch in Deleu and Theys, *Urbi et Orbi,* pp. 140–142.

Once one gets rid of idealistic representations about the 'nature', 'origin' or 'necessity' of architecture, only this is left: the awareness that architecture is destined to stand in reality (as it is devoted to the accommodation of men's environment), and that it is thus also fated to represent reality. When this double-essential condition of architecture is conflated into 'imitative' practice, it effects (to put it in Jean Baudrillard's words) a 'collapse into hyperrealism.' Maybe one could say that *The Unadapted City* represents just that: a 'simulation [that] envelops the whole edifice of representation as itself a simulacrum.' But here, representation gears to exposure. At any rate, it does not try 'to absorb simulation by interpreting it as false representation.'[61] In our case the 'exposition' is not of the kind that endeavors to 'absorb' anything. It aims at total undressing: reality and simulation stripped down, and simulacrum brandished before the public. Obviously, this 'work of architecture' exceeds the terms of what Colin Rowe called 'an advertisement of a point of view.' The (intrinsic) property of a project (virtually any project) to convey surreptitiously (or 'illicitly') something about an 'attitude taken up with regard to (...)' reality is here toughened into an explicit, bold declaration: *The Unadapted City* is a manifesto.

61 Jean Baudrillard, 'The Precession of Simulacra', in: *Simulations,* trans. Paul Foss, Paul Patton and Philip Beitchman (New York: Semiotext[e], 1983), p. 11. The unaltered phrase is: 'Whereas representation tries to absorb simulation by interpreting it as false representation, simulation envelops the whole edifice of representation as itself a simulacrum.'

Reyner Banham noted that megastructures proceed from 'the ancient architectural dream of imposing a grand order on a disorderly world,' and he quoted Cesar Pelli saying that 'the only reason for megastructures, is the ambition of architects.'[62] Undoubtedly, unbridled ambition can beget monsters. But cities are human makings, and the aspiration of architects to comprehend them is as commendable as their unconcern would be outrageous. Deleu asserts: 'urban space is makeable, urban life is not.'[63] While this is a fair pronouncement, the purpose to bring those two conditions in resonance confronts practice with an aporia. Since for the disciplines of architecture, urban design and city planning the capabilities of making are ultimately situated in the register of space and its delineation, each practice pretending to match social morality (e.g. to dedicate its efforts to the making of valuable space for a good and liberated life) will have to deal with this impediment.

62 Banham, *Megastructure,* p. 209.

63 Deleu, *U&O,* p. 43.

Theory should help here, and it is perhaps time to evaluate which claim *The Unadapted City* makes on theory. The project is centered on a case, and endeavors to make a case. The given case is the city, or rather, the challenge of its formation. The case to make is for the role of architectural practice: how (being bereft of power) can it deal with ruling contingency and resist the sway of commodification? How can it reeve obstruction? Of course this is far more demanding than providing some comment (or critique, or lament, etc.) about the conjuncture.

The project of *The Unadapted City* is rendered by rehearsal: its discourse is polysemic, and all proceeds are credentials of exercise. Yet, a conceited theoretical discourse would have been univocal. Moreover, the project suspends the common expectation that a purposive venture taken in the 'master form' of the city should bring forth some fundamentals, imitable exemplars, perhaps an outset of typology or method. *The Unadapted City* is marked by the awareness that practice stands alone before the aforementioned aporia. It acknowledges the bare reality that there isn't any theory to signpost a passage. This dearth is comprehensibly due to the fact that architecture is no scientific discipline that can legitimately devise a theory to conduct its practice (there is no truth to start with). Neither does it work the other way around, as practice does not beget knowledge except from its object, and since anyway all of its products are determined by the outlook of the practitioner (hence are inescapably bound to ideology).[64] This is not to say, however, that the proceeds of practice cannot relate to knowledge or convey an awareness of reality. As Louis Althusser puts it (speaking about art), the outcome of practice can 'give to see,' or 'to perceive,' or 'to feel' something which is 'allusive' to reality.[65] That is, the piece of work (or an oeuvre), imbued as it is with the ideology from which it stems, can offer 'a view from within' on ideology.[66] But this demands of the 'practitioner' (the architect, 'orbanist', artist, writer, narrator, etc. — but let us conditionally think of him as an 'author' now) to take a step back, to take up 'an inner distance on the very ideology that holds him.'[67] Everything that has to do with the qualification of (the outcome of) a practice is thus bound to the 'specific form' of the 'subject/object' relation.

64 Cfr. Louis Althusser, *Idéologie et appareils idéologiques d'Etat* (http://classiques. uqac.ca [1970] 2008), pp. 34–55, and Louis Althusser, 'Lettre sur la connaissance de l'art' (1966), in: *Ecrits philosophiques et politiques: Tôme 2* (Paris: Stock/IMEC, 1995), p. 582.

65 Althusser, 'Lettre sur la connaissance de l'art' p.582.

66 Ibid. Althusser refers to Balzac and Solzhenitsyn.

67 Ibid. Althusser, 'Lettre sur la connaissance de l'art'.

An (Unsettled) Position

In *Machiavel et nous*, Althusser (leaning on Gramsci) construes *The Prince* as a manifesto (an 'utopian revolutionary manifesto'). He undertakes to analyze its mechanism starting from the provisional statement that it is 'a specific apparatus establishing particular relations between the discourse and its *object*, and between the discourse and its *subject*.'[68] Doing this he demarcates it from theoretical discourse: 'The manifesto is centered on a case, a situation: it uses theory but it considers practice. The case to be made is not *about the conjuncture*, but *under the conjuncture*. And to think under the conjuncture is literally to submit to the problem induced and imposed by its case. The *theoretical* propositions made, or to be made, are thus unsettled. They have to *shift* because they are compelled to *change their space*. Indeed, a space of pure theory would not have any subject (truth is valid for every possible subject), whereas the space of practice has no meaning but through its possible or requested subject. For the manifesto to be effective, that is, to become itself the

68 Louis Althusser, 'Machiavel et nous' (1972–1986), in: *Ecrits philosophiques et politiques: Tôme 2* (Paris: Stock/IMEC, p. 56; trans. by Gregory Elliot as *Machiavelli and Us* (London and New York: Verso, 1999), p. 14.

agent of the practice that it endeavors to instate, it must be inscribed somewhere in the field of practice.'[69] In our case, that is why *The Unadapted City* had to be a project. Therefore, Althusser contends, the manifesto has to lay out a place: an empty space to be filled up, or where the problem of practice can be deployed.[70]

Vipcity is such a place: an uninhabited city (only populated by numbers), a vacant floor, a 'free space'. A place instituted by the step back of the 'author' as he sought to convene allies; the void created as he took an inner distance, as he tried to rid himself of his ideological costume; a place adrift. Roland Barthes (again), an author pondering about authorship, trying out all positions of enunciation and all enunciative strategies, writing himself *'Roland Barthes'*, describes this place, or rather points at its image (only a fragment laying apart, a debris washed ashore): *'Indexed*: I am indexed, assigned to a place (an intellectual locus), to a residence of caste (if not of class). Against which, one inner doctrine: that of *atopia* (of the drifting abode). Atopia is superior to utopia (utopia is reactive, tactical, literary, it proceeds from sense and makes it run).'[71]

Utopia is suspect since it is subdued to all of the subject's sticky determinations. Atopia stands for the awareness of that problem, for the 'inner doctrine' of the author's obligatory retreat once he has crafted his braid. For its part, *Vip-city* (hypostasis of the void) is not a denunciation, rather an enunciation of the necessary 'im-posture' of authorship.[72] Its vacancy is a precondition for an 'authorized' address to the world ('urbi et orbi', to use Deleu's phrasing). It is T.O.P. office's 'free space' for practice, and a post of enunciation; conspicuously, the prerequisite for *The Unadapted City* to be uttered as a manifesto.

69 This entire passage is entirely compiled and paraphrased from Althusser, 'Machiavel et nous', pp. 61–66 and trad. Elliot, *Machiavelli and Us*, pp. 18–22.

70 Ibid.

71 My translation of: 'Fiché: je suis fiché, assigné à un lieu (intellectuel), à une résidence de caste (sinon de classe). Contre quoi une seule doctrine intérieure: celle de l'atopie (de l'habitacle en dérive). L'atopie est supérieure à l'utopie (l'utopie est réactive, tactique, littéraire, elle procède du sens et le fait marcher).' In: Roland Barthes, *Roland Barthes par Roland Barthes* (Paris: Editions du Seuil, 1975), p. 53.

72 For his first exhibition, Deleu himself pointed at this void: 'Luc Deleu leaves architecture in the vacuum for New Dimensions', February 1970. More than I can indicate here, I am indebted to Serge Doubrovsky, 'Roland Barthes, une écriture tragique', in: *Parcours critique II (1959–1991)* (Grenoble: Ellug, 2006); the essay about Barthes was previously published in: *Poétique* 47 (September 1981).

An (Aleatory) Encounter

The whole issue about authorship ultimately throws us back upon the question regarding the legitimacy of (authored) architecture to control the city's formation. Equipped with a highflying megastructure, *Vip-city* is an excellent case to bring this forth. Indeed, megastructure failed and its very concept was abandoned when it occurred to everybody that the entrusting of the 'form' of the collective to a sole specialized agency is the best underwriting for the production of an inadequate environment. Banham pointed to *Thamesmead New Town* (1967) as the 'ultimate tombstone' of this 'run-down concept': 'even architects originally excited at the idea of a three-mile building from a single hand (or group of

73 Greater London
Council Architect's
Department,
Thamesmead New Town,
project model, 1967.
Banham, *Megastructure,*
p. 190. The last quote
is from a caption to
the photograph of the
model.

75 Siegfried Kracauer,
'Cult of Distraction:
On Berlin's Picture
Palaces' (1926), in:
*The Mass Ornament:
Weimar Essays,* trans.
and ed. Thomas Y.
Levin (Cambridge, MA,
and London: Harvard
University Press, 1995), p.
327. For the transposition
to architecture, see
Walter Benjamin, *Das
Kunstwerk im Zeitalter
seiner technischen
Reproduzierbarkeit*
(1935); I used the
Dutch translation *Het
kunstwerk in de tijd
van zijn technische
reproduceerbaarheid,*
trad. Henk Hoeks
(Nijmegen: SUN, 1985),
cfr. esp. XIV and XV,
pp. 35–40.

76 Althusser, 'Machiavel
et nous', p. 66; trad.
Elliot, *Machiavelli and
Us,* p. 22.

hands) now seem to doubt whether the result would be tolerable.'[73]

The design exercises on simulated contingent situations exerted on the *Vipcity* megastructure are certainly not meant to find whatever solution for this quandary. They rather intend to deepen acquaintance with this potential of architecture that was perceived as a promise in the simple contraposition of the Barcelona Towers (perceived, then grasped and worked to the bone in all the parts of its assemblage).[74] That promise holds for the capacity to engender things and places that are 'celebratory' for the collective: things and places standing aside of the continuous flow of depletion, unenticing but effective in just being there, and bearing 'moral significance' through their availability to 'disclosure in distraction'.[75] When actualized in architecture, this 'celebratory' value is not to be contemplated. In fact, there is nothing to contemplate as there was nothing written beforehand. Architecture 'makes' sense by 'being there', responsive to use and giving something 'to perceive, to see, to feel' about reality. The promise of architecture springs from its virtue to bear witness to the attitudes of men. Its truth is in its effective presence. Like Machiavelli (and Althusser), we know 'that there is no truth — or rather, nothing true — other than what is *actual,* that is to say, borne by its effects, nonexistent outside them; and that the effectiveness of the true is always merged with the activity of men (…).'[76]

74 *The Unadapted City:
Vipcity,* one nautical
mile, 2004.

77 In the 1980s Althusser
worked on the theme of
'aleatory materialism'.
He only left some notes
about it. A substantial
piece was published in:
*Ecrits philosophiques
et politiques* (Paris:
Stock/IMEC, 1994)
under the title 'Le
courant souterrain
du matérialisme de la
rencontre', pp. 553–594.

The accomplishment of the Prince's historical destiny was subjected to the existence of a void (in that case a political void), where his Virtù could encounter Fortune.[77] Correspondingly, the existence of a void is the precondition for the accomplishment of architecture's promise. But the world seems fully occupied already. Architectural practice is in preparation of coincidence, attending to virtù as to set up for an aleatory encounter. *Vipcity* is the 'free space' where T.O.P. office deployed the issue of practice and where it practiced the virtù of architecture.

Yet, entering this space did not imply any renouncement. Seen from there, the world outside resurfaces as ever aborning, and it finally recurs as a viewshed for action. With sovereign confidence Luc Deleu points once again to the example of Le Corbusier who drew the features of *La Ville Radieuse* as 'pure theoretical products' and said that 'they helped to establish the principle of things, ideally, above the fray.' A provisional retreat from the 'true events of life' was needed in order to acquire dependable guidelines. 'In the following years these views of the *Radiant City* confronted the materiality of events: the plan for Algiers, Stockholm, Barcelona, Nemours, etc.'[78]

78 Le Corbusier, *La Ville Radieuse: élé- ments d'une doctrine d'urbanisme pour l'équipement de la civilisation machiniste* (Paris, 1933, reprint 1964) p. 156.

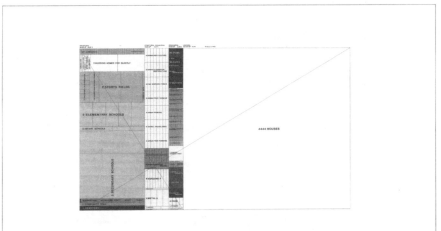

HOUSING GENERATOR 20000
A SURFACE-ARRANGEMENT FOR A BUILDING DEVELOPMENT FOR 20000 PEOPLE / SA STANDARD
9616.03

D.O.S. XXI - VIPCITY # 7 revisit

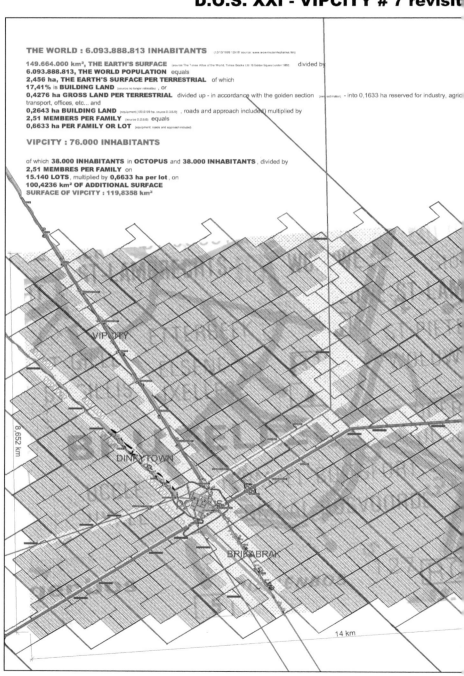

THE WORLD : 6.093.888.813 INHABITANTS (12/10/1999 12h18 source: www.ecomodernplanet.nl/en)

149.664.000 km², THE EARTH'S SURFACE (source: The Times Atlas of the World, Times Books Ltd 15 Golden Square London 1989) divided by
6.093.888.813, THE WORLD POPULATION equals
2,456 ha, THE EARTH'S SURFACE PER TERRESTRIAL of which
17,41% is BUILDING LAND (source: no longer retrievable) , or
0,4276 ha GROSS LAND PER TERRESTRIAL divided up - in accordance with the golden section (own estimation) - into 0,1633 ha reserved for industry, agric
transport, offices, etc... and
0,2643 ha BUILDING LAND (equipment (100,6109 ha, source D.O.S.0) , roads and approach included) multiplied by
2,51 MEMBERS PER FAMILY (source D.O.S.0) equals
0,6633 ha PER FAMILY OR LOT (equipment, roads and approach included)

VIPCITY : 76.000 INHABITANTS

of which **38.000 INHABITANTS** in **OCTOPUS** and **38.000 INHABITANTS** , divided by
2,51 MEMBRES PER FAMILY on
15.140 LOTS , multiplied by **0,6633 ha per lot** , on
100,4236 km² OF ADDITIONAL SURFACE
SURFACE OF VIPCITY : 119,8358 km²

8,652 km

14 km

A STANDARD LOT
0,6185 ha NET
(equipment, roads and approach excluded)

SCALE 1/2.000

SCALE 1/20.000

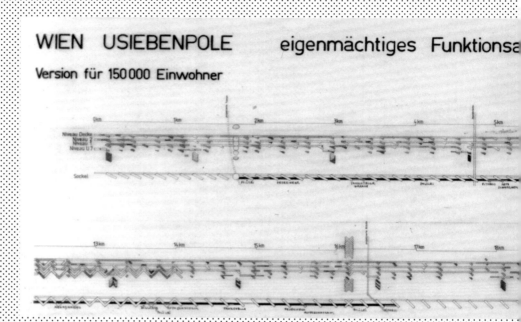

ment

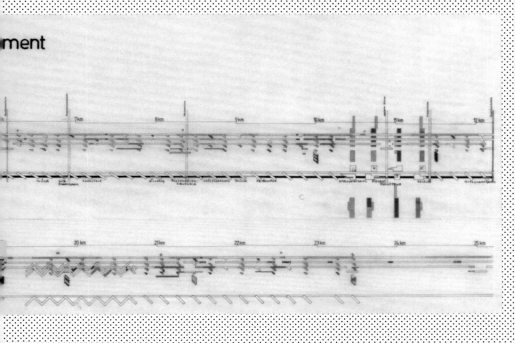

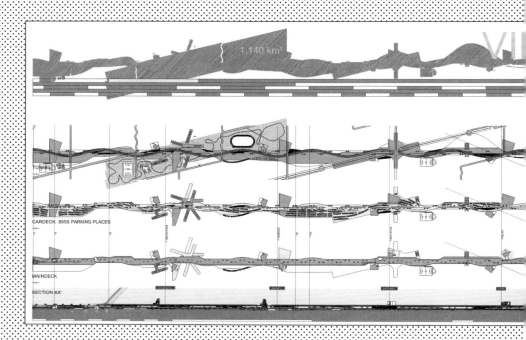

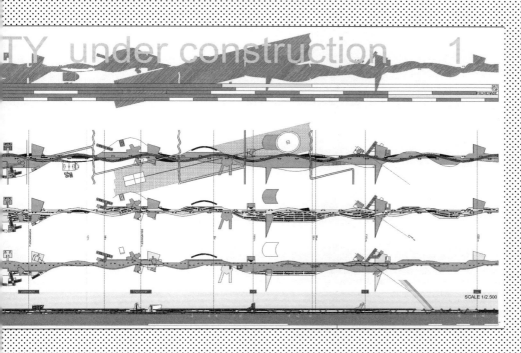

XLIV

TY under construction   1

SKY
TOP
PROMENADE

SCALE 1/2.500

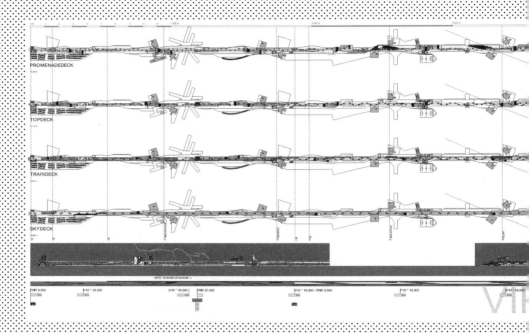

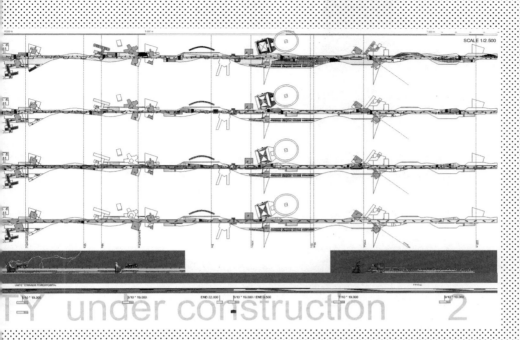

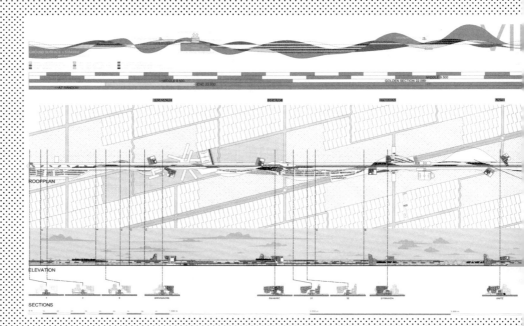

XLVI

ROOFPLAN

ELEVATION

SECTIONS

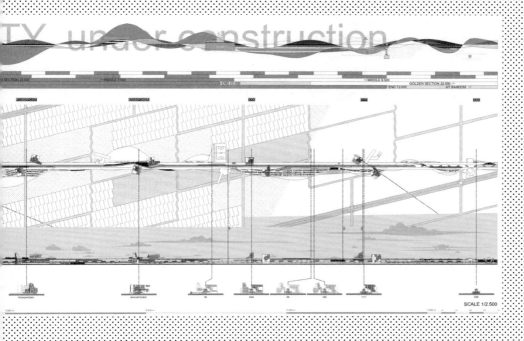

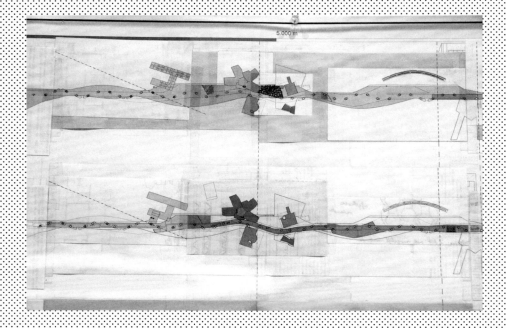

5.000 m

T.O.P. office: a Portrait

 T.O.P. office: Works – Exhibitions – Writings (1967–2011)

 T.O.P. office: Future Prospects
A Conversation between Isabelle De Smet, Steven Van
den Bergh, Wouter Davidts, and Hans De Wolf

 T.O.P. office: Excerpts from Print Maps 1997–2012

T.O.P. office:
a Portrait

O F F I C E

is an architecture and urban planning firm with many faces
and multiple personalities. Founded by Luc Deleu and his wife
Laurette Gillemot in 1970 in their house *Les Nénuphars* in the
stately Cogels Osylei street in Antwerp, one year after Deleu's
graduation as an architect from the Hoger Instituut Sint Lucas
in Brussels, it has known a horde of long- and short-term collaborators, assistants and interns over the past four decades.
Based on the recognition that 'it takes a team to deal with the
complexities of architecture,' Deleu conceived both the mode
and the environment of his commencing prac-   **1** Luc Deleu, *Ethics of
tice as collaborative and dialogical.[1] The young   Architecture*, April 1988,
practitioner made a clear statement against   (unpublished), p. 1.
modernist architecture's culture of 'masters', an assertion that
would gain full resonance within the flourishing cult of star-
architects since the late 1980s. The logo of T.O.P. office further
underscored the ethical stance taken by Deleu: a globe upside-down and in reverse, the emblem represented the willful
shift from local preoccupations towards a global consciousness. With the concept of *Orban Planning*, Deleu further developed an architecture and urban planning practice that took
the earth as its yardstick. T.O.P. office made an imaginative
plea for a tolerant urbanism for a tolerant society, an ecological perspective, true citizen participation, and, *avant la lettre*
as it were, sustainability. The profound changes in the organization of public space, transport and dwelling combined with
the steady increase of the world population, Deleu wrote in
his *Orban Planning Manifesto* of 1980, forced the architect-

2 Luc Deleu, *Orbanistisch*   town-planner to define new priorities: '"In-
Manifest/Manifeste   formation" (reduction of uncertainty) is now
d'Orbanisme/Orban   an important part of the "momental" orban
Planning Manifesto, in: planner's activities: he is a medium, a trend-
Vrije Ruimte–Espace Libre–   setter and/or town fool, etc. ... He designs,
Open Space, Antwerp: publishes, performs, shows, realizes or plays,
Internationaal Cultureel   etc. ... '[2]
Centrum (ICC)/Ministerie
van Nationale Opvoeding
en Nederlandse Cultuur,
1980, pp. 20-26 (p. 26).

T.O.P. office
*Present-day team
members:*
Luc Deleu, Architect and
Urbanist—Founder
Laurette Gillemot, Office
administration—Founder
Isabelle De Smet,
Architect
Steven Van den Bergh,
Architect
Tijana Lukovic, Intern

T.O.P. office was set up based on two distinct convictions: first, that it would be better to reduce the spatial impact of building and hence to build *less*, and second, that future developments in communication media would enable new modes of nomadic life. The ensuing early works emphasized mobility versus the immobilism of real estate and questioned the exclusive privilege of buildings as living and working accommodation. The assertion that '[t]he orban planner has become primarily a theoretician, who in rare cases realizes his visionary views on space of the planet earth,' has constituted the core of T.O.P. office's mission ever since. By means of a consistent formal research and multi-layered design strategies it investigated such dichotomies as order and chaos, or new and existing.

Partly due to his many friendships with local artists, Deleu primarily gained visibility in the art world in the 1970s and early 1980s with performances, sculptures and installations of large-scale objects that shifted the scale and perspective of both urban and natural settings. Rather than being acknowledged as an architect and urban planner in charge of an office, Deleu built up an international reputation as an artist. However, Deleu's claim that 'building' is not the only available mode to express ideas on architecture and urban planning should by no means be regarded as grounds to portray him as a mere visionary or even utopian architect. To Deleu, the sphere of the arts just

3 Luc Deleu, *Schaal & Perspectief, Zwitserland '86*, 1986 (unpublished). This position is echoed by Deleu's aphoristic statement that 'I am an artist because I'm an architect.'

served as an additional platform to make his work public, or as he formulated it in a short unpublished statement on scale and perspective in 1986, 'to put his ideas up for discussion.'[3] His ambitions, Deleu has never failed to stress, have always been situated squarely in the realm of architecture and urban planning.

Even though Deleu engaged in several collaborative projects during the 1970s, both artistic and architectural, it were the various studies for High Speed Rail (HST) lines in Brussels (1986–89), Utrecht (1989–90), Antwerp (1989–93), and Rotterdam (1990–91), the *Housing (&) the City* public housing contest (1989), the design for the reconversion of the 'De Hef' bridge in Rotterdam into a sky plaza and civil offices (1989–90), or the cruise terminal for Antwerp (1998), that marked a new phase in the structure and activities of T.O.P. office. These large-scale and elaborate architectural and infrastructural design projects required a collective mode of research and a novel degree of shared efforts. In this period the office grew considerably and employing an ever varying number of collaborators. The shift in the late 1980s to the design of large-scale urban projects encouraged the office in the mid-1990s to add a bottom-up approach to the conventional top-down method.

The Unadapted City, an ample study for the development and organization of urban infrastructure and amenities initiated by T.O.P. office in 1995, was a new pinnacle in this development. Idiosyncratically labeling it as 'design by research' T.O.P. office invested in a long-term mode of research and in the development of more sophisticated concepts. This new development moved into a higher gear in 1997, when Isabelle De Smet and Steven Van den Bergh joined T.O.P. office and soon after became permanent staff members. In little less than a decade, the new team developed a unique model of collaborative practice centered upon aleatory techniques and engaging stochastic processes that led to autopiloted design. As they worked together, and often simultaneously, on one single computer drawing for *The Unadapted City*, all the while combining high technology and chance principles, T.O.P. office merged authorship to a large degree. Parallel to an adherence to strict rationality, T.O.P. office tried more and more to get hold of the synchronicity of things in the processes of creation.

T.O.P. office has always cherished its position as an independent research team that develops an autonomous format for urban research by design. On many occasions T.O.P office has participated in debates on the present state and the future of architecture and urban planning. Yet the drive behind the work and practice of T.O.P. office has never been merely theoretical. The many and varied activities of the past four decades have resulted in a distinct understanding of the design challenges of very large and complex programs and meanings, this from a planetary point of view and bearing the earth's scale in mind. They have developed a unique sensibility for oversized monumentalism and advanced the strategy of imaging concepts. Yet the conceptual vocation of T.O.P. office has always been coupled with the sincere desire to consolidate the built-up expertise and the acquired knowledge in the very practical realm of building. The claim to build less is all too often mistaken for a refusal to build.

Orban Space, the latest and ongoing project by T.O.P. office, investigates the design of urban space in a global context.

T.O.P. office
Former team members
(1970–2011):
Addy De Boer, Anna Sochocka, Anna Wójtowicz, Annelies De Mey, Anne-Marie Morel, Anne-Marie van der Meer, Anne-Sophie Moors, Anoek De Smet, Aurore Lieben, Ben van Hoorn, Bianca Verbeeck, Boris Sverlow, Charlotte Geldof, Chris Mys, Daniela Verwilt, David Reffo, Dimitri Meessen, Dmitry Sakhno, Douglas Allard, Els Vervloesem, Emilio Lopez-Menchero, Erwin Vangenechten, Filiep Decorte, Francis Jonckheere, Frank Theyssen, Geert Blervacq, Geert Bosch, Gialt Latte, Guan Ursi, Gunther Slagmeulder, Hanneke Van Hassel, Herbert Staljanssens, Ignace Pollentier, Ilke Van den Brempt, Ilse Berghmans, Ines Keersmaekers, Ivo Vanhamme, Jan Croenen, Jan Verheyden, Jef Verbeeck, Joachim Walgrave, Joaney Korevaar, Johan Voorhans, Jonas De Rauw, Joost Vandendriessche, Joris Hendrickx, Joris Van Reusel, Judith Peeters, Jurgen Ceuppens, Karel Lowette, Kathleen De Bodt, Koen Heene, Koen Pauwels, Koen Raes, Kris Elsen, Kristof Vermeir, Lien Moens, Lieve Sysmans, Lieven De Boeck, Luc Buelens, Mariella Peterse, Mark Kramer, Mark Polman, Marlies Lenaerts, Mattias Vroom, Michel van Achterberg, Monique Beumers, Myrka Wiesniewski, Nadine Vandendriessche, Nathalie Leysen, Nel Janssens, Olivier Claeys, Patrick Moyersoen, Peter de Rijck, Peter Goemans, Peter Savenije, Peter Swinnen, Pieter De Clercq, Pieterjan Gijs, Ramses De Pauw, Raymond Franke, Remko Schultheiss, Roeland Vergouwen, Roman Selyuk, Rudolf Kallenbach, Saskia Baetens-Van Gils, Saskia Kuijpers, Stan Jacobs, Tal Huberman, Thierry Berlemont, Thierry Denoiseux, Walter Grasmug, Wannes Deprez, Werner Van Hoeydonck, Wietse Vermeulen

T.O.P. office:
Works – Exhibitions – Writings (1967–2011)

1970

Crossed-out Collage
Mixed media

Plan for a Terrace House
Free distribution of a plan for a terrace house
Performance with drawing

Inktpot
Performance, installation with bunker, and video (with Filip Francis and De Nieuwe Koloristen)

Complete Land-saving Houses
Architectural design for houses withoutland use
Drawing

'Luc Deleu says farewell to architecture', Vacuum voor nieuwe dimensies, Antwerp, Belgium (solo)

'Group Exhibition (Karl Bungert, Luc Daems, Gilbert De Bontridder, Luc Deleu, Harry De Schepper, Filip Francis, Georges Smits, Nico Van Daele, Frans van Roosmaelen, Wout Vercammen', Vacuum voor nieuwe dimensies, Antwerp, Belgium

1971

Villa Tournesol
Architectural design for a holiday park residence in Tenerife, Spain
Drawings and model

Flagging of the Cogels Osylei
Installation with flags
Antwerp, Belgium

1967

Cultural Center
Architectural design for a cultural center in Duffel, Belgium (student project)
Model and photomontage

1968

Church in the Dunes
Architectural design for a house for prayer in Koksijde, Belgium (student project)
Drawings and model

1969

Untitled (Project for Left Bank)
Urban design (with Filip Francis and L. Van Looy)
Drawings, photocollages, and text

Library
Architectural design for a library in Duffel, Belgium (student project)
Model

Europakruispunt
Urban design for the site in front of Central Station, Brussels, Belgium (student project)
Drawings, model, and photos

'Vaga', Koninklijk Museum voor Schone Kunsten, Antwerp, Belgium

Villa Verbaenen
Architectural design for a villa commissioned by architect F. Verbaenen
Drawings

1971–72
Artworker Star
Screen-printed magazine (no. 1 *Common Medium* (1971), printed by Wout Vercammen and Hugo Heyrman; no. 2 *Brainwashing Medium* (1972), printed by Wouter Vercammen and Filip Francis; no. 3 *Art at Work* (1973), printed by Hugo Heyrman, Luc Deleu and Filip Francis) with contribution by Deleu to no. 1 (*Art is art is not*) and no. 3 (*Mobile Medium University*). Published by *Artworker Foundation*, Antwerp

1972

Mobile Medium University
Architectural competition design for a new campus for University Institute Antwerp (UIA), Belgium
Drawings and model

1972–73
Situations (Journal)
Super8 film
In the context of De Koninklijke Filmclub van Antwerpen
(Luc Deleu, Filip Francis, Hugo Heyrman, and George Smits)

1972–73
Police
Super8 film

T.O.P. office Multi Mixed Media Show (with Filip Francis and George Smits)
Schoten, Belgium
Performance, Super–8 film, and video

1972–75
Tribune
Collage book

1972–80
Proposals
(revisited in 2000 and 2002)
Drawings, photocopies, photomontages, and texts

'Art Worker Star 3', Multi Art Gallery, Antwerp, Belgium
'Man and Architecture', Sablon, Brussels, Belgium

1973

Packed Antwerp
Installation proposal for 8ème Biennale des Jeunes Artistes, Paris, France (with Jan Putteneers)
Text

Mobile Medium Architecture Promotion
Refurbished ambulance, performance, photos, and photomontages
Europe

De Ooievaar
Interior design
Realization
Antwerp, Belgium

Van Erp House
Preliminary architectural design for a private dwelling in Tervuren
Drawings

1973–75
De Skipper
Architectural reconversion to pub De Skipper, Antwerp, Belgium (in collaboration with George Smits [wallpaper and front window decoration] and Luc Carlens [front window decoration])
Drawings, model, and realization (demolished)

'Luc Deleu, Filip Francis en Wout Vercammen', Ercola, Antwerp, Belgium
'Internationale Kunst- und Informationsmesse', Düsseldorf, Germany
'Group Exhibition (Karl Bungert, Joost De Brune, Luc Deleu, Filip Francis, Jan Putteneers, Georges Smits, Bernd Urban, Wout Vercammen, Ercola, Pieter Celie, Laurent Lauwers', Empire Shopping Centre, Antwerp, Belgium

1974

Manure Heap
Mixed media
Internationaal Cultureel Centrum (I.C.C.), Antwerp, Belgium

Een land zoek zijn evenwicht
Set design for tv program E*en land zoekt zijn evenwicht* by Belgian Radio and Television (BRT)
Mixed media

1974–
Recyclage
First exhibited in 1988
Mixed media

'Mobile Medium Architecture', Estro Armonico, Brussels, Belgium (solo)

'Kunst aus Belgien', Survival Art, Galerie Linsen, Bonn, Germany
'Aspekten van de Aktuele Kunst in België', I.C.C., Antwerp, Belgium
'Tendenzen der aktuellen Kunst in Belgien (Luc Deleu, Filip Francis, Wout Vercammen)', Galerie Von Kolczynski, Stuttgart, Germany

1975

Boutique Babylon
Architectural remodeling of fashion store
Drawings and realization (demolished)
Antwerp, Belgium

Cafeteria U.I.A.
Architectural design for the cafeteria of the University Institute Anwerp (U.I.A.), Antwerp, Belgium (with Filip Francis)
Drawings

1975–79
De Wollewei
Architectural reconversion of a former cloister into a youth center in Turnhout, Belgium (with Jan Croenen)
Drawings
Turnhout, Belgium

'Agora Studio Travelling Exhibition 1975', Galerij Agora, Maastricht, the Netherlands; traveling to: C.A.Y.C., Buenos Aires, Argentina; Estudio Actual, Caracas, Venezuela; Museo de Arte Contemporanea, São Paolo, Brasil

1976

Rothiers House with Studio
Architectural design for the reconversion of a house into a house with studio, Antwerp, Belgium
Drawings

'Fifth International Open Encounter on Video', I.C.C., Antwerp, Belgium

1977

Bentley House
Interior design for bar Bentley House
Drawings and realization (demolished)
Malaga, Spain

Antwerp Caravan City
Proposal for the Rubens Year (1977)
Photos

Psychiatric clinic Borsbeek
Preliminary study for the reconversion of a former farmhouse into a rehabilitation center for psychiatric patients, Borsbeek, Belgium
Drawings

1977–83
Lego Constructions
Models and photos

1977–
Situations Trouvées
Photos

'Spectrum 77–78', Spectrum Gallery, Antwerp, Belgium

'Luc Deleu: 20 futuristieke voorstellen voor stedelijke agglomeraties (26.6.77)', A+ no. 7–8 (1977), pp. 52–53

1978

House Bekaert
Preliminary study for the remodeling of a private dwelling, Ekeren, Belgium
Drawings

Bird's Nest
Mixed media

Museum for Broken Art
Waterworks building, mixed media, performance, photomontages, photos, texts, and video
Turnhout, Belgium

Electric Fireplace Video
Black–and–white video

Aquarium Vide
Black–and–white video

Video Comic
Black–and–white video

De Group House
Remodeling of private house
Drawings and realization
Antwerp, Belgium

'Voorstel tot afschaffing van de wet van 20 februari 1939' [Proposal for abolishment of the law of February 20, 1939], Spectrum Gallery, Antwerp, Belgium (solo)

'Luc Deleu, Filip Francis, Wouter Vercammen', Cultuur– en Ontmoetingscentrum De Warande, Turnhout, Belgium

1979

Super–superposition
Video (with Filip Francis and Wout Vercammen)

The Last Stone of Belgium
Installation in reinforced concrete and performances; permanent installation in the Municipal Museum for Contemporary Art (S.M.A.K.) Ghent, Belgium in 2010

1979–80
Idée pour la transformation du chantier 'Les Halles' en paysage urbain en évolution
Urban competition design for the 'Quartier des Halles', Paris, France
Drawings, photomontages, and text

Neo–natural Space
Investigation of the former CBR factories in Ravels, Belgium (with Bernd Urban)
Photos

Elderly Center Hoogstraten
Architectural competition design for an elderly center in Hoogstraten, Belgium (with Jan Croenen)
Drawings and text

1979–85
*Ready-made Housing Architecture (Luc Deleu
Manifesto to the Board)*
Drawings, model, performance, photos,
purpose-built dwellings
(guided self-realizations), and texts

 'JP 2', Palais des Beaux-Arts,
Brussels, Belgium

1980

Ponds for the I.C.C.
Installation proposal for the Internationaal
Cultureel Centrum (I.C.C.), Antwerp,
Belgium
Drawing

Golden (Section) Triangle
Drawings and printed plexi-glass

Scale & Perspective
Design by research/Research by
design

*Principle of a Lesson in Perspective
Featuring the World's Tallest Twin
Towers*
Drawing

*Principle of a Lesson in Scale with
Two Buildings (An idea-design
for a global center for interracial
communication showing a lesson
in scale with twin buildings)*
Drawing

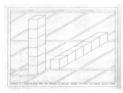

*Principle of a Lesson in Scale with
Two Buildings of Identical Volume
Featuring the World's Tallest Tower*
Drawing

Big Triumphal Arch
Model, mixed media

1980–81
*Principle of a Lesson in Perspective
Featuring the World's Tallest Twin
Towers*
Model

 'Vrije Ruimte—Espace Libre—Open
Space', I.C.C., Antwerp, Belgium
(solo)

'Ruimte Z', Antwerp, Belgium

 Luc Deleu, *Vrije Ruimte—Espace
Libre—Open Space*, Antwerp:
Internationaal Cultureel
Centrum (I.C.C.)/Ministerie
van Nationale Opvoeding en
Nederlandse Cultuur, 1980
(exh. cat.), including *Orbanistisch
Manifest/Manifeste d'Orbanisme/
Orban Planning Manifesto*,
pp. 20–26

1981

*Principle of a Lesson in Scale with Two
Identical Buildings Featuring Queen
Elizabeth I and II*
Model

*Principle of a Lesson in Scale with Two
Buildings of Identical Volume Featuring
the World's Tallest Tower*
Model

*Proposal for a Worldwide Windmill
Network*
Drawing

Gentils House
Preliminary study for the architectural
remodeling of a private dwelling,
Antwerp, Belgium (bathroom and
veranda extension)
Drawings

1981–82
*Scale & Perspective with
Tower Crane*
Drawing, installation with
tower crane, and photos
Montevideo warehouse,
Antwerp, Belgium

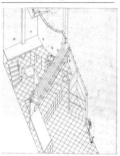

1981–82
Flower Shop Mergits
Architectural remodeling and interior
design of a flower shop
Drawings and realization
Antwerp, Belgium

'Perspectief & Schaal', Zeno X,
Antwerp, Belgium (solo)
'Schaal & Perspectief', Montevideo,
Antwerp, Belgium (solo)

'Echelle 1:1981 Schaal', Gallerij vzw
ERG, Leerlooierij Belka, Ateliers,
Raffinerie du Plan K, Brussels,
Belgium
'Naar en in het landschap', I.C.C.,
Antwerp, Belgium
'Kunst in/als vraag', Provinciaal
Museum voor Moderne Kunst, Ypres,
Belgium

1982

Montevideo Entrance
Architectural design for an entrance for the
Montevideo warehouse, Antwerp, Belgium
Drawings

Belgian Highway Sanitation
Architectural competition design for sanitary houses
alongside Belgian highways (with Jan Croenen and
Peter Goemans)
Drawings and text

1982–83/1987
*Antique Shop and Penthouse for Bernard
Blondeel*
Architectural remodeling and interior design
of an antique shop and a private dwelling
Drawings and realization
Antwerp, Belgium

'Insthal', Hallen van Schaarbeek, Brussels,
Belgium
'Interieur 82: 8e Internationale Biënnale van
woonkreativiteit', Kortrijk, Belgium

Luc Deleu, 'Tekst voorgedragen voor de Orde
van Architecten te Antwerpen, op 2 december
1982' (unpublished)

1983

Two Small Triumphal Arches
Installation proposal for two
triumphal arches on an unfinished
highway exit in Basel, Switzerland
Drawing

Obelisk
Installation proposal for Basel,
Switzerland
Photomontage

Small Triumphal Arch
Drawing, installation with containers,
and photo
Basel, Switzerland

Big Triumphal Arch
Drawing, installation with containers,
and photo
Neuchâtel, Switzerland

Golden Gate
Model, mixed media

Arcade
Model

Obelisk
Installation proposal for the Schuman
roundabout, Brussels, Belgium
Drawing

Obelisk
Installation proposal for the South Pole,
Antarctic
Drawing

Belgian Gate
Model

The Museum of Architecture
Architecture competition design for a
architecture museum in Ghent, Belgium
Photocollage

1983–86
*Scale & Perspective with Two Electricity
Pylons*
Drawings

'Selected work', Art–Info, Antwerp, Belgium
(solo)
'1 m3 Lego = obélisque', Galerie Média,
Neuchâtel, Switzerland (solo)

'Das Prinzip Hoffnung', Museum Bochum,
Germany
'Portfolios in Architecture', Storefront for Art
& Architecture, New York, USA
Montevideo, Antwerp, Belgium

Luc Deleu, 'Lezing bij opening van de
tentoonstelling van Eugeen Liebaut',
9 December, 1983 (unpublished)
Luc Deleu, *Luc Deleu Manifest aan de Orde*,
Antwerp: Guy Schraenen, 1983

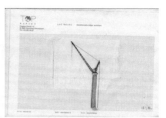

*Untitled (Installation with Crane on top of a
Chimney in the 'Quartiere S. Marta')*
Installation proposal for the 1984 Venice
Biennale, Venice, Italy (rejected)
Drawing

Untitled (Installation with Scaffolding)
Installation proposal for the 1984 Venice
Biennale, Venice, Italy (rejected)
Drawing

Containers in Bulk
Model, installation with containers, and
photos
Montevideo, Antwerp, Belgium

'Schaal & Perspectief', St. Lukas Gallery,
Brussels, Belgium (solo)
'Voorstellen—theorieën—modellen' (with
Guy Rombouts), Het Apollohuis, Eindhoven,
the Netherlands (solo)

'Torens van Babel', Montevideo, Antwerp,
Belgium
'Espace Libre', 41st Venice Biennale, Venice,
Italy

Luc Deleu and Marc Hostettler, *Luc Deleu:
Prototype d'un Monument Mobile*, Brussels:
Sint–Lukasstichting/Neuchâtel: Editions
Media, 1984
Luc Deleu and Marc Hostettler, *Luc Deleu:
Urbild eines beweglichen Denkmales*,
Brussels: Sint–Lukasstichting/Neuchâtel:
Editions Media, 1984

1984

Big Triumphal Arch
Installation proposal
for the 1984 Venice
Biennale, Venice, Italy
(rejected)
Drawing

1985

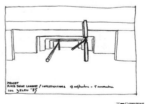

Scale & Perspective with Two Lampposts
Drawing, installation with lampposts, and photos
Liège, Belgium

Scale & Perspective with Two Lampposts
Installation with lampposts and photos
De Fabriek, Eindhoven, the Netherlands

Ponte dell'Accademia
Architectural competition design for Ponte dell'Accademia, Venice, Italy
Drawings

Pantacom Container Depot
Plan for Pantacom container depot
Drawings and realization (altered)
Antwerp, Belgium

Santa Maria della Scala
Study for the re-use of the Santa Maria della Scala Hospital, Siena, Italy
Drawing

Promenade Pier
Architectural design for a promenade pier in Flushing, the Netherlands
Drawing, model, and text

1985–86
House Vandewalle
Purpose-built private dwelling
Drawings and realization
Hove, Belgium

'Schaal & Perspectief 2', De Fabriek, Eindhoven, the Netherlands (solo)

'Investigations', Liège, Belgium

Luc Deleu, *Over de belangrijkheid en onbelangrijkheid van de architectuur*, February 1985 (unpublished)

1986

Scale & Perspective with Two Electricity Pylons
Drawings, installation with containers, and photos
Ghent, Belgium

Scale and Perspective with Electricity Pylon
Installation proposal for the New Museum, New York, United States
Drawing

Small Triumphal Arch (With Armored Tank)
Installation with containers and armored tank
Tielt, Belgium

Obelisk (unfinished)
Installation with containers (unfinished)
Liège, Belgium

Untitled (Installation with Crash Barriers)
Installation with crash barriers
Claire Burrus Gallery, Paris, France

Crane Ballet in front of the 'Opéra La Bastille'
Photo

Untitled (Installation with Windsocks and Rulers)
Installation with windsocks and rulers
Furkapass, Switzerland

Big Card House Castle
Drawings and installation with glass plates

1986–87
SATO
Interior design with Japanese elements of a
Japanese restaurant
Antwerp, Belgium

Untitled (Krems)
Architectural design proposal for a panoramic tower
around the chimney of the Stein tobacco factory in
Krems, Austria
Drawing

TGV Spectaculair Boven Brussel
Artist's pages
Newspaper print
De Antwerpse Morgen, Thursday 7 August, 1987, pp. 1–2

1986–87
Antique shop J. Dirven
Architectural remodeling and interior design of an
antique shop
Drawings and realization
Antwerp, Belgium

1986–89
Tent for Napoleon
Installation proposal for Waterloo, Belgium; model and
realization in La–Roche–sur–Yon, France
Drawings, models, multiple, text, and realization
La–Roche–sur–Yon, France

1986–97
Atelier Hofraum
Architectural remodeling of the dépendance of Hotel
Furkablick
Drawings, models and realization
Furkapass, Switzerland

1986–89
*'Europe Central Station' (HST
Brussels)*
Urban design for a HST line and
station in Brussels, Belgium
Drawings and model

'Une semaine avec Luc Deleu
à Neuchâtel', Galerie Média,
Neuchâtel, Switzerland (solo)
'Luc Deleu', Galerie Claire Burrus,
Paris, France (solo)

'Beelden Buiten', Tielt, Belgium
'Initiatief 86', Ghent, Belgium
'Architectuur als imaginaire
werkelijkheid', Forum, Middelburg,
the Netherlands

Luc Deleu, 'Towards Re–use', in:
ILA&UD: Annual Report 1985–86,
Milan 1986
Luc Deleu, *Schaal & Perspectief*,
Zwitserland '86, 1986 (unpublished)

1987

Obelisk
Installation with containers
Antwerp, Belgium

Big Triumphal Arch
Drawings and installation with containers
Barcelona, Spain

*Design for Visual Augmentation of Scale with
''t Kofschip' model*
Design for the visual augmentation of scale of
the Grindtsveen sand quarrel with a model of 't
Kofschip, a five–funnel passenger vessel
Drawing

Lesson in Scale
Drawings and installation with tree and
scaffolding
Slochteren, the Netherlands

Tracés Régulateurs on Villa Schwob (Le Corbusier)
Drawing and installation with climbing rope
La-Chaux-de-Fonds, Switzerland

Pictura Antiquairs Nationaal
Master plan for antiques art fair, RAI Amsterdam
Drawings and exhibition display design
RAI, Amsterdam, the Netherlands

1987–89
Panamarenko House
Architectural remodeling of the residence and studio of Panamarenko
Drawings and realization
Antwerp, Belgium

1988
Cornerhouse A
Architectural remodeling and consolidation of a historical house (one of the oldest of Antwerp)
Drawings and realization
Antwerp, Belgium

'Luc Deleu Postfuturismus?', deSingel, Antwerp, Belgium (solo; traveling to La Monnaie, Brussels, Belgium)

'Beeld en land '87', Slochteren, the Netherlands
'19de Biënnale voor beeldhouwkunst', Openluchtmuseum Middelheim, Antwerp, Belgium

Luc Deleu, *Luc Deleu Postfuturismus?*, Antwerp: deSingel/Wommelgem: Den Gulden Engel, 1987 (exh. cat.)

1988

Glass Containers in Bulk
Installation with glass containers
Museum am Ostwall, Dortmund, Germany

ORBINO
Drawing

Scale and Perspective with Small Triumphal Arch
Installation with containers
Watou, Belgium

Untitled (Installation with Windsocks)
Installation with windsocks
Zoetermeer, the Netherlands

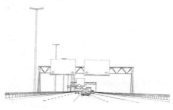

Signposting for Amsterdam
Public art competition proposal for the signposting of the A1 Amsterdam ring–road
Drawings, models, mixed media, and text

Tonalité
Remodeling of monumental housing lot and reconversion into a shop
Amsterdam, the Netherlands

Ø Gate '84–'88
Souvenir for the Maritime Museum, Amsterdam, the Netherlands
Paper model

'Luc Deleu Postfuturismus?', Technische Universität, Berlin, Germany (solo)
'Central Station Europe', Brussels, Galerie Etienne Ficheroulle, Brussels Belgium (solo)

'Stellproben', Museum am Ostwall, Dortmund, Germany
'Exhibition with Richard Serra', Provinciaal Museum, Hasselt, Belgium
'Visualia '80', Watou, Belgium
'Kunst Maritiem', Het Scheepvaartmuseum, Amsterdam, the Netherlands

Luc Deleu, *De kracht van de visionair*, 1988 (unpublished)
Luc Deleu, *The Ethics of Architecture*, April 1988 (unpublished)

1989

Scale & Perspective: Barcelona Towers (Housing (&) the City)
Urban competition design for two towers in Barcelona, Spain (honorable mention)
Drawings and models

Scale & Perspective: Monument for the Ending of the Delta Works
Public art competition proposal for a Delta Works monument in Noarderleech, the Netherlands (1st prize)
Drawings and model

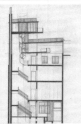

The Illusion
Architectural design for the reconversion of a residence into artist's center in Rotterdam, the Netherlands
Drawing

Big Triumphal Arch
Installation with containers
Hamburg, Germany

Glass Containers in Bulk
Installation with glass containers
Villa Arson, Nice, France

Lampposts in Bulk
Installation with lampposts
École des Beaux–Arts, Mâcon, France

Wind Turbine Bering Strait
Installation proposal for a wind turbine and power transport over the Bering Strait, Diomede Islands, USSR/Russia; Call for Entries, Storefront for Art and Architecture, New York
Drawing

Untitled (Tent Construction)
Installation proposal for a tent construction over a bridge in Gateshead, United Kingdom
Drawing

Sint-Joost Academy
Architectural design for the reconversion of a convent into the Sint-Joost Academy, Den Bosch, the Netherlands
Drawings

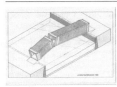

Bridge
Installation proposal for a container bridge in Leiden, the Netherlands
Drawing

Mobile Medium University Revisited
Photograph of 1972 model with space exploration poster

Annie Gentils Gallery
Design for the art fair booth of Annie Gentils at the Kunstmesse, Cologne
Drawings and exhibition display design
Cologne, Germany

1989–90
Untitled (Installation with windsocks and glass containers)
Proposal for an installation with windsocks and glass containers in Haarlem, the Netherlands

1989–90
HST Hoog Catharijne
Urban design for a HST line and station in Utrecht, the Netherlands
Drawing and model

1989–90
HST Hoog Catharijne, Utrecht
Urban design for a HST line and station, and a housing level in Utrecht, the Netherlands
Drawings and model

1989–93
Koude Brug
Urban design for a HST line and station in Antwerp, Belgium
Drawings

'Central Station Europe', Galerie Montevideo, Brussels, Antwerp, Belgium (solo)
'Schaal & Perspectief', Ecole des Beaux-Arts, Mâcon, France (solo)
'Schaal & Perspectief', Galerie Claire Burrus, Paris, France (solo)
Helan Arts, Bornem, Belgium (solo)

'Parallel Views', Arti et Amicitiae, Amsterdam, the Netherlands
'En mai, fais ce qu'il plaît', Ecole d'art de La Roche-sur-Yon, France
'Pas à côté, pas n'importe où 4', Villa Arson, Nice, France
Biënnale Kunst & Architectuur, The Hague, the Netherlands
'D&S Ausstellung', Kunstverein, Hamburg, Germany
Nicole Klagsburn Gallery, New York, United States

Luc Deleu, *Ethique de l'architecture* (Collection Point de Vue), Saint–Benoît du Sault: Tarabuste Editions, 1989
Luc Deleu, *Luc Deleu: Stellproben*, Dortmund: Museum am Ostwall, 1989 (exh. cat.)

1990

Scale & Perspective (Mail Sorting Center)
Public art competition design for a mail sorting center in Antwerp, Belgium
Drawing

Scale & Perspective (Public sculpture for University of Twente)
Public art proposal for a public sculpture for the University of Twente campus, Twente, the Netherlands
Model

Scale & Perspective (Eine Skulptur für die Landspitze)
Public art competition proposal for an installation for Skulpturenweg Nordhorn, Projekt Landspitze, Stiftung Niedersachsen, Hanover, Germany
Drawings and photomontage

Scale & Perspective (Lenbachhaus)
Installation with lampposts
Städtische Galerie in Lenbachhaus, Munich, Germany

Antwerp, Your Next Cruise Stop! (AYNCS)
Urban competition design for a bridge over the river Scheldt in Antwerp, Belgium
Drawings and model
Competition Stad aan de Stroom

Untitled (Installation with windsocks)
Installation with windsocks
Zoersel, Belgium

Section d'or
Drawings and installation with wood and plastic film Château de Magny, Normandy, France

Studs
Installation with metal studs and photos
École Supérieure d'Art Visuel, Geneva, Switzerland

Untitled (Red-white Mast Project)
Proposal for an installation in a sculpture park in Tel Hai, Israel
Model

Container Bridge over the Venidse
Drawings and installation with containers
Hoorn, the Netherlands

Allotment Gardens Antwerp X
Public art competition proposal for the
arrangement of allotment gardens
alongside the former mail sorting center
Antwerp, Belgium
Drawing and model

Annie Gentils Gallery
Architectural remodeling and extension
of the attic of the Annie Gentils Gallery,
Antwerp, Belgium
Drawings

Untitled (Installation with windsocks)
Installation with windsocks
Lommel, Belgium

*Untitled (Apartment Building with
Satellites)*
Public art competition, proposal for an
integrated communication system on top
of the Hillekop flat (Mecanoo Architects),
Rotterdam, the Netherlands
Drawings

Container Bridge
Model (multiple)

1990–91
De Hef (HST Rotterdam)
Architectural proposal for the HST line in
Rotterdam on the old railroad track (De
Hef study III)
Drawings

1990–97
Les Nénuphars
Remodeling, restoration, and consolidation of
own house
Drawings and realization
Antwerp, Belgium

'De Hef Rotterdam', RAM Galerie, Rotterdam,
the Netherlands (solo)
'Luc Deleu', Provinciaal Museum, Hasselt,
Belgium (solo)
'Luc Deleu', Lumen Travo, Amsterdam, the
Netherlands (solo)
'Antwerpen Welles–Nietes', Galerie
Montevideo, Antwerp, Belgium (solo)
'Échelle & Perspective', Galerie Christine & Isy
Brachot, Brussels, Belgium (solo)

'Echange de procédés', Sous–sol, Galerie
de l'Ecole Supérieure d'Art Visuel, Geneva,
Switzerland
'Three Belgian Artists', Union of Architects,
Moscow, USSR
'Zoersel '90', Domein Kasteel van Halle,
Zoersel, Belgium
'Antwerpen-Haarlem', Vleeshal, Haarlem, the
Netherlands
'For Real Now', Stichting De Achterstraat,
Hoorn, the Netherlands
'Kunstproject 1', Lommel, Belgium
'Tel Hai '90', Tel Hai, Israel
'Paradoxes des Alltags', Städtische Galerie im
Lenbachhaus, Munich, Germany

Luc Deleu, *Drijvende vliegvelden en andere
infrastructuren/Floating Airports and Other
Infrastructures*, special issue of *Forum* 34, no. 1
(March 1990)

1991

*Scale & Perspective: Barcelona
Towers (Apartment)*
Detail, apartment in Barcelona
Towers
Model

*Scale & Perspective: Barcelona
Towers (Staircase)*
1:1 mockup of apartment staircase
Installation
Kröller–Müller Museum, Otterlo, the
Netherlands

Porte Ø
Installation with containers
FIAC art fair, Grand Palais, Paris, France

Untitled
Drawings, model, installation with canvas and
scaffolding
Bienne, Switzerland

Untitled (Installation with 14 windsocks)
Installation with windsocks
Museum of Contemporary Art (MuHKA), Antwerp,
Belgium

A Wall for MuHKA
Exhibition wall for the Museum of Contemporary
Art (MuHKA)
Exhibition design of 'Luc Deleu & T.O.P. office
1967–1991'
Antwerp, Belgium

William
Stage design for theater show William by De
Nieuwe Snaar
Drawings and realization

*Barcelona (Tumbling) Apartments: A project for
Artforum by Luc Deleu*
Artist's pages
Artforum International XXX (October), no. 2, pp.
91–93

Scale & Perspective: Barcelona Towers (Staircase)
Multiple

Journey Around the World in 80 Days
Very first model

'Luc Deleu: Schaal en perspectief', Rijksmuseum
Kröller–Müller, Otterlo, the Netherlands (solo)
'Luc Deleu: Scale & Perspective', Storefront for Art &
Architecture, New York, United States (solo)
'Luc Deleu & T.O.P. office 1967–1991', MUHKA,
Museum of Contemporary Art, Antwerp, Belgium
(solo)
'Luc Deleu & T.O.P. office 1967–1991', Galerie Andata/
Ritorno/Galerie Moï Farine, Geneva, Switzerland (solo)
'Luc Deleu', Vlaams Cultureel Centrum 'De Brakke
Grond', Amsterdam, the Netherlands (solo)
'Luc Deleu & T.O.P. office : FRI–ART', Centre d'Art
Contemporain, Fribourg, Switzerland (solo)

'Dialogue sur l'herbe: Een keuze van Luc Deleu
en Alexander Vos', De Tuin, Museum Boijmans
van Beuningen, Rotterdam, the Netherlands
'V Mostra Internazionale di Architettura:
Architetti (della Fiandra)', Belgian Pavilion,
Venice, Italy
'Luc Deleu—Guy Rombouts & Monica
Droste—Narcisse Tordoir', Rijksmuseum
Kröller-Müller, Otterlo, the Netherlands
'Tabula Rasa', Fondation Exposition Suisse de
Sculpture, Bienne, Switzerland

Luc Deleu, *Associatief ontwerpen*, 21
November, 1991 (unpublished).
Luc Deleu, *Luc Deleu & T.O.P. office, 1967–
1991*, Antwerp: Museum voor Hedendaagse
Kunst, 1991 (exh. cat.), including 'Een hefboom
voor Orbanisme/Un levier pour l'Orbanisme/A
driving force for Orbanism', pp. 37–39

1992

*Scale & Perspective: Barcelona
Towers (Swimming Pool)*
Detail of the swimming pool in
Barcelona Towers
Model

Untitled (Signposting Geneva)
Public art competition proposal
for RN1 and RN1A ring-roads of
Geneva, Switzerland
Drawings

Rietveld Exhibition
Display design competition
entry for Rietveld exhibition at
the Centraal Museum, Utrecht,
the Netherlands
Drawings

Lux Aeterna, 5000 Lights
Light installation proposal for Edinburgh,
United Kingdom
Drawings

Antipodal World map
Pencil on photocopy

Vuelta al mundo 'Madrid–Weber–Madrid' en ochenta dias
Drawing on The World, Physical Map
(Kümmerly+Frey, Bern; Van der Grinten projection)
Scale 1:32.000.000
Mixed media

Jumbo Twin Flight
Mixed media

1992–93
Journey Around the World in 80 Days (Madrid–Weber–Madrid)
Drawing on globe (3 versions) and photo

1992–94
Untitled (Public sculpture for the Hogeschool van Amsterdam)
Public sculpture for the Hogeschool van Amsterdam
(1st prize in competition; in collaboration with Karin Daan)
Installation with lampposts, trees and bench

1992–95
Hôtel Stok
Purpose–built private dwelling
Drawings, models and realization
Poortugaal, the Netherlands

'Echelle & Perspective', Galerie Catherine &
Stéphane de Beyrie, Paris, France (solo)
'Continue De Hef Rotterdam', RAM Galerie,
Rotterdam, the Netherlands (solo)

'Unbuilt Belgium 1950–1990', Fondation pour
l'Architecture, Brussels, Belgium
Kunstfort Asperen, Asperen, the Netherlands

1993

Scale & Perspective: Rheinturm
Public art competition proposal for the
Rheinuferstrasse tunnel, Düsseldorf, Germany
Drawings and model

Scale & Perspective: Chapel Analysis
Preliminary study for a workshop in Lyon, France
Drawings

Around the World, Madrid 40°25N 3°43W–Weber 40°22S 176°20E–Madrid, in 80 days,
Drawing on The World, Physical Map
(Kümmerly+Frey, Bern; Mercator projection)
Mixed media

Tours du monde Madrid–Weber–Madrid
Drawing on The World, Political Map (Kümmerly+Frey, Bern; Van der Grinten projection)
Scale 1:23.000.000
Mixed media

Tours du monde Madrid–Weber–Madrid
Drawing on manipulated version of The World, Physical Map (Kümmerly+Frey, Bern; Van der Grinten projection)
Scale 1:23.000.000
Mixed media

Around the World in 80 days
'Weber–Madrid–Weber'
Drawing table, lamp, globe,
Buckminster R. Fuller Dymaxion map,
paint
Mixed Media

Madrid–Madrid en 80 jours par son
antipode, 40°25S 176°17E (Weber),
(triptych)
Drawing on *Carte générale du monde*
(Institut Géographique National, Paris;
Mercator projection)
Mixed media

Journey Around the World (Dordrecht–
Dordrecht via the Pacific)
Public sculpture
Kalkhaven, Dordrecht, the Netherlands

Journey Around the World in 80 Days
Multiple (Museum Dhondt-Dhanens,
Deurle)

Heerlijckheid de Hollain (The Red
House)
Architecture competition design for
social housing on the site of the former
Hollain barracks, Ghent, Belgium
Drawings and model

Massstabstudie für Grossen
Hamburger Triumphbogen
Drawing

1993–99
Medical Practice A.P.C.
Purpose-built medical practice
Drawings and realization
Hoogvliet, the Netherlands

Galerie Etienne Ficheroulle, Brussels, Belgium (solo)

'51°48'—04°40'', Kalkhaven, Dordrecht, the Netherlands
'Limerick', Museum van hedendaagse kunst, Gent,
Belgium
'9ème Bourse d'Art Monumental d'Ivry', CREDAC/
Galerie Fernand Léger,
Ivry-sur-Seine, France
'Kunst in België na 1980/L'Art en Belgique après 1980',
Musée d'Art Moderne, Brusssels, Belgium

Luc Deleu, 'Een andere taak voor de architect', in:
Architectuur in de Provincie: Realisaties in Oost-
Vlaanderen 1963–1993, Ghent: Provincie Oost-
Vlaanderen, 1993, pp. 11–14
Luc Deleu, 'The Blanlin-Evrard Lecture', 1993 (lecture
delivered on the occasion of the Blanlin-Evrard Award
ceremony; unpublished)
Luc Deleu, *Over Open Ruimte*, July 1993 (unpublished)
Luc Deleu, 'Public Space', 2 July, 1993 (lecture delivered
on the award ceremony of the 'Plein Problemen'
competition, Roosendaal–Bergen-op–Zoom, the
Netherlands; unpublished)

1994

Untitled (Jakominplatz)
Public installation for Jakominplatz
Model and installation with painted
lamppost and masts
Graz, Austria

Meridian Minute (Nautical Mile)
Public sculpture proposal for Hoorn,
the Netherlands
Drawing

Construction X
Drawings, model, and installation
with containers
Limerick, Ireland

Untitled (Container Installation)
Proposal for temporary installation
at Cité des Sciences et de l'Industrie,
Parc de la Villette, Paris, France
Drawing

Neu Bratislava
Preparatory urban design study for a
summer school in Vienna
Drawing

1994–96
Usiebenpole
Urban design for a new city
quarter on the Donau Insel,
Vienna, Austria
Drawings and models

'Luc Deleu—Willy De
Sauter—Isa Genzken—
Langlands & Bell', Museum
Dhondt-Dhaenens, Deurle,
Belgium
'EV+94 Biennial of Visual Art',
Limerick, Ireland
'Bouwen in het buitenland',
ARCAM, Amsterdam, the
Netherlands
'Translokation', Haus der
Architektur, Graz, Austria

Luc Deleu, 'Lezing naar
aanleiding van de ontvangst van
de Prijs Blanlin-Evrard', *A+* no. 128
(1994), pp. 55–56.

1995

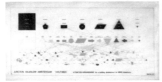

Halfweg
Urban analysis
Drawings

Takeitainer/Bambootainer
Installation with container and bamboo trees
Minimata, Japan

Takeitainer/Bambootainer
Installation with container and bamboo
tree
Tokyo, Japan

Project Uni Dufour
Public art competition proposal for
Geneva, Switzerland
Drawings and model

1995–2006
*The Unadapted City—De Onaangepaste
Stad (D.O.S.)*
Research by design/Design by research
Drawings, models, texts

1995–99
The Unadapted City: Ten Plates
Analysis, datascapes
Mixed media

Witte Zaal, Hoger Architectuurinstituut
Sint-Lucas, Ghent, Belgium (solo)
'In 80 days around the world', RAM
Galerie, Rotterdam, the Netherlands
(solo)

'Memoria e desejo : 9 artistas
contemporaneas de Flandres', Palacio
National de Sintra, Sintra, Portugal
'Ripple Across the Water', Watari-um,
The Watari Museum of Contemporary
Art, Tokyo, Japan

Luc Deleu, 'Alles ist Architektur', in:
Das letze Haus im Steir, Graz: Haus der
Architektur, 1995, pp. 36–48
Luc Deleu, 'A Task for Contemporary
Architecture', in: *Sites & Stations:
Provisional Utopias* (Lusitania 7), ed. by
Stan Allen with Kyong Park, New York:
Lusitania Press, 1995, pp. 234–242

1996

*Scale & Perspective: The Luxor
Obelisk*
Sand drawing
École de Beaux–Arts, Nîmes,
France

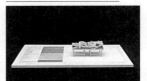

The Unadapted City: BingBong
Analysis and formal study
Drawing and model

Housing Generator
Urban planning competition proposal
for Cato Manor, Durban, South Africa (in
collaboration with Jan Verheyden)
Drawings and model

New Small Triumphal Arch
Model and installation with containers
École de Beaux-Arts, Nîmes, France

SEGHERS engineering N.V.
Architectural competition design for
office and housing development in
Willebroek, Belgium
Drawings

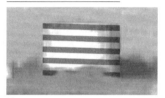

Zoom
Project proposal for exhibition 'Beeld &
Land', Avere Vloeivelden, the Netherlands
Drawings and models

'De Onaangepaste Stad', Netherlands
Architecture Institute, Rotterdam, the
Netherlands (solo)
'De Onaangepaste Stad', Sint-Lucas,
Brussels, Belgium (solo)

'De rijkdom van de eenvoud/L'éloge de la
simplicité: Architecture contemporaine en
Flandre', Fondation pour l'Architecture,
Brussels, Belgium
'Winter Festival: Luc Deleu, Peter
Downsbrough, Bernd Lohaus, Philippe
Van Snick and Marthe Wéry', National
Gallery, Sarajevo, Bosnia-Hercegovina
'De Rode Poort', Museum van
Hedendaagse Kunst, Ghent, Belgium
'Elsewhere', John Hansard Gallery,
University of Southampton,
Southampton, United Kingdom
'Nouvelle architecture en Flandres', Arc
en rêve centre d'architecture, Bordeaux,
France
École des Beaux Arts, Nîmes, France

Luc Deleu, *The Unadapted City*, 1996
(unpublished)

1997

1997–2001
Niebuur House
Purpose-built private dwelling for three
generations
Drawings, models, and realization
Poortugaal, the Netherlands

MACBA Piece
Installation with containers
Museum of Contemporary Art
(MACBA), Barcelona, Spain

De Meerminne, UIA
Architecture competition design for a
new campus for University Institute
Antwerp (UIA) in Antwerp, Belgium
Drawings and model

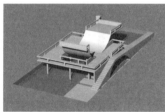

Untitled (Skate ramp)
Public art competition proposal for
Bruges, Belgium
Drawings

Proposal for Carfree Afternoons
Installation
Salzburg, Austria

Fruitcontainer
Installation with container and fruit tree
Louvain, Belgium

1997–99
Untitled (Installation with lampposts)
Public artwork for the Landeskrankenhaus
Installation with lampposts
Hartberg, Bundesland Steiermark, Germany

1997–99
Cabinet of the Minister-President of the
Flemish Community
Architectural remodeling and photo
decoration of the cabinet of the Minister-
President of the Flemish Community
Drawings and realization
Brussels, Belgium

Hogeschool voor Wetenschap & Kunst, Hoger
Architectuurinstituut Sint–Lucas, Brussels,
Belgium (solo)

'Asymptoot', Arti et Amicitiae, Amsterdam,
the Netherlands
'Nature Morte', Cultureel Centrum Leuven,
Louvain, Belgium
'Un toit pour tout le monde', Künstlerhaus
Bethanien, Berlin, Germany
'Sel', Museu d'Art Contemporani de Barcelona
(MACBA), Barcelona, Spain
CIPRA, France

Luc Deleu, Spaceship Earth, 18 July, 1997
(unpublished)

1998

Scale & Perspective with
Three Towers
Model

The Unadapted City: TOPDOS
Research by design/Design by research
Excel application

The Unadapted City: Brikabrak
Urban design
Drawings and model

The Unadapted City: Dinky Town
Urban design
Drawings and model

Artificial Horizon for Ostend
Public artwork for traffic infrastructure
De Bolle
Drawings and realization (unfinished)
Ostend, Belgium

Untitled
Installation with Jerseys
Speelhoven, Belgium

Pentagon Square
Public art competition proposal for
Almelo, the Netherlands
Drawing

1998–2001
Clinckx House and Studio
Architectural renovation and
extension of private dwelling and
artist's studio
Drawings, model, and realization
Ekeren, Belgium

Soleil du Nord
Architecture competition design for
a community house in Schaarbeek,
Belgium
Drawings and model

Container with Birch Bush
Installation with container and birch
trees
Liège, Belgium

Cruise Terminal
Architectural competition design for
a cruise terminal in Antwerp, Belgium
Model

1998–2005
Casa Roja
Purpose-built private dwelling
Drawings, model and realization
Tervuren, Belgium

'Speelhoven '98', Speelhoven,
Aarschot, Belgium
'L'arbre qui cache le fôret', Musée
d'Art Moderne et d'Art Contemporain,
Liège, Belgium
'Stations en hun omgevingen',
Centrum voor Architectuur & Design,
Kortrijk, Belgium
'Fotohof', Galerie 5020, Initiative
Architektur, Internationale
Sommerakademie für Bildende Kunst,
Salzburger Kunstverein, Salzburg
Galerie Vera Van Laer, Antwerp,
Belgium
MUKA Gallery, Auckland, New Zealand

1999

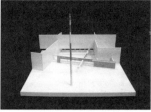

*Scale & Perspective (Installation with 3 red-
white masts)*
Public art competition design for Ter Linden
rest house in Gits, Hooglede, Belgium (first
prize)
Model

The Unadapted City: Octopus
Urban design
Drawing and model

1999–2002
Ventilation chimney
Architectural design for a ventilation shaft
Drawings, models and realization
Petuelring, Munich, Germany

The Equator W100°28'679
Photo taken aboard the cargo ship
the Speybank Photo

Journey Around the World in 72 Days
40° 24' 904S 176° 17' 551E over its antipode
40° 24' 904N 3° 24' 449W (ERNSLAW ONE
TTD, WEBER, NEW ZEALAND over its
antipode PLAZA MAYOR, MADRID, SPAIN)
Doubled photo

Journey Around the World in 72 Days:
Auckland, New Zealand
Photo

Speybank
Construction design for an
installation with containers
Model

FFI Triumphal Arch
Infrastructure for 'Vitrine 99' exhibition
by Flanders Fashion Institute (FFI) on the
Scheldt river quai, Antwerp, Belgium
Exhibition display design

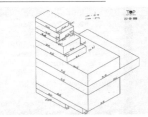

MAS (Museum aan de Stroom)
Architecture competition design for
the Antwerp City Museum, Antwerp,
Belgium
Drawings and model

Untitled (Installation with GSM mast)
Public art competition proposal for
Breda, the Netherlands (first prize)
Drawing

Villa Hermosa
Architectural design for the remodeling
of Gallery Christine & Isy Brachot,
Brussels, Belgium
Drawings and model

*Urban planning competition design for
Meulestede-Noord, Ghent, Belgium*
(in collaboration with MONaRCH, Jan
Verheyden)
Drawings

*Architecture competition design for
social housing, Wevelgem, Belgium*
(in collaboration with MONaRCH, Jan
Verheyden)
Drawings and model

Galerie Annie Gentils, Antwerp,
Belgium (solo)

'Horta and After: 25 Masters of
Modern Architecture in Belgium',
4a Biennial Internacional de
Arquitetura de São Paolo, São
Paolo, Brasil

2000

Surfing Sail
Installation with surfing sail and mast on
De Kaai apartment building (Willem Jan
Neutelings, 1988–92), Antwerp, Belgium
(demolished)

Ghent University
Architecture competition design for a new
aula, offices and amenities for the Faculty
of Engineering, Ghent University, Ghent,
Belgium
Drawings and model

Telepolis
Preliminary design for a public artwork for
Telepolis, Antwerp, Belgium
Drawing

2000–03
St Camillus Boiler Room
Purpose-built boiler room for psychiatric clinic
Sint-Camillus (in collaboration with Hugo
Deleu)
Drawings and realization
Sint-Denijs-Westrem, Belgium

'La ville inadaptée', Centre d'art contemporain
Chapelle Saint-Jacques, Saint–Gaudens,
France (solo)
'Luc Deleu: Le tour du monde en 80 jours',
Galerie Martine & Thibault de la Châtre, Paris,
France (solo)
'Luc Deleu: The Undapted City. Works in
Progress 1995–99', Galerie Aschenbach,
Amsterdam, the Netherlands (solo)

'Horta and After: 25 Masters of Modern Architecture in Belgium', National Gallery, Prague, Czech Republic
'Mo(u)vements', NICC/Koninklijk Museum voor Schone Kunsten, Antwerp, Belgium
'Recycling = another chance', Sint-Lukasarchief, Brussels, Belgium

2000–2001
Luc Deleu, *Theorie van de Architectuur*, Hogeschool voor wetenschap voor wetenschap en kunst, Departement Architectuur Sint-Lucas Brussel-Ghent

2001

Kennedy Belvédère
Public art proposal for the remodeling and refurbishment of the Kennedy Belvédère viaduct, Nancy, France
Drawings, photomontages and model

2001/2004
Old Harbor of Antwerp
Proposal for the reshuffling of the Old Harbor of Antwerp, Antwerp, Belgium
Photomontage and print on dibond (2004)

2001–02
The Unadapted City: Vipcity House of Prayer
Architectural design
Drawings and models

2001–02
The Unadapted City: Vipcity Necropolis
Architectural design
Drawings and models

2001–03
The Unadapted City: Vipcity
Urban design
Drawings and models

2001–03
Elysium
Executive architect of the construction of an apartment building by the late Alfons Hoppenbrouwers
Genk, Belgium

2001–03
Millenium
Executive architect of the construction of an apartment building by the late Alfons Hoppenbrouwers
Genk, Belgium

2001–05
Vertigo at the Scheldt
Architectural remodeling of a private dwelling
Drawings, model and realization
Ter Platen, Ghent, Belgium

Competition for an artistic intervention for the House of the Flemish Parliament,
Brussels, Belgium
Drawing

Brugge Vismijn Boogaard
Proposal to plant fruit trees at the site of the fish market in Bruges, Belgium
Drawing

Architecture competition design for an office building, Rijswijk, the Netherlands
Drawings

'The Unadapted City', Galerie Zwart Huis, Knokke, Belgium (solo)
'L'oeuvre collective', Centre d'art contemporain Chapelle Saint-Jacques, Saint–Gaudens, France (solo)
'La ville inadaptée', Centre d'art contemporain de Brétigny, Brétigny-sur-Orges, France (solo)

'Horta and After: 25 Masters of Modern Architecture in Belgium', Ruimte voor Actuele Kunst, Mechelen, Belgium
Galerie Média, Neuchâtel, Switzerland

2002

Sundial
Public art proposal for a sundial, Breda, the Netherlands
Photomontage

Gielen-Briers House
Architectural remodeling of a private dwelling
Drawings and realization
Genk, Belgium

Masson House
Self-realized architectural remodeling of private dwelling after drawing by Luc Deleu on photograph
Drawing on photograph and realization
Antwerp, Belgium

ORBINO
Installation with containers; with interior
presentation of The Unadapted City (1995–2002)
(1st realization)
Drawings and realization
Nauerna, Amsterdam, the Netherlands

2002–03
*Journey Around the World (Academical Upgrade
2&3 Setenil over Auckland)*
5,6 km north-west of SETENIL, SPAIN, N 36° 52.
683' W 5° 14. 126' 2003 June 19, 18H 47' 54'' to 18H
50' 16'' UNIVERSAL TIME OVER MOUNT EDEN,
AUCKLAND, NEW ZEALAND, S 36° 52. 683' E 174°
45. 874' 2002 DECEMBER 20, 6H 47' 54'' to 6H 50'
16'' UNIVERSAL TIME
Doubled photo

'VIPCITY en De Onaangepaste Stad', Galerie
Mercator, Antwerp, Belgium (solo)

'Antwerp & the world, Antwerp & the planet',
MuHKA, Antwerp, Belgium
'Luc Deleu & Niels Donckers', Cultureel Centrum,
Strombeek, Belgium
'Van IJ tot Zee—Van Halfweg tot Nauerna',
Stichting Kunst en Cultuur Noord-Holland,
Noorzeekanaalregio, the Netherlands
'Le Petit Cabinet d'un Amateur de Ruines', Orion Art
Gallery, Oostend, Belgium
ABC, Haarlem, the Netherlands

Luc Deleu and Hans Theys, *Urbi et Orbi: De
Onaangepaste Stad*, Ghent: Ludion, 2002
Luc Deleu, *EU*, 6 August, 2002 (global urban
concept for the European Quarter in Brussels,
motivation of candidacy; unpublished)

2003

Container Triangles
Installation with containers
Middelburg, the Netherlands

Urbi et Orbi
Poster for Utopia Station, 50th Venice
Biennale, Venice, Italy
Poster

Museum of Fine Arts (KMSK)
Architecture competition design for a
master plan for the Royal Museum of Fine
Arts (KMSK), Antwerp, Belgium
Drawings

Montyplan
Cover images for the monthly agenda
and newsletter of the Monty Theater,
Antwerp, Belgium
Photomontages and print

2003/2004
Untitled (windmill-grid-park)
Proposal for a windmill-grid-park for the
Antwerp Harbor, Belgium
Drawing and print on dibond (2004)

Speybank
Installation with containers (exhibition
ensemble of 5 container installations)
Middelheim Open Air Museum, Antwerp,
Belgium

Glass containers in Bulk
Installation with glass containers
Middelheim Open Air Museum,
Antwerp, Belgium

New Big Triumphal Arch
Installation with containers (exhibition
ensemble of 5 container installations)
Middelheim Open Air Museum,
Antwerp, Belgium

Untitled (L)
Installation with containers (exhibition
ensemble of 5 container installations)
Middelheim Open Air Museum,
Antwerp, Belgium

Construction X
Installation with containers (exhibition
ensemble of 5 container installations)
Middelheim Open Air Museum,
Antwerp, Belgium

Obelisk
Installation with containers (exhibition
ensemble of 5 container installations)
Middelheim Open Air Museum,
Antwerp, Belgium

Parasite Paradise
Design layout for the exhibition
'Parasite Paradise' Leidsche Rijn,
Utrecht, the Netherlands
Drawings, model and realization
Leidsche Rijn, Utrecht, The
Netherlands

2003–04
The Unadapted City: Nautical Mile
Urban design
Drawings, model, film and photomontages

2003–07
Belpaire House
Architectural remodeling and extension of
a private house
Drawings and realization
Steenhuize, Belgium

2003
Luc Deleu & Niels Donckers
Exhibition design
Drawings and realization
Cultural centre Strombeek-Bever, Belgium

2003
Untitled
Public art competition design, proposal for an
installation with windmills on a roundabout
Blixembosch, the Netherlands
Drawing

2003–2004
*Architecture competition design for a bicycle
and pedestrian bridge between the Seawall
and the nature reserve, Heist aan Zee, Belgium*
Drawings 'Luc Deleu', Middelheimmuseum,
Antwerp, Belgium (solo)
Galerie Média, Neuchâtel Switzerland (solo)

Kunst aan de Stroom vzw, Oudenaarde,
Belgium
Beeldenpark Geert Verbeke, Kemzeke,
Belgium
'De collectie Luc Deleu', MuHKA, Antwerp,
Belgium
'Utopia Station', 50th Venice Biennale, Venice,
Italy
'ParasiteParadise', Utrecht, the Netherlands
'Citizen Game', Le Quartier, Quimper, France

Luc Deleu, *Luc Deleu*, Antwerp:
Openluchtmuseum voor beeldhouwkunst
Middelheim, 2003 (exh. cat.)
Luc Deleu and Hans Theys, *La Ville Inadaptée*,
Toulouse: Éditions Ecocart, 2003

2004

Dageraadplaats
Urban competition design for
'Dageraadplaats' square, Antwerp,
Belgium
Drawings

Waerzeggers-Van Cauwelaert House
Architectural remodeling of a private
dwelling
Drawings and realization
(unfinished)
Dilbeek, Belgium

Middelheim Promenade Walk
Landscape design of a new terrain at
Middelheim Open Air Museum
Drawings and realization
Antwerp, Belgium

ORBINO
Installation with containers
(permanent)
Middelheim Open Air Museum,
Antwerp, Belgium

Kromme Hoek
Architecture competition design
for a yacht harbor in Nieuwpoort,
Belgium (in collaboration with
Studiegroep Omgeving)
Drawings

*Double Deck Quai with Photovoltaic
Cells*
Architectural proposal for new
warehouses for Antwerp harbor,
Antwerp, Belgium
Photomontage and print on dibond

Ecoharbor with Parking Garage
Architectural proposal for the
Antwerp harbor, Antwerp, Belgium
Photomontage and print on dibond

2004–10
Belle Epoque Center
Architectural restoration and remodeling
of three Belle Epoque villas into a cultural
center (in collaboration with Sint Lukas
Archives)
Drawings, model, and realization
Blankenberge, Belgium

'Luc Deleu: Travel', RAM Galerie, Rotterdam,
the Netherlands (solo)
'De onaangepaste stad (VIP-City) 1', RAM
Galerie, Rotterdam, the Netherlands (solo)
'Luc Deleu & T.O.P. office: VALUES',
Museum for Contemporary Art MuHKA,
Antwerp, Belgium (solo)
'Luc Deleu & T.O.P. office: A la recherche de
la ville inadaptée', Espace-architecture La
Cambre, Brussels, Belgium (solo)

'Small Works X', RAM gallery, Rotterdam,
the Netherlands
'Dear ICC', MuHKA, Antwerp, Belgium
Chateau de Jehay, Liège, Belgium

Luc Deleu, 'Concept global d'urbanisme
pour le quartier européen à Bruxelles',
in: *Change: Brussels Capital of Europe*,
Brussels: Prisme Editions, 2004

2005

The Fifth Façade
Architectural design for the Bozar,
Brussels, Belgium
Drawing and model

Solar Umbrella
Mixed media

Petrol
Architecture competition design for
Elia electricity cabin on site Petrol,
Antwerp, Belgium
Drawings

Noeud de Chaise
Study
Models

Speybank
Installation with containers
Yokohama, Japan

Bridge
Installation with containers
Gorinchem, the Netherlands

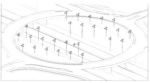

Kyoto 1
Proposal for installation with wind turbines on a
roundabout in the Waaslandhaven, Antwerp, Belgium
Drawings

Containers in Bulk
Proposal for installation with containers on a roundabout
in Waaslandhaven, Antwerp, Belgium
Drawings

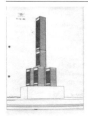

Obelisk
Proposal for installation with containers on a roundabout
in Waaslandhaven, Antwerp, Belgium
Drawings

V.RL.
Proposal for installation with
containers on a roundabout in
Waaslandhaven, Antwerp, Belgium
Drawing

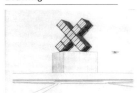

Construction X
Proposal for installation with
containers on a roundabout in
Waaslandhaven, Antwerp, Belgium
Drawings

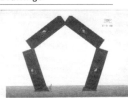

Speybank XL
Installation with containers
Drawing

2005
Kyoto 3
Public art competition design for
Sint-Jans-Molenbeek, Belgium
Drawings

'Façade 5, Luc Deleu', BOZAR/Palais
des Beaux-Arts, Brussels, Belgium
(solo)
'De onaangepaste stad (VIP-City)
2', RAM Galerie, Rotterdam, the
Netherlands (solo)

'Talking Cities', Zeche Zollverein,
Essen, Germany
'Luc Deleu en Thomas Schats', RAM,
Rotterdam, the Netherlands
'Horta and After: 25 Masters of
Modern Architecture in Belgium',
Facultad de Arquitectura y
Urbanismo, University of Caracas,
Caracas, Venezuela
'International Triennial of
Contemporary Art', Yokohama, Japan
'Nancy 2005, le temps des Lumières',
Nancy, France
'Visionair België/La Belgique
Visionnaire: C'est arrivé près de
chez nous', Palais des Beaux–Arts,
Brussels, Belgium
'Different Dimensions', RAM,
Rotterdam, the Netherlands (solo)
NDSM Wharf, Amsterdam, the
Netherlands

Luc Deleu, '31 overpeinzingen omtrent architectuur (Academical Upgrade 05, Deel I)'/'31 reflections on architecture (Academical Upgrade 05, Part I)', in: Bart Bulter and Arjen Oosterman (eds.), *A/S/L Architectuur/Stedenbouw/ Landschapsarchitectuur: Jaarboek Academie van Bouwkunst Amsterdam 2004–2005/A/U/L: Architecture/Urbanism/Landscape Architecture: Yearbook Academy of Architecture 2004–2005*, Rotterdam: 010 Publishers, pp. 269–279

2006

Competition design for the infrastructure for the creation of a manifestation of contemporary art in Rennes
Drawings
40m3, Rennes, France

Sluizen Houses
Preliminary architectural design for four purpose-built dwellings in Tongeren, Belgium
Drawings

Refuel Vespucci
Proposal for exclusive fuel stations for expensive fuel (analogous to Louis Vuitton, Prada, et cetera)
Photograph

From Mobile Medium University to Orban Space
Print

2006–
Orban Space
Research by design/Design by research (work in progress)

2006–09
Orban Space: Passage to the Antipodes
Orban research during a voyage from Palermo (Italy) to Richards Bay (South Africa) on board of the sailing yacht *La Malu II*
Remote work by satellite, videoconferences, cartography, drawings, and photographs

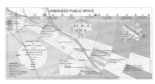

2006–
Orban Space: Panels
Analysis of public space on earth
Drawings, S, M, L, XL, prints (work in progress)

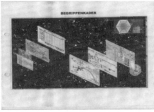

2006–
Orban Space: Terminology
Classification of the analysis of public space on earth
Text and photos (work in progress)

2006–07
Quay Jacques Brel
Architectural competition design for the new Quay Jacques Brel in Zeebrugge, Belgium
Drawings

2006–10
Dolce Vita
Architectural design for 2 purpose-built dwellings
on common property
Drawings and realization
Genk, Belgium

'Luc Deleu: VIPCITY', Technische Universiteit,
Eindhoven, the Netherlands (solo)

5th Shanghai Biennale, Shanghai Art Museum,
Shanghai, China

Luc Deleu, *Antwerp Ontwerpen*, 5 May 2006
(unpublished)

2007

Speybank
Permanent installation with containers
Ghent, Belgium

Troubleyn
Installation in a theater in Antwerp,
Belgium
Photomontage and realization

ORBINO
Temporary artist's studio
Installation with containers
Alkmaar, the Netherlands

Spoornoord
Architecture competition design for
a bicycle and pedestrian bridge at
Noorderplaats, Antwerp, Belgium
Drawings

'Orban Space: Work in Progress 2006–2010',
Galerie Micheline Szwajcer, Antwerp, Belgium
(solo)

'The Moss Gathering Tumbleweed Experience:
A Growing Exhibition Composed by Hans
Theys', NICC, Antwerpen, Belgium; Lokaal_01,
Breda, the Netherlands; Galeria Klerckx,
Milan, Italy

2008

2008–
House Panamarenko
Architectural remodeling
(installation of helicopter
platform) and the reconversion
of the house and studio of
Panamarenko to patrimonium
Drawings and realization in
progress
Antwerp, Belgium

Antwerp Sculpture Show
Masterplan for an open air
sculpture show
Drawings and realization
Antwerp, Belgium

Pacific
Container installation
Drawings

2008–
Royal Conservatory of Brussels
Architectural design for the
remodeling of the Royal
Conservatory of Brussels,
Brussels, Belgium
Drawings on 5 CD covers (in
progress)

Brussels Biennial
Architecture remodeling of former metro
station Anneessens into exhibition space,
Brussels, Belgium
Drawings, model and realization

Less is Less
Graffito
Anneessens Metro Station, Brussels,
Belgium

'Works 1970–2008', Rossicontemporary,
Brussels, Belgium (solo)
Brussels Biennial, Centre Anneessens,
Brussels, Belgium (solo within Biennial)

'Antwerp Sculpture Show', Antwerp,
Belgium

2009

The Container
Public art competition
proposal for Boekhoute,
Belgium
Photomontage

Quebec, Manitoba, Montreal
Public art competition
proposal for Lembeke,
Belgium
Photomontage

Under Milk Wood
Temporary theater with
containers
Drawings and realization
Zeeland, the Netherlands

Construction X
Installation with containers
Model and realization
Antwerp, Belgium

ORBINO
Installation with containers; with interior
presentation of *Orban Space* (2006–09)
Zeebrugge, Belgium

'Luc Deleu: MuHKA collectie', public library,
Sleidinge, Belgium
'Beaufort03', Beaufort Triennial of
Contemporary Art, MUZEE, Ostend,
Belgium
'Coups de coeur & Audioguides',
Rossicontemporary, Brussels, Belgium
'Después del Arte: Colección del M HKA',
Centro de Arte Contemporáneo Wifredo
Lam, Havana, Cuba

2010

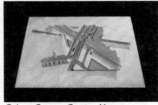

Orban Space: Sector X
Formal study
Drawings and models

*International Idea Contest for the Court House
Brussels*
Architectural competition design for the Brussels
Court House, Brussels, Belgium (first prize;
with EXPO 68 and Jos Vandenbreeden Heritage
Architects)
Drawings

2010–11
Spiretec
Architecture competition design for an I.C.T.
campus in Greater Noïda, Delhi, India (with 1:1
architects)
Drawings

2010
Het Avontuur
Architecture design for the
transformation of a service
building into primary school
in Antwerp, Belgium (in
collaboration with Professionele
Architectenvennootschap
Joachim Walgrave bvba)
Drawings

2010-2011
Small X
Installation with containers
Model and realization
Antwerp, Belgium

'Sector X', Rossicontemporary,
Spiretec, Brussels, Belgium
(solo)

'Kristof Van Gestel & Luc Deleu',
Campo & Campo, Antwerp,
Belgium
'X Highway to reflexion',
Cultureel Centrum, Strombeek-
Bever, Belgium
Festival Mawazine, Galerie
Nationale Bab Rouah/Musée
des Oudayas, Rabat, Morocco
'Curators' Series #3: History of
Art, The', The David Roberts Art
Foundation Fitzrovia, London,
United Kingdom

Luc Deleu, 'Panamarenko's
Biekorfstraat 2, from terrace
house to monument', in:
*Panamarenko, Workstation
Biekorfstraat?*, Antwerp:
Linkeroever Uitgevers, 2010

2011

Tervuren
Built heritage research study (in collaboration
with Jos Vandenbreeden and Sint Lukas
Architecture Archives)
(work in progress)
Tervuren, Belgium

House of the Province of Antwerp
Architectural competition design for the House
of Province of Antwerp, Antwerp, Belgium (with
1:1 Architects)
Drawings and video

'Orban Space', Librairie Evasions 2, Brussels,
Belgium (solo)

'Spirits of Internationalism: 6 European
collections, 1956–1986', Van Abbemuseum,
Eindhoven, the Netherlands
'Vis-à-vis', Rossicontemporary, Brussels,
Belgium
'Museum of Affects', Museum of Contemporary
Art Metelkova, Ljubljana, Slovenia

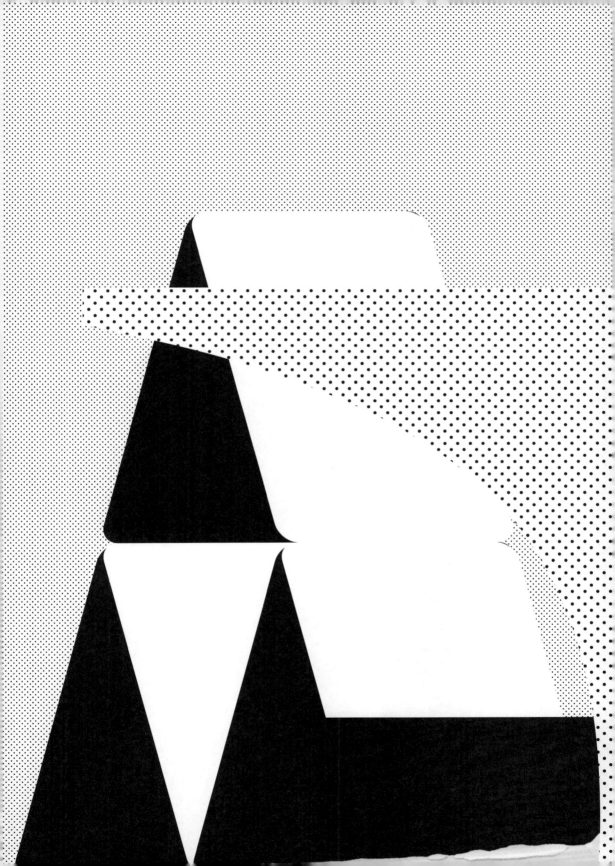

T.O.P. office:
Future Prospects

A Conversation between Isabelle De Smet, Steven Van den Bergh, Wouter Davidts, and Hans De Wolf

Concepts & Methods

Hans De Wolf (HdW) We would like to discuss with you T.O.P. office's present position as an office and think tank for urbanistic reflection and get a general idea of its current activities. In the minds of many people, the studio is closely related to the person and ideas of Luc Deleu. How would you, as staff members of the studio for fifteen years now, describe T.O.P. office's current position? What are your guiding principles? What do you stand for today? And, especially, how do you see T.O.P. office's future, related to its undeniable history?

Isabelle De Smet (IDS) The earlier work, such as the *Proposals*, the various installations and the *Orban Planning Manifesto* have of course laid down a solid foundation. The studio has its own particular, specific way of doing things, which evolved over the years, long before we came on board. Luc Deleu's concepts have a history of forty years by now.

Steven Van den Bergh (SVdB) Then again, nowadays they also go in a new direction, partly because we have been working here for fifteen years now, partly because of Luc himself. Or rather, we haven't so much taken a new direction but are continuing a development. The original work has too often been regarded as purely conceptual, sometimes even in a negative way. One could say that we are trying to consolidate the ideas and the approach, looking for ways to introduce them into the wider social discourse in a concrete manner.

IDS Through research projects such as *The Unadapted City* we have developed these historical concepts into a number of tools.[1] While we use these tools in tackling larger projects, the development of those projects has also led to new design methods of our own.

1 *The Unadapted City (D.O.S.), Plate VIII: Culture and Entertainment*, 1995.

HdW Those are two points I would like to explore more specifically. Firstly, the conceptual principle and especially how it is developed further. Secondly, the methodology and how it provides the means to connect to the daily reality of urban planning.

IDS To begin with, we don't separate the two. We firmly believe that the elements we develop in our research projects can be used in realizations or concrete projects. Our practicing of architecture and urban planning on paper indeed has a lot to do with the studio's orbanistic approach.

HdW Are you saying that orbanism generates some sort of organic program, an approach that guides and validates everything the studio does? That the products actually bear the signature of the method?

2 *The Unadapted City: Vipcity, One Nautical Mile (Structure 1)*, 2004

SVdB Orbanism is certainly a constant at the studio, both in thinking and in working. The studio's orbanistic way of thinking includes careful consideration of limited space and limited means, besides aiming for natural development and design. We never present anything saying, 'this is it'. We try to make a design grow organically by using drawings and models. In other words, orbanistic thinking also manifests itself in the way our studio works. In short, I don't think that *The Unadapted City* could have been produced in a year, even with a bigger team.[2] It took ten years—not so much because we are a small studio, but because we chose to let the project evolve and mature slowly. We firmly believe that this approach not only suits us, but that it was necessary.

IDS To us, this is not a critical statement in itself, as we realize we can't and probably shouldn't work on every project for ten years. However, because we did spend ten years on *The Unadapted City* we are now able to design architecturally completely innovative office buildings in a few months.[3] In other words, the results and insights from *The Unadapted City* are our stock in trade.

3 *House of the Province of Antwerp (facade 1)*, 2011.

HdW Could we say that this principle of letting things mature somehow guarantees the quality and value of T.O.P. office's output, while at the same time it exposes a sharp contrast with the present-day haste in urban planning?

IDS Well, of course we sometimes feel that reality is catching up with us. But that is just one more reason for us to try and apply the developed skills in commissioned projects. This is very important to us, as we don't want our research to be gratuitous. It is certainly not research for the sake of research only. We feel that research is very important—after all, it doesn't use up space—but we do wish to propagate our fifteen years of thinking about the city, and that includes giving it concrete shape in projects.

Research

HdW Research is a very popular word these days and has been at the forefront of quite a number of practices in art, architecture and urban planning. What is T.O.P. office's position in this development?

IDS Our work is all about data and how these are manipulated. Our practice is at the intersection of the rational ordering of data and controlled randomness. For each design, we start collecting all sorts of data. It can be figures we compiled ourselves or the preconditions for competitions or information about a location. We subject this input to consciously formal processes and also let randomness run its course.

SVdB We never know what the results will be and we don't really want to know. But what happens between the data and the results, and what it takes to get from one to the other, is something we are very good at. We've practiced long and hard to master that.

IDS In this way, the design almost grows by itself, and very often the result is something we could not have designed without that randomness. This 'aleatory' design can be found in all of our projects: it is a form of controlled chance. We do aim for a certain result but we don't impose a form on it beforehand. This is in line with the orbanistic way of thinking. We aim to design a public space that is flexible and that can be adapted and changed in many different ways. This ambition is a connecting thread throughout *The Unadapted City* but is equally discernible in all of our concrete projects.[4] We feel that not only are we using a sort of natural design process, but also that we end up with

4 *The Unadapted City: Vipcity, One Nautical Mile (3 D model),* 2004.

a natural space as a result of that, almost regardless of who makes up the design team. We have learned to work together as a team in such a way that our different competencies converge. With that in mind, we always work from a central data model in which all the various layers of data are accommodated and which is also accessible to various people and even teams. It is also an expertise that we wish to disseminate. As we can't do everything on our own, this method is exactly right for collaborating with others and taking that research further. It would be regrettable if the research stopped with the end results of the models.

Wouter Davidts (WD) Is the research primarily aimed at optimizing architectural and urban planning design processes? Or do you regard research as a way of generating distance from

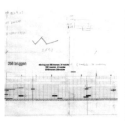

5 *The Unadapted City: Brikabrak (Arrangement)*, 1998.

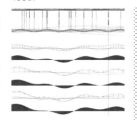

6 *The Unadapted City: Dinky Town (Arrangement)*, 1998.

7 *The Unadapted City: Vipcity (Arrangement Model)*, 2004.

10 *House of the Province of Antwerp (facade 2)*, 2011.

8 *Casa Roja*, Tervuren, Belgium, 2005.

9 *Belle Epoque Center*, Blankenberge, Belgium, 2010.

a practice that traditionally relates to the world in a very goal-oriented manner? How, in other words, does research relate to the daily routine of the studio?

SVdB I think we use research to study things; it's as simple as that. We're not looking to demonstrate what kind of manipulations we are capable of. While research gives us 'exercise', it should also take that exercise further. The cause is often a simple one: we need certain data. Pretty soon, however, you have to conclude that no one is looking into this or gathering this data. So the only thing for it is to start doing it yourself. With the 'design by research' done in *The Unadapted City* the trigger was mundane enough: data for designing urban equipment just didn't exist. In other words, we started *The Unadapted City* to get a grip on urban planning research.

IDS Besides, the research does not manifest itself only in the larger, abstract projects. While working on *The Unadapted City*, we also realized some very concrete architectural projects and urban competitions in which we explicitly tried to implement this constantly evolving methodology. The evolution of those projects was parallel to that of *The Unadapted City*, in which there is a clear evolution from *Brikabrik* [5] to *Dinkytown* [6] and to *Vipcity* [7]. Whereas this analog development perhaps manifested itself somewhat randomly at the time, we now do so with much more focus. That is reflected in the methodology, but also in the desire to create and develop a good public space. Projects such as *Casa Roja* [8] in Tervuren, the *Belle Epoque Center* [9] in Blankenberge or the *House of the Province of Antwerp* [10] express this notion.

Design practice

HdW The House of the Province of Antwerp is one of the most recent large projects, and one on which you have worked very intensively. Can you tell us the extent to which the final design bears the signature of the theoretical meta-work?

SVdB First of all we entered the design competition because we were especially interested in this location. It is by far *the* green site in the city. Of course our interest in nature in the city goes back to the *Proposals*.

And again, we started with classifying all the data we were getting and becoming very familiar with that information. In relation to the overall duration of the project, we took ample time to do this. I think that most studios would not spend that much time on this. Next, we used various techniques to build something from the data. The method we control best, is putting out the data on a line. Those linear scores or arrangements are written in such a way that clusters emerge.[11] We then adapted and manipulated this scheme to different parameters. In fact, one could say that the manipulations designed the building: in the end the facade was presented to us by the manipulations of the office spaces. We could never have implemented such a design procedure without the experience from *The Unadapted City*.

11 *House of the Province of Antwerp (Arrangement)*, 2011.

HdW Let's be very concrete. A House of the Province is a government building where a few hundred people work, preferably under the best conditions. They arrive at nine and leave at five. What is the fundamental difference in T.O.P. office's thinking about these very basic functions?

IDS Our main goal is to design a good public space, both outside and inside the office building. We regard the office building as a public space where people go to work. The design of the various offices came second and took shape only during and through the extensive ordering process. The result is not a long stretch of office cubicles, but a public space that meanders through the offices, alternating between larger and smaller spaces, etc. Just as in *The Unadapted City*, the design of the space in between was our main concern.

WD How important are aesthetic choices in the design process of T.O.P. office? You are currently describing the activity of designing as primarily an organizational process here, in which proper management of the public space provides an inherent quality. Surely, aesthetic decisions are inevitably part of that process?

SVdB Of course aesthetics are important. Our methodology doesn't go as far as to make us accept an ugly result at any cost, just because it is our way of doing things. If we did that, we would produce more ugly buildings than good ones! Of course we are also driven by aesthetic considerations. We feel, however, that by allowing those manipulations we can design a building that exceeds personal aesthetics and therefore will not be ruined even if it is renovated within ten years. In a sense we hope that further manipulations in the future will only improve the building. No, our methods are primarily aimed at designing natural and flexible things.

A Conversation between Isabelle De Smet, Steven Van den Bergh, Wouter Davidts, and Hans De Wolf

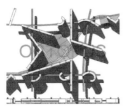

12 *The Unadapted City: Octopus (model drawing)*, 1999.

IDS And it is not like we don't know until the very end if the design is beautiful or ugly. Again, this is about controlling randomness. The aesthetics are guided by the drawings. Drawings don't lie, we strongly believe that. We learn from the drawings.

WD Could you explain a little more about the status of the many schemes, plans and drawings for the research projects?

SVdB When a project is finished, the many documents should be regarded as intermediate deadlines. They are always moments in which everything comes together, and from which a product is then made. For instance, with *The Unadapted City* we also didn't know exactly when the end point would arrive. It actually stopped at *Vipcity*,[12] while another model had been planned on top of that: *NotForYou*. It would have meant another doubling of the number of inhabitants.

Orban space

WD *The Unadapted City* has always fascinated me by the way in which the ordering of abstract data translated itself into a concrete architectural and urban design. There is something incredibly powerful in the way in which you suddenly move from 'datascapes' to a built shape, a leap that is far from simple, after all. What's happening in this regard with *Orban Space*, your current 'research by design' project? Is there a shape looming on the horizon?

IDS *Orban Space* is all about public space, and the research is of course guided by our orbanistic thinking. At the moment we are still at the stage where we are trying to understand the various scales, networks, spaces and the relationships between all these different elements.

13 *The Unadapted City: Brikabrak (model)*, 1998.

SVdB Actually, *Orban Space* is a continuation of *The Unadapted City*, or, more specifically, a further exploration of urban space. *The Unadapted City* also began as a continuation of the *Usiebenpole* design. The starting point is that not houses but facilities make up a city. *Brikabrak* is a literal expression of that proposition.[13] During the next phase, *Dinkytown*, we started to realize that in fact the space between the facilities, in other words the public space, is even more important.[14] So we wrote ar-

14 *The Unadapted City: Dinky Town (model)*, 1998.

rangements and scores that unconsciously shaped the public space. With *Dinkytown* the approach was rather formal, as we were still mainly focused on manipulating the facilities. With *Vipcity*, by contrast, we started designing the public space itself, so it was no longer the formal end result of the posi-

15 *The Unadapted City: Vicpcity, One Nautical Mile (Structure 2)*, 2004.

tioning of the facilities.[15] The arrangement and scores in this case were largely written for the public space. *Orban Space* is the continuation of this. With *Orban Space*, the study of public space goes much further than formal analysis. We are trying to register the acts and networks that define public space, along with all that they entail.[16]

HdW Could one say that, with *Orban Space*, a temporal dimension has been added to the study of public space? Are you now trying to map movement and displacement, in particular the dynamics governing public space?

SVdB Yes, I think one could certainly say that.

WD Can you identify the design challenge of *Orban Space*?

SVdB No, but with *The Unadapted City* we couldn't initially either.

16 *Orban Space: Panel Urbanized Public Space*, 2006–.

WD With *The Unadapted City*, it looks as if you are trying to design the city. And the city's public space has a scale that is still related to bodies and buildings. But what happens when you shift the focus to the scale of the Earth, when you want to make statements about designing public space on a global scale? Wouldn't such a task run the risk of becoming intangible? In other words, how can you still connect such an ambition with architectural and urban design?

IDS The goal of *The Unadapted City* wasn't to design the city. Rather, our aim was to map and understand the various scales and spaces within the city and then decide how this could bring about a good public space.

17 *Orban Space: Terminology*, 2006–.

SVdB Of course the scale became larger with *Orban Space*. On the other hand however, in the *Glossarium*, the basic document of the project, we don't investigate, for instance, the movement of tectonic plates, as that can hardly be related to mankind in either size or time.[17] By contrast, the *Sector X* project does produce a number of initial works, including the first formal results of *Orban Space*.[18] One crucial and intentional quality of that project is that it has no scale. By taking an intersection as study object we have zoomed in on a site that is even smaller than *Brikabrak*'s surface area, but we can register the networks we wish to explore in *Orban Space* at this site.

18 *Orban Space: Sector X*, 2010.

HdW With *The Unadapted City*, it is obvious that you are elaborating on a development in urban planning that is based on anything but traditional principles. By systematically exploring those principles you have been developing very specific applications and projections. Has *Orban Space* yielded any results so far that point in the same direction?

IDS Besides the *Sector X* project mentioned earlier, we are currently working on a project in Tervuren together with the Sint-Lukas Archive, at the invitation and under supervision of Jos Vandenbreeden. We have been asked to make a statement about how a city can and should treat its heritage. This research exposes the various layers of public space in a way that is similar to what happens in *Orban Space*. We collect data from various fields: topography, urban structures, and heritage. At the moment, we are still processing all this information in order to combine the data in practical drawings of high graphical quality. Inevitably these will lead to insights that can be processed into a statement about public space. This commission is a good example of how the research of *Orban Space* is directed by practice but in turn also guides practice. By following the same methods, concrete projects determine how *Orban Space* proceeds and incorporates the results. It is a constant process of mutual influences. Sometimes in a very practical, but quite often in a sort of in-between way.

WD Can these methods be articulated? After all, methodology presupposes some system. Could the methodology for instance be formalized in a 2012 update of the *Orban Planning Manifesto*?

SVdB Although *The Unadapted City* is about urban planning and about designing public space, it hasn't really produced a method. We never wanted to posit or produce a method. All we did was use a precise and rational method that enabled us to approach the project as a team. Things one is not conscious of then play a leading role. The problem is that the establishment expects a clear definition of the 'alternative' urban planning that we are developing. When such a clear definition is consciously not provided, the project is all too soon dismissed as fooling around. But it's far from that. Our ambition is to constantly link our thinking to reality and to the urban planning issues of today, but this doesn't mean that we always want to apply *The Unadapted City*. We do hope, though, that when a studio such as ours engages in a proj-ect like this, it will result in the introduction of 'newness' in contemporary urban planning – an ambition in which we are not alone, by the way. This project fits into a wider trend in architectural culture and its principles are shared by other designers as well.

Art
HdW Finally, we'd like to discuss the rather complex but also very positive and productive triangle between architecture,

urban planning and visual art that has always been central to T.O.P. office. Much of the studio's work is also shown in museums and in different art contexts.[19] What is your position at present? How would you like to situate yourselves within that triangle, today, but especially in the future?

19 T.O.P. office, anno 2012 (f.l.t.r. Steven Van den Bergh, Isabelle De Smet, Laurette Gillemot, and Luc Deleu).

SVdB Somewhere in the middle, surely? Over the past fifteen years we have always more or less occupied the middle ground in this, sometimes leaning one way and then again somewhat the other way. I guess your question has to do with the possibility that at some point in the future Luc Deleu may leave the studio and that the art element would disappear with him. We are not thinking too much about that, to be honest.

WD As I see it, it has more to do with the instrumental way in which T.O.P office has been using the various stages and platforms associated with the three domains to not only present its work but especially to develop it further and give it a new boost. It has always been one of the hallmarks of T.O.P. office to have a broad approach of both the work and the practice.

SVdB That is why I say we wish to remain in the middle of that triangle. These are three niches, but we don't want to be claimed by any of them exclusively. We never develop a project with the idea of subsequently being able to sell it as art. Each product primarily serves as a way to bring focus to the studio. For instance, we immediately put a high degree of 'product' into the initial drawings, which gives us an idea of the project very early on. We must always take care to avoid that each one of us sticks to his or her own computer and spreadsheets and that we then suddenly have to produce a result. We have our own way of communicating within the studio and it is in our nature to present everything in attractive documents.

T.O.P. office:
Excerpts from Print Maps
1997–2012

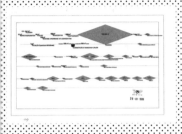

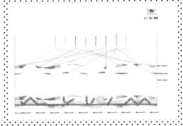

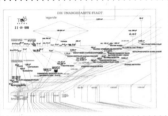

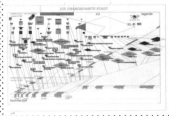

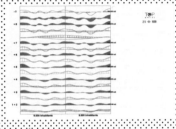

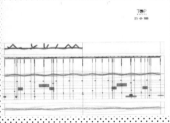

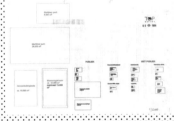

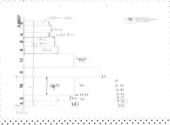

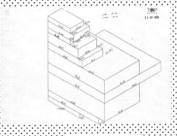

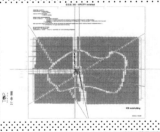

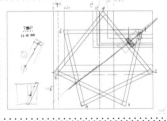

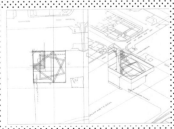

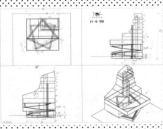

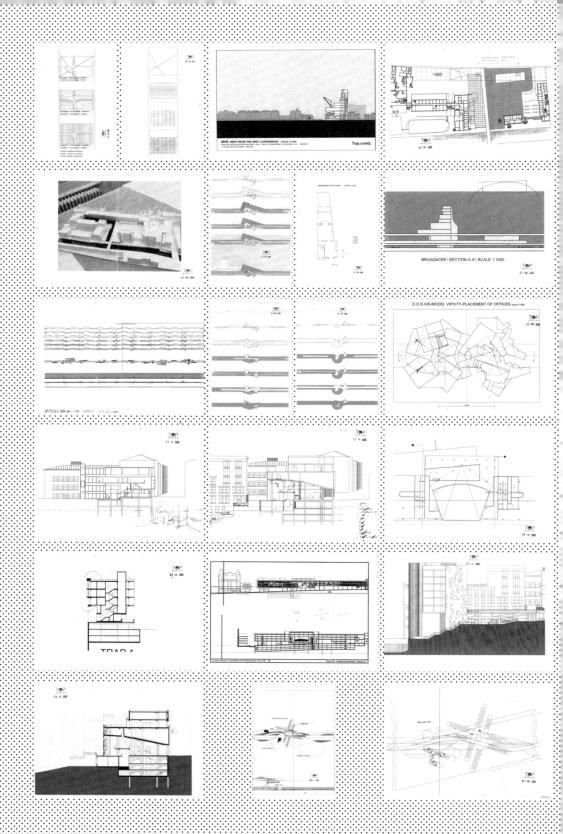

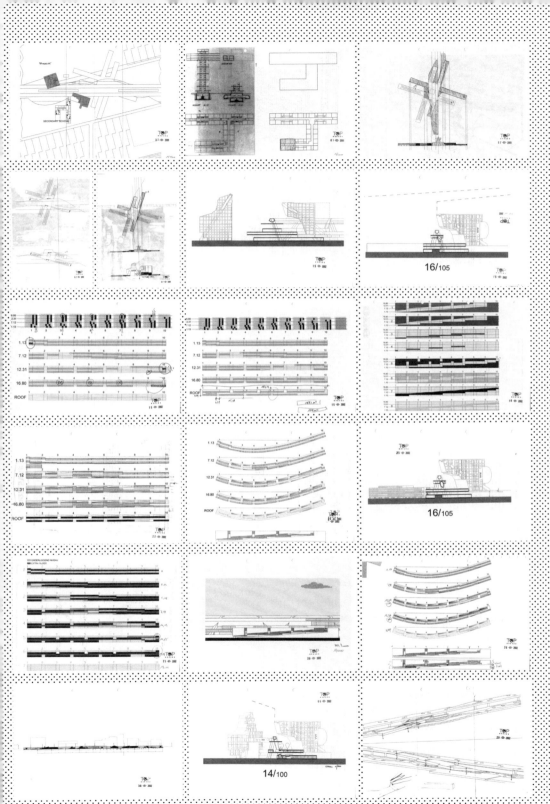

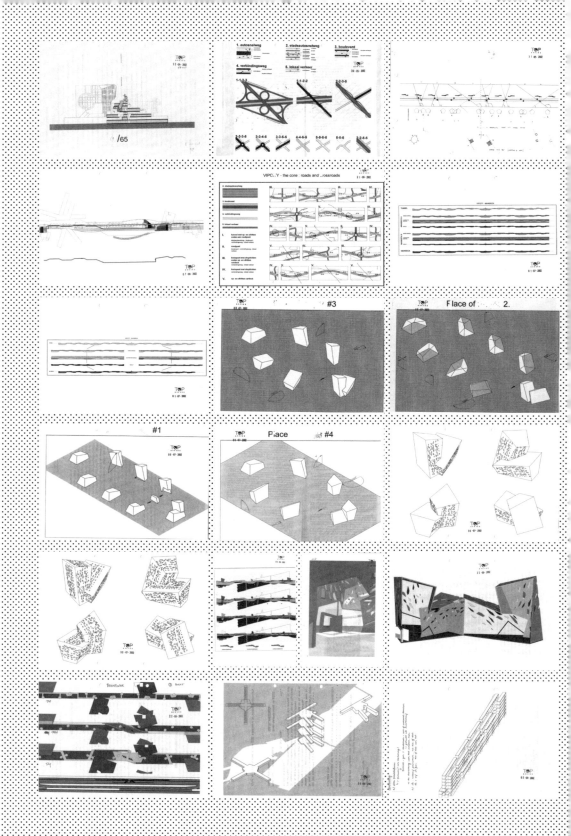

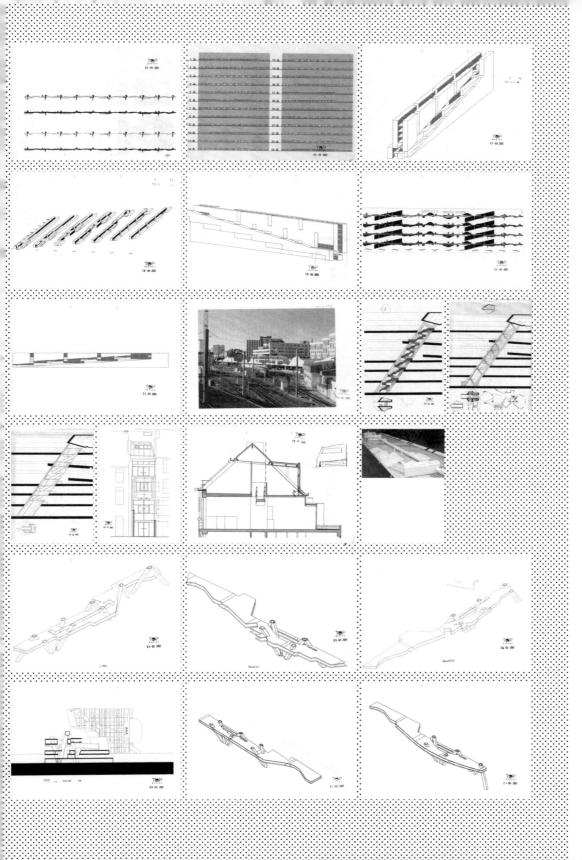

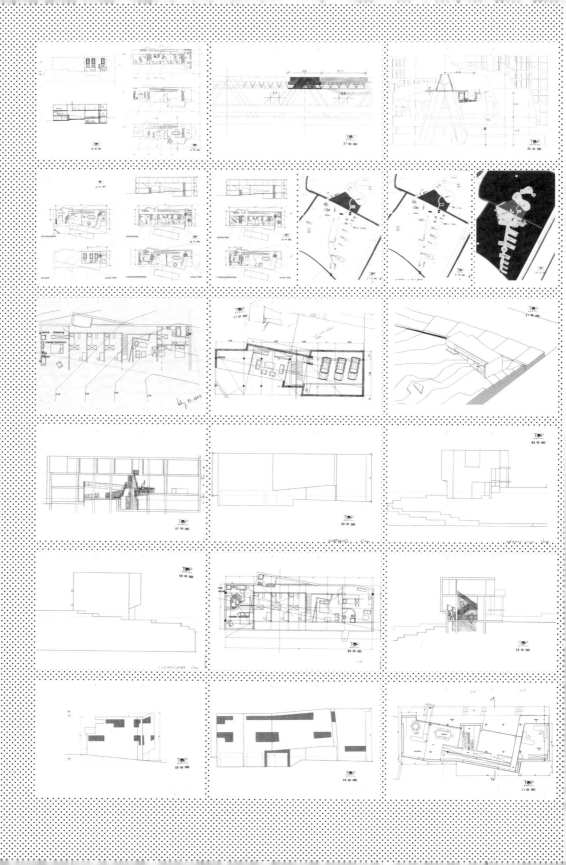

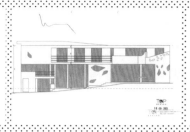

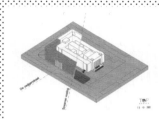
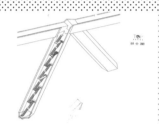
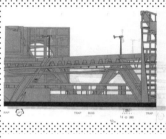

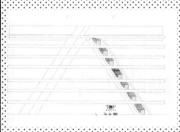
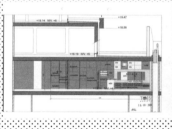
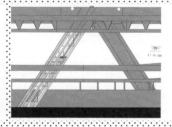
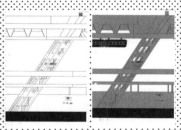
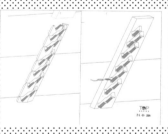
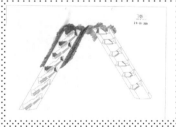
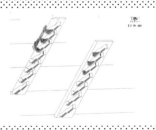
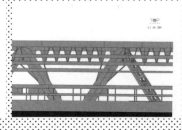

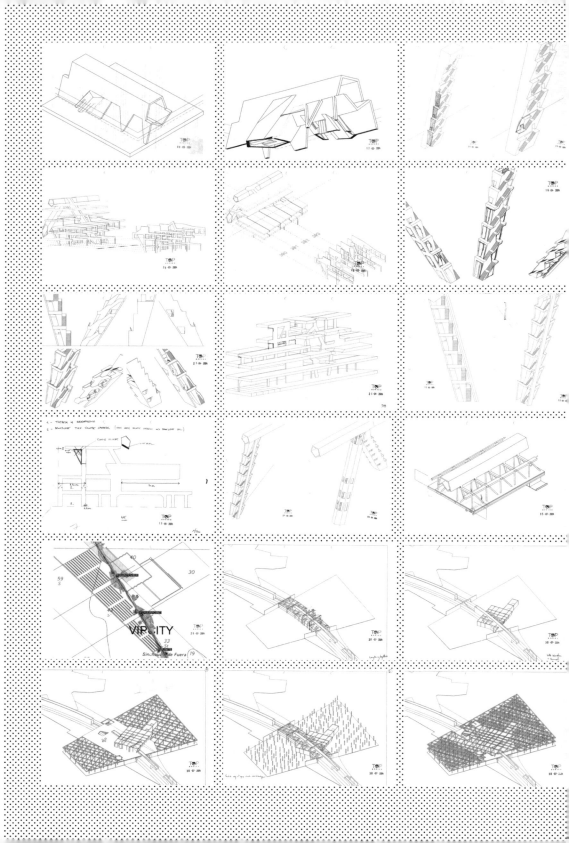

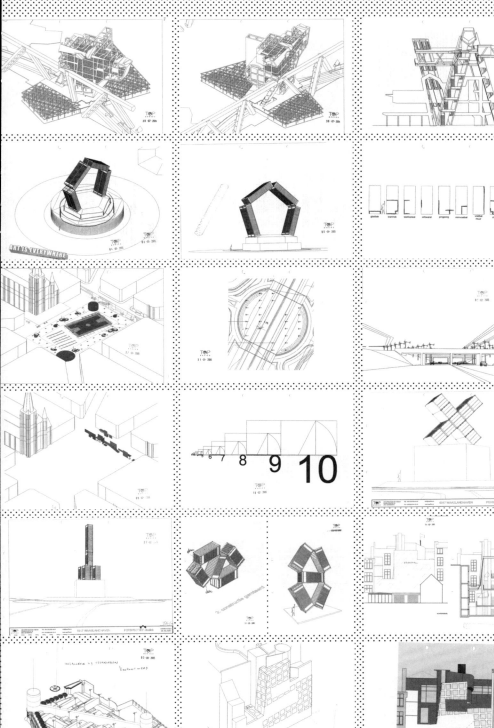
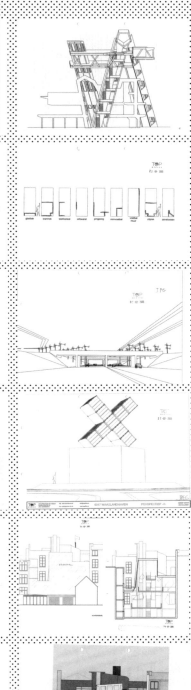

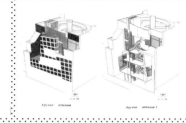

RESIDENTIE DOLCE VITA
ZICHT VANUIT HET OOSTEN

RESIDENTIE DOLCE VITA

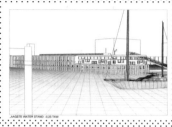

LAAGSTE WATER STAND -0,25 TAW

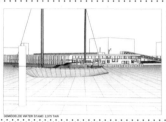

GEMIDDELDE WATER STAND 2,375 TAW

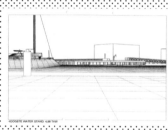

HOOGSTE WATER STAND 4,98 TAW

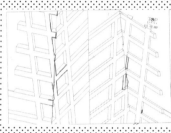

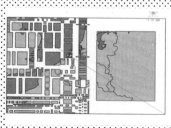

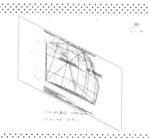

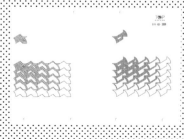

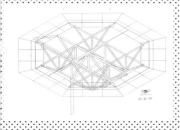

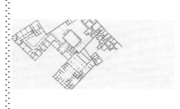

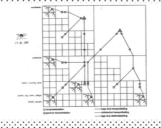
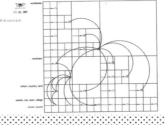

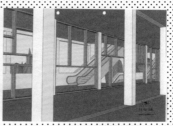

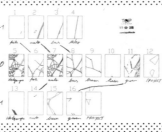
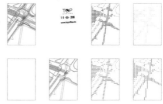
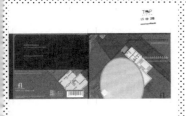

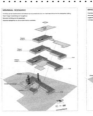
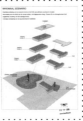

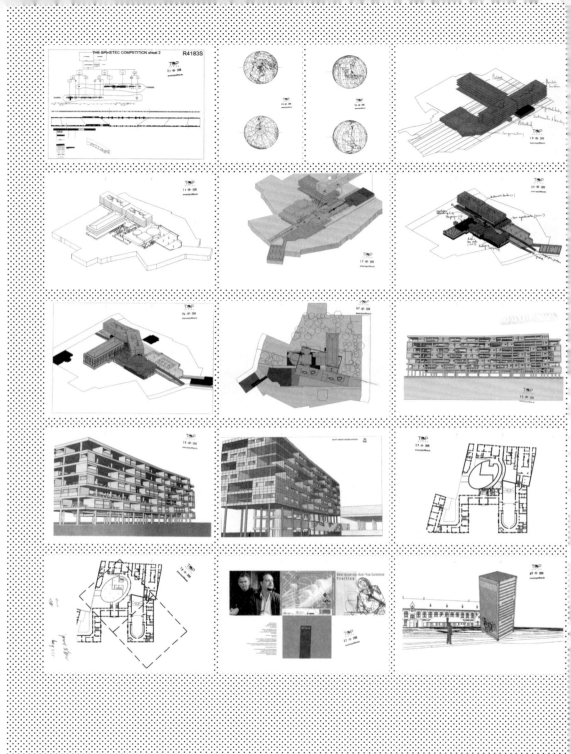

Contributors

Guy Châtel (Ghent, B) is an engineer-architect and Associate Professor in the Department of Architecture & Urban Planning, Ghent University. As a practicing architect he was laureate of the competition *Minister P. Akkermans* in 1987 and has won the Belgian Architectural Award 2000. His work has been published in (among others) *A+, Abitare, de Architect, Flanders Architectural Yearbook, DW&B, OASE, World Architecture Magazine* and exhibited (*Homeward, Contemporary Architecture in Flanders,* Antwerp, Bordeaux, Rome, Venice, Plymouth). He founded the office *ssa/xx* in 2000 and frequently works in association with engineer-architect and landscape architect Kris Coremans. Their project for the Central Control Station on the Canal Louvain-Dyle in Kampenhout-Sas was selected for the Belgian Architectural Awards 2005 and the Provincial Architecture Award of Province Flemish-Brabant 2008 and was also nominated for the triennial Prix Georges de Hens 2004 and for the biennial European Union Prize for Contemporary Architecture—Mies van der Rohe Award 2007.
As a tutor he participated in several international design workshops (AIL—Politechnico di Milano, Academie van Bouwkunst Amsterdam) and since 2003 he is the national coordinator of the *International Concrete Design Competition.* Since 2009 he is principal of Lab A—Ghent University, which conducts applied research and fulfills service assignments on design-oriented issues. He has published on architecture and visual arts in books and journals (including *A+, Janus, DW&B, AS, MDD, Cahiers Thématiques AVH, Interstices, OASE, San Rocco*).

Wouter Davidts (Antwerp, B/Amsterdam, NL) is critic and writer. From 2009 to 2012 he was Professor of Modern and Contemporary Art at the VU University in Amsterdam. Between 2003 and 2008 he was a postdoctoral researcher in the Department of Architecture & Urban Planning of Ghent University, where he obtained a PhD on museum architecture in 2003. In the fall of 2006 he was a British Academy research fellow at Goldsmiths, University of London. He was a research fellow with the Research Group of Visual Arts, Academie voor Kunst en Vormgeving| St Joost, Avans Hogeschool between 2007 and 2008, and a visiting research fellow at the Henry Moore Institute, Leeds in the fall of 2008.
He is the author of *Bouwen voor de kunst? Museumarchitectuur van Centre Pompidou tot Tate Modern* (A&S/books, 2006) and has published on museums, contemporary art and architecture in journals such as *Afterall, Archis, De Witte Raaf, Footprint, Kritische Berichten, Metropolis M, OASE* and *Parachute,* and in books and exhibition catalogues. He recently edited *The Fall of the Studio: Artists at Work* (Valiz, 2009; with Kim Paice) and *CRACK: Koen van den Broek* (Valiz, 2010). His exhibition reviews have appeared in, among others, *Artforum, Camera Austria, Sculpture* and *OPEN.*
He curated the shows 'Philippe Van Snick: Undisclosed Recipients', BK SM, Mechelen (2006), together with Hilde Van Gelder), 'Beginners & Begetters', Extra City, Antwerp (2007) and 'Abstract USA 1958—1968: In the Galleries', Rijksmuseum Twenthe, Enschede (2010). In parallel with this publication, he has curated the exhibition 'Orban Space: The Work & Practice of Luc Deleu — T.O.P. office', Stroom Den Haag, The Hague (2011) and Extra City|VAi, Antwerp (2012).

Hans De Wolf (Brussels, B) studied Art History and Archaeology at the Free University of Brussels, Belgium (VUB) and Columbia University, New York. He obtained his PhD with a revolutionary study about *La Mariée mise à nue par ces célibataires, même* by Marcel Duchamp, one of the most complex art works of the 20th century. He published several papers on this and related subjects in international magazines. For several years he worked at the Hamburger Bahnhof, the Berlin museum of contemporary art, and simultaneously lectured at the Kunsthochschule Berlin Weissensee. In 2005 De Wolf accepted the position of Professor of Art History at the VUB. He founded The Platform, the Brussels institute for a PhD in the Arts. He is a consultant for the Centre for Fine Arts in Brussels, where he recently co-curated an extensive Jeff Wall exhibition and catalogue.

Maarten Delbeke (Brussels, B) is Associate Professor with the department of Architecture and Urban Planning of Ghent University, where he studied and received his doctorate in 2001. In 2001—03 he was the Scott Opler fellow in Architectural History at Worcester College (Oxford), and in 2004 a visiting scholar at the Canadian Center for Architecture. From 2003 until 2009 he was a postdoctoral research fellow with the Research Foundation Flanders (F.W.O.). He has been teaching in Ghent and at the Art History Department of Leiden University since 2005.
Currently he leads the project 'The Quest for the Legitimacy of Architecture in Europe 1750—1850' at Leiden University, funded by a Vidi grant from the Netherlands Organisation for Scientific Research (NWO). His research concerns early modern art and artistic theory, architectural theory and contemporary architecture. With Evonne Levy and Steven Ostrow he has edited *Bernini's Biographies: Critical Essays* (Penn State UP, 2006), and with Minou Schraven *Foundation, Dedication, and Consecration in Early Modern Europe* (Brill, 2011). His monograph *The Art of Religion: Sforza Pallavicino and Art Theory in Bernini's Rome* is forthcoming with Ashgate.
He was the co-curator of the Belgian exhibition at the Venice Architecture Biennale in 2000, as well as of 'Piranesi: De prentencollectie van de Universiteit Gent', Museum voor Schone Kunsten, Ghent (2008). His essays have appeared in many collective volumes and journals, such as *Journal of Architecture, Art History, Word and Image, OASE, El Croquis, AA Files, Archis* and *A+.*

Luc Deleu (Antwerp, B) is an architect/urbanist, graduated from the Hoger Instituut Sint-Lucas, Brussels in 1969. In 1970 he founded his studio T.O.P. office. In 1973 he started to develop the concept *Orbanism* (cfr. *Orban Manifesto & Proposals*) and in 1980, after visiting the US, he started the series *Scale & Perspective.* He set up a series of designs for infrastructures in 1988 and in 1991 initiated a study for *Journey Around the World in 80 Days,* followed by *The Unadapted City,* a design by research study, set up in 1995. In 2006, he launched *Orban Space,* a further design by research study including a 'mobile medium' research project during a journey around the world on board of the sailing yacht *La Malu II.* Since 1983 Luc Deleu has realized container installations in Switzerland, Belgium, France, Germany, Ireland, Japan, and the Netherlands.
Deleu has taken part in international exhibitions such as 'Horta and After: 25 Masters of Modern Architecture in Belgium', São Paolo (1999), Prague (2000), Tokyo (2001), 'Van IJ tot Zee — Van Halfweg tot Nauerna', the Netherlands (2002), 'Le temps des Lumières', Nancy (2005), 'Talking Cities', Zeche Zollverein, Essen (2006) and 'Curator's Series #3: History of Art, The', The David Roberts Art Foundation Fitzrovia, London (2010).

Solo exhibitions of Deleu's work have been organized by Storefront for Art & Architecture, New York (1991), Netherlands Architecture Institute, Rotterdam (1996), Centre d'Art Contemporain, Brétigny-sur-Orges, France (2001), Open Air Sculpture Museum Middelheim, Antwerp (2003), MuHKA, Antwerp (2004), Palais des Beaux-Arts, Brussels (2005), and Technical University Eindhoven (2006). His work has also been included in other major exhibitions such as the International Triennale of Contemporary Art, Yokohama, Japan (2005), 5th Shanghai Biennale, Shanghai (2004), Brussels Biennial, Brussels (2008), and 'Beaufort 03', Ostend (2009).

Luc Deleu's work is represented in the collections of the Ministerie van de Vlaamse Gemeenschap, Brussels; Musées royaux des Beaux-Arts de Belgique, Brussels; Museum voor Hedendaagse Kunst (MuHKA), Antwerp, Stedelijk Museum voor Aktuele Kunst (S.M.A.K.), Ghent; Fonds Régional d'Art Contemporain de la Corse; Musée Château d'Annecy; Fonds Régional d'Art Contemporain Languedoc-Roussillon; Fonds Régional d'Art Contemporain Franche-Comté, France; Kröller-Müller Museum, Otterlo; Collection d'estampes et de dessins de l'Ecole Polytechnique Fédérale, Zurich; Nederlands Architecture Institute (NAi), Rotterdam.

From 1981 to 2009 he taught Theory of Architecture at Hogeschool Sint-Lukas Brussels and from 1991 to 2009 at Hogeschool voor Wetenschap & Kunst, Brussels/Ghent. Luc Deleu is a fellow of The Platform, doctorate in the arts, the Brussels model.

Marjolijn Dijkman (Brussels, BE) graduated from the free media department at the Gerrit Rietveld Academy in Amsterdam in 2001, finished a postgraduate course at the Piet Zwart Institute in Rotterdam in 2003 and for two years was a researcher at the Jan van Eyck Academy in Maastricht, until 2008. She has been a tutor at the Fine Art Department of the MFA AKV St. Joost since 2009. Her work has been exhibited internationally in independent art spaces, centers for contemporary art and museums of modern art. Recent solo exhibitions include 'Comma 02', Bloomberg SPACE, London (2009), 'MATRIX 234', BAM/PFA, Berkeley (2010), and 'Theatrum Orbis Terrarum', IKON Gallery, Birmingham and Spike Island, Bristol (2011). Recent group exhibitions include 'Still Life, Art, Ecology and the Politics of Change', Sharjah Biennial 08, United Arab Emirates (2007), 'Neue Konzepte', Bonner Kunstverein (2007), 'Decollecting', FRAC NPDC, Dunkerque (2007), 'The Order of Things', MuHKA, Antwerp (2008), 'Now JumP', Nam June Paik Museum, Yongin-si (2008), 'The Uncertainty Principle', MACBA, Barcelona (2009), 'Screaming and Hearing', Mercosul Biennial 07, Porto Alegre (2009), 'Ondertussen', Noord-Holland Biënnale, the Netherlands (2010), and 'Portscapes', Boijmans Van Beuningen Museum, Rotterdam (2010).

Kersten Geers (Brussels, BE) graduated in Architecture and Urbanism at the University of Ghent and at the Escuela Tecnica Superior de Arquitectura in Madrid. He was a project leader for Maxwan Architects and Urbanists in Rotterdam and for Neutelings Riedijk Architects in Rotterdam (2001–05). He is currently visiting professor at the University of Ghent, and at the School of Architecture in Mendrisio. In 2002, together with David Van Severen, he founded the award-winning architecture firm Office Kersten Geers David Van Severen.

Aglaia Konrad (Salzburg, A) is an artist living and working in Brussels. She studied at the Jan van Eyck Academy in Maastricht. Her work focuses on the exploration of urban space as the central form of organization of contemporary cultures through photography, film and video. In the course of her projects, she travels to numerous cities and urban agglomerates in order to research the structure of these urban spaces and architectural and urban planning concepts of the past modern age as a global form of appropriating space and society.

The vast archive she has created constitutes a particular body of contemporary, documentary photography and now forms a subject in its own right and the starting point for most of her projects, exhibition contributions and installations. Her work could be considered as a form of visual research.

Up until now Konrad has been known for her photographic work through books and publications and her spatial interventions. She has had solo shows in Siegen, Antwerp, Geneva, Graz, Cologne, Florence, New York, etc. and participated in international group exhibitons like Documenta X (1997), 'Cities on the Move', (traveling exhibition, 1998–1999); 'Orbis Terrarum', Antwerp (2000); 'Talking Cities', Zeche Zollverein, Essen (2006); 'Rencontres Internationales', Centre Pompidou, Paris (2011), 'Ways of Worldmaking', National Museum of Art, Osaka (2011), 4. Fotofestival Mannheim (2011), and 'The Way It Wasn't', Culturgest, Porto (2011). Her published books: *Elasticity*, (NAi Publishers, 2002); *Iconocity*, (Verlag der Buchhandlung Walther König/deSingel, 2005); *Desert Cities* (JRP-Rignier, 2009); *Carrara*, ROMA (Publications, 2011).

She has been advising researcher at the Jan van Eyck Academy, Maastricht, and currently is teaching at the Sint-Lukas Brussels University College of Art and Design.

John Macarthur (Queensland, AUS) is Professor of architecture and Dean of the School of Architecture at the University of Queensland, Australia. He directs the research group ATCH (architecture, theory, criticism, history). He writes on the cultural history and aesthetics of architecture, and is an active critic of contemporary work. His work has appeared in *Assemblage, Architecture Research Quarterly, The Journal of Architecture, Architectural Theory Review*, and *OASE*. His book *The Picturesque: Architecture, Disgust and Other Irregularities* was published by Routledge in 2007. With his colleagues in ATCH he is currently working on projects on the 20th-century reception of Baroque architecture, on criticism and aesthetics, and on the architecture of Queensland.

Metahaven is a studio for design and research, founded by Vinca Kruk and Daniel van der Velden. Metahaven's work—both commissioned and self-directed—reflects political and social issues in provocative graphic design objects. Metahaven released *Uncorporate Identity*, a book on politics and visual identity, published by Lars Müller in 2010. Solo exhibitions include 'Affiche Frontière', CAPC musée d'art contemporain de Bordeaux (2008) and 'Stadtstaat', Künstlerhaus Stuttgart/Casco (2009). Group exhibitions include 'Forms of Inquiry', AA, London (2007), Manifesta 8, Murcia (2010), the Gwangju Design Biennale 2011, Gwangju, Korea, and 'Graphic Design: Now In Production', Walker Art Center, Minneapolis (2011). Daniel van der Velden is a Senior Critic at the Yale University MFA program in graphic design. He is a tutor with the design department of the Sandberg Institute in Amsterdam and lecturer with the University of Amsterdam School of Media Studies. Vinca Kruk teaches Editorial Design at ArtEZ Academy of the Arts in Arnhem and graphic design at Otis College of Arts and Design in Los Angeles.

In 2011, Metahaven was selected by *Rolling Stone Italia* as one of the world's 20 most promising design studios. Their forthcoming book, *Black Transparency*, is to be published in 2013.

Manfred Pernice (Berlin, DE) studied at the Institut für Bildende Kunst in Braunschweig from 1985 to 1986 and at the Universität der Künste in Berlin from 1988 to 1993. Soon after his solo exhibition at the Galerie NEU in Berlin in 1995, Pernice was invited to participate in international exhibitions such as the Lyon Biennale of 1997 and Berlin Biennale of 1998.

Later solo exhibitions of Pernice's work have been organized by Musée d'art moderne de la Ville de Paris (1998), Portikus, Frankfurt (2000), Hamburger Bahnhof, Berlin (2000), Sprengel Museum, Hanover (2001), Pinakothek der Moderne, Munich (2003) and Neues Museum, Nuremberg (2008). His work has also been included in major exhibitions such as the Lyon Biennale (1997), Berlin Biennale (1998), Manifesta 3 (2000), Documenta 11 (2001), Venice Biennale (2001 and 2003), BIACS2, Biennale Sevilla (2006), Skulptur-Projekte Münster (2007), and Carnegie International (2008). Pernice currently teaches at the Academy of Fine Arts Vienna and lives and works in Berlin.

Felicity Scott (New York, US) is director of the program in Critical, Curatorial and Conceptual Practices in Architecture (CCCP) at the Graduate School of Architecture, Planning and Preservation, Columbia University. She is also a founding co-editor of *Grey Room*, a quarterly journal of architecture, art, media, and politics. She is the author of *Architecture or Techno-Utopia: Politics After Modernism* (MIT Press, 2007) and *Living Archive 7: Ant Farm* (Actar, 2008). She recently completed the manuscript for a book *Cartographies of Drift: Bernard Rudofsky's Encounters with Modernity*. Her next book, *Outlaw Territories: Environments of Insecurity, Architectures of Counter-Insurgency*, will investigate the relation of architecture to 'human unsettlement' and territorial insecurity. Scott's writing on modern and contemporary art and architecture has appeared in numerous magazines and journals including *Texte zur Kunst*, *Artforum*, *October*, the *Journal of the Society of Architectural Historians*, *Volume*, and *Quaderns*, as well as in many catalogs and edited volumes. She is currently working on an exhibition of the early video, media, and environmental works of artist Les Levine.

Teresa Stoppani (London UK) studied architecture at the Institute of Architecture of the University of Venice (MArch Iuav) and at the University of Florence (DrRic Arch&UD). She is Reader in Architecture at the University of Greenwich in London, where she coordinates the postgraduate Architecture History and Theory courses. She has taught architectural design and theory at the Iuav in Venice, the Architectural Association in London, the RMIT University in Melbourne and the University of Technology in Sydney. Stoppani's research focuses on re-readings of the city through unorthodox approaches to urbanism and architecture, and includes: considerations on the significance of dust in the work of Walter Benjamin and Georges Bataille (in *The Journal of Architecture*; Log); studies on the grid (in *Architecture Research Quarterly*) and the map (in *Angelaki*), in relation to the architectural project; a study of the complex relation of architecture with the artificial disaster (in *Space & Culture*); the book *Paradigm Islands: Manhattan and Venice. Discourses on Architecture and the City* (Routledge, 2010); and a series of essays on the work of G. B. Piranesi, proposing how this may engage

with contemporary spatial practices, in: *Haecceity Papers*, *Footprint*, *The Journal of Architecture*, M. Frascari et al. (eds.), *From Models to Drawings* (Routledge, 2007); I. Wingham (ed.), *Mobility of the Line* (Birkhäuser, 2012).

UP (Koenraad Dedobbeleer & Kris Kimpe) (Brussels — Antwerp, BE) is a fanzine focusing on 'interesting architecture', published by artist Koenraad Dedobbeleer and architect Kris Kimpe since 2006. Each issue is presented in A5, stapled or concertina folded, and features photography by Dedobbeleer, Kimpe and others of a single work of architecture that inspires them. The publication 'appears regularly with an irregular interval.' Koenraad Dedobbeleer is an artist, living and working in Brussels. Kris Kimpe is an architect, living and working in Antwerp.

Stefaan Vervoort (Ghent, B/Amsterdam, NL) graduated as an architect-engineer at Ghent University in 2009 and finished the research master VAMA (Visual Arts, Media and Architecture) at VU University, Amsterdam, in 2011. His research focuses on the exchange between art and architecture in the postwar era, as well as on the material formation of modern and contemporary art museums. He writes for the art and architecture magazines *De Witte Raaf*, *Metropolis M* and *OASE*.

In October 2011 he started as FWO PhD candidate in the Department of Architecture & Urban Planning, Ghent University, with a research project entitled 'Model as Sculpture'. He is assistant curator of the exhibition 'Orban Space: The Work & Practice of Luc Deleu — T.O.P. office', Stroom Den Haag, The Hague (2011) and Extra City|VAi, Antwerp (2012).

C

D

E

F

T

U

V

W

X

Y

Z

N

O

P

R

W

Colophon

Editors
Wouter Davidts, Guy Châtel, Stefaan Vervoort
Visual Essays
Luc Deleu, Koenraad Dedobbeleer & Kris Kimpe, Marjolijn Dijkman,
Kersten Geers, Aglaia Konrad, Metahaven, Manfred Pernice
Textual Essays
Guy Châtel, Wouter Davidts, Maarten Delbeke, John Macarthur,
Felicity D. Scott, Teresa Stoppani, Stefaan Vervoort
Interview
Hans De Wolf, Wouter Davidts
Design
Metahaven
Copy-editing
Els Brinkman, Leo Reijnen
Translation
Leo Reijnen with Jane Bemont (Dutch-English)
Production and Publicity
Valiz, Liesbet Bussche, Pia Pol, Astrid Vorstermans
Paper inside
Munken Pure Rough, Arctic Volume White
Paper cover
Arctic Volume White
Typeface
Univers
Lithography and Printing
die Keure, Bruges
Binding
Catherine Binding, Bruges
Publisher
Astrid Vorstermans, Valiz, Amsterdam

The publication *Luc Deleu –T.O.P. office:
Orban Space* was made possible
through the generous support of

Stroom Den Haag
www.stroom.nl

Luc Deleu – T.O.P. office, Antwerp
www.topoffice.to

The Netherlands Architecture Fund
www.archfonds.nl

SNS Reaal Fonds
www.snsreaalfonds.nl

Fonds BKVB / Mondriaan Fund
www.mondriaanfonds.nl

The Flemish-Dutch House deBuren
www.deburen.eu

VU University Amsterdam,
Faculty of Arts

Ghent University,
Faculty of Architecture, Ghent

Vlaamse Overheid

www.valiz.nl
Distribution:
BE/NL/LU: Coen Sligting, www.coensligtingbookimport.nl;
Centraal Boekhuis, www.centraal.boekhuis.nl
GB/IE: Art Data, www.artdata.co.uk
Europe/Asia: Idea Books, www.ideabooks.nl
USA: D.A.P., www.artbook.com
Individual orders : www.valiz.nl; info@valiz.nl

ISBN 978 90 78088 60 8
NUR 648, 640
Printed and bound in Belgium / EU

The editors wish to the thank:
T.O.P. office (Luc Deleu, Laurette
Gillemot, Isabelle De Smet and Steven
Van den Bergh), the contributors, the
team of Valiz (Astrid Vorstermans,
Pia Pol, Liesbet Bussche), and the
team of Stroom Den Haag (Arno
van Roosmalen, Francien van
Westrenen, Jane Huldman and all of
the staff members); the Masterclass
participants (Stijn Rybels, Pieter de
Walsche, Nathan Wouters, Olivier
Cavens, Bram Denkens, Jonas
Apers, Janik Beckers, Roel Griffioen,
Evelien Livens, Tine Segers, Sarah
Melsens, Lyndsey Housden, Vincent
Schipper, Marijke Goeting, Alexander
van Straten, and Florence Himpe;
Carmen Van Maercke, Hong Wan Chan,
Thomas Montulet, Mathieu, and Bea
Delannoy, for doing the preparatory
work for the survey); Andrea Cinel,
Bart De Baere, Evi Bert, Christine
Clinckx, Francesco Rossi, ZENO X
Gallery, Els Brinkman, Jean-Pierre Le
Blanc, Godfried Verschaffel, Dorian
van der Brempt, Leo Reijnen, Frits
Erkens, Dries Vandevelde, Hans De
Wolf, Laura Hanssens, Miek Monsieur,
Eline Dehullu, Sonja van der Oord, Jan
Storms, WeTransfer, Rosa Vandervost,
Mihnea Mircan, Christoph Grafe,
Katrien Reist, Caroline Van Eccelpoel.